The Rational Guide To

Monitoring and Analyzing with Microsoft® Office PerformancePoint Server 2007

PUBLISHED BY

Rational Press - An imprint of the Mann Publishing Group
710 Main Street, 6th Floor
PO Box 580
Rollinsford, NH 03869, USA
www.rationalpress.com
www.mannpublishing.com
+1 (603) 601-0325

ISBN-10: 1-932577-41-6
ISBN-13: 978-1-932577-41-9
Library of Congress Control Number (LCCN): 2007936575
Printed and bound in the United States of America.
10 9 8 7 6 5 4 3 2 1

Credits

Authors:	Nick Barclay, Adrian Downes
Technical Reviewer:	Corey Hulen
Editorial Director:	Jeff Edman
Production Editor:	Kimberly Meurillon
Production Assistant:	Scott Gardenhire
Indexer:	Christine Frank
Series Concept:	Anthony T. Mann
Cover Concept:	Marcelo Paiva

All Mann Publishing Group books may be purchased at bulk discounts.

Rational Press is not affiliated with IBM Corporation or Rational Software.

The Rational Guide To

Monitoring and Analyzing with Microsoft® Office PerformancePoint Server 2007

Nick Barclay
Adrian Downes

RATIONAL PRESS

An imprint of the mann PUBLISHING GROUP
www.mannpublishing.com

About the Authors

Adrian Downes (MCITP: BI) is Director and co-founder of B(iQ) Pty Ltd (`www.b-iq.org`) and has spent over 10 years delivering Business Intelligence and Performance Management solutions for customers in Canada, the U.S., and Australia. A graduate of Sheridan College in Oakville, Ontario, Adrian earned a masters degree in IT from Charles Sturt University, and is currently completing his MBA studies with the Australian Institute of Business Administration. Adrian lives just outside Adelaide in sunny South Australia with his wife Mary and daughter Christine, and, when time permits he posts blogs on BI subject matter at `http://adriandownes.blogspot.com`. He has also co-authored *The Rational Guide to Microsoft® Office Business Scorecard Manager 2005* and *The Rational Guide to Planning with Microsoft® Office PerformancePoint Server 2007*, both available from Rational Press (`www.rationalpress.com`).

Nick Barclay is a Principal Consultant at B(iQ) in Australia and has been delivering solutions in the business intelligence and performance management space for over 7 years. He holds Microsoft Certified IT Professional (MCITP) certifications as a DBA, database developer and BI developer and has presented at TechEd and SharePoint conferences in the Asia Pacific region. Nick resides on Sydney's northern beaches with his wife Angela and daughter Olivia and maintains a blog at `http://nickbarclay.blogspot.com`. Nick has also co-authored *The Rational Guide to Microsoft® Office Business Scorecard Manager 2005* and *The Rational Guide to Planning with Microsoft® Office PerformancePoint Server 2007*, both available from Rational Press (`www.rationalpress.com`).

Acknowledgements

We'd like to thank Tony Mann and the team at Mann Publishing for giving us the opportunity to write another Rational Guide. Sincere thanks are also due to our editor Jeff Edman and technical editor Corey Hulen for their attention to detail and helpful advice. Last but not least, thanks to all members of the PerformancePoint Monitor and Analyze team for building such a fantastic product; it's been a pleasure writing about it.

Adrian Downes: Once again, my love and gratitude to Mary and Christine for allowing daddy to hide in his study and write, when he really should have been outside playing with his favourite girls. Thanks again to Nick for his positive energy and resolve throughout our little venture. Also, a great deal of thanks are due to our readers for their positive feedback and support. I dedicate this volume to my parents Pamela and Malcolm, who always challenged me to continuously exceed my own expectations.

Nick Barclay: Thanks again to my wonderful wife, Angela, who has noted on several occasions that I've spent more time talking with Adrian than her over the last few months. Thank you to my daughter, Olivia, who reminded me where my real priorities lie when she took her first steps recently. Lastly, thanks to my co-author, colleague, and friend who started us down this path that has now led to us to completing yet another book; it really has been a lot of fun.

RATIONAL PRESS™

Rational Guides for a Fast-Paced World™

About Rational Guides

Rational Guides, from Rational Press, provide a no-nonsense approach to publishing based on both a practicality and price that make them rational. Each Rational Guide is constructed with the highest quality writing and production materials—at an affordable price. All Rational Guides are intended to be as complete as possible in a compact size. Furthermore, all Rational Guides come with bonus materials, such as additional chapters, applications, code, utilities, or other resources. To download these materials, just register your book at `www.rationalpress.com`. See the instruction page at the end of this book to find out how to register your book.

Who Should Read This Book

This book details the features and functionality of the Monitoring and Analyzing aspects of Microsoft Office PerformancePoint Server 2007 (PPS). Step-by-step exercises cover the installation, design, and deployment steps necessary to create an interactive dashboarding solution. This book is aimed at technical business analysts, business intelligence consultants, and DBAs who wish to get up to speed with features and functionality provided by this product. People with experience managing or querying structured data stores (particularly OLAP) will benefit most. An understanding of, and access to, server technologies such as SQL Server 2005, SharePoint Services 3.0, and Office 2007 applications will be necessary in order to complete all step-by-step exercises throughout the book.

Conventions Used In This Book

The following conventions are used throughout this book:

- *Italics* — First introduction of a term.
- **Bold** — Exact name of an item or object that appears on the computer screen, such as menus, buttons, dropdown lists, or links.
- `Mono-spaced text` — Used to show a Web URL address, computer language code, or expressions as you must exactly type them.
- **Menu1⇨Menu2** — Hierarchical Windows menus in the order you must select them.
- ➲ — Code wrap icon.

Tech Tip:

This box gives you additional technical advice about the option, procedure, or step being explained in the chapter.

Note:

This box gives you additional information to keep in mind as you read.

FREE Bonus:

This box lists additional free materials or content available on the Web after you register your book at `www.rationalpress.com.`

Caution

This box alerts you to special considerations or additional advice.

Contents

Contents

Contents

Contents

Part I

Introduction

Chapter 1

Introducing Performance Management

Remember learning about the scientific method in high school? In case you don't, here's a brief review of the four major steps involved:

1. Observe something.
2. Come up with a hypothesis to explain it.
3. Use the hypothesis to predict the results of further observation.
4. Conduct experiments to test the hypothesis.

If the results of the experiments prove the hypothesis, then it is probably accepted as common knowledge—if not, then the hypothesis probably needs to be modified, or rejected altogether.

So what does the scientific method have to do with Microsoft Office PerformancePoint Server 2007? Plenty! It all starts with a maturing discipline in business known as *performance management.*

This book explains what PerformancePoint Server 2007 (PPS 2007) is and how it applies to performance management. Like other books in the Rational Guide Series, this one does not attempt replace the product help files. However, this book is actually the first part of a two part series describing the performance management cycle you will learn more about in this chapter. *The Rational Guide to Planning with Microsoft® Office PerformancePoint Server 2007* is a complementary title which fulfills another part of the cycle. Think of these books as your supplement to the existing help files and whitepapers available from Microsoft, which should be read and referenced often. The goal of these books is simple: to quickly bring you up to speed on how PPS 2007 works and how you can make it work for your business needs.

The first part of this book provides the necessary grounding essential for later "click-intensive" chapters. Chapter 1 describes performance management and its association to the concept of Business Intelligence, the key terms and elements of a performance management system, as well as what PPS 2007 provides to build such systems. In Chapter 2, we are formally introduced to the Monitoring components of PPS 2007 at a fairly high level by reviewing its architecture of components and how it relates to PPS 2007 Planning components (not covered in this book).

The practical examples in this book begin in Part II. Chapter 3 shows you how to perform a basic installation of PPS 2007 Monitoring, and provides a sneak-preview of the final solution you will develop over the course of this book for a certain fictitious company. Chapter 4 introduces us to Dashboard Designer, the central port-of-call for crafting your dashboards (and the elements that comprise them) and the main application you will work with throughout the remainder of the chapters.

Part III delves further with the Dashboard Designer application, progressively growing your knowledge and skills with key elements as you build the solution. Chapters 5 through 10 cover basic data source, indicator, and KPI elements to more complex scorecards, reports and dashboards.

Part IV helps us to wrap up your solution for delivery. Chapter 11 demonstrates how to export your dashboard to Windows SharePoint Services 3.0 and work with PPS web parts, while Chapter 12 details Monitoring security.

Downloadable chapters are available in the bonus content of this book. Bonus Chapter A covers the topic of managing dashboard elements and metadata.Bonus Chapter B provides some guidance on designing an effective solution while Bonus Chapter C details how score values are actually calculated and rolled up in PPS 2007 Monitoring. Bonus content is available after you register your book online at `www.rationalpress.com`. See the instructions page at the end of this book to learn how to register.

The Role of Performance Management in Organizations

Performance management is an emerging and quickly maturing business discipline. Like its better known siblings—Sales, Human Resources, Operations, and Finance—performance management has a key role to play in improving the overall value of an organization. Wayne Eckerson of The Data Warehouse Institute defines performance management as *"a series of organizational processes and applications designed to optimize the execution of business strategy."* Although this book focuses on the application-side of the definition, it is important for you to first understand how the organizational process works.

The Balanced Scorecard Method

In 1992, Robert S. Kaplan and David Norton proposed the concept of a Balanced Scorecard (BSC), an approach for measuring the performance of a business strategy. Balanced Scorecards emphasise the association of corporate activities to important performance metrics, grouped into four main business perspectives:

- **Financial Perspective** — Objectives and measurements which are focused on the financial state of a given business. Some examples of financial metrics include return on assets, cash flow from operating activities, and profitability.

- **Internal Business Process Perspective** — Objectives and indicators aimed at specific business processes, such as time spent with prospective customers, tender success rate, or length of time between product sale and product delivery.

- **Customer Perspective** — Customer impact is emphasised, with measurements dedicated to average customer service satisfaction surveys, or number of repeat customer complaints.

- **Learning and Growth Perspective** —Measurements that focus on how an organization learns, changes, and improves—for example, the number of employee suggestions or the total hours spent on staff training.

Within each of the perspectives, specific performance measurements are selected to reflect key influences (or "drivers") for a given organization. The Balanced Scorecard method helps companies systematically perform the following actions:

1. Communicate business strategy, objectives, and goals.
2. Monitor metrics aligned with objectives, comparing them to stated goals.
3. Analyze and communicate issues with respect to metrics reflecting a condition that warrants greater attention. Performance metrics under such conditions are generally said to be "in exception."
4. Take action based on outcomes from analysis.
5. Conduct reviews into continuous performance improvement, sometimes warranting adjustments to strategies or objectives.

Note:

Although the Kaplan-Norton approach encourages a broad view of an organization, it should come as no surprise that for certain organizations, a performance management solution may only reveal measurements associated to some of the perspectives. The examples built throughout the course of this book are based on a single perspective for the sake of brevity and clarity.

From Mission to Measurements

Businesses of all sizes have more than a few things in common, and pretty much all business schools and books tell us that it usually starts with a *mission statement.* The mission statement is the single reason for getting up in the morning; it summarizes (among other things) what a business does, whom it serves, and how it differs from other similar companies. A sample mission statement might read:

- *"to design, build and market <insert your product here> for sale, driven by certain key features to meet the needs of <insert your target customer segments> along specific channels of distribution in <insert your target market or geography>"*

Another trait exhibited by most businesses is the organic phenomena of *strategy*. Corporate strategies are often qualitative in nature, and reflect the mission of the company. Corporate strategy warrants a broad view of internal and external factors, and is often subject to change as the business itself changes over time. An example corporate strategy supporting our vague mission statement could be:

- *"Improve <Your Target Customer Segment> Satisfaction"*

In most cases, a given corporate strategy is supported by one or more *objectives*. An objective is expressed as a results-oriented statement, indicating where a company would like to be. Objectives, like strategies, may be adjusted over time. Building on our enigmatic corporate strategy, we may include the following objectives:

- *"Increase Repeat <Your Target Customer Segment> Store Sales"*
- *"Increase <Your Target Customer Segment> Satisfaction Survey Scores"*

Objectives, expressed in quantitative terms, present opportunities for businesses to measure specific activities—these measurements are typically referred to as *key performance indicators* or *KPIs*. KPIs are of particular importance to us because they serve as a window into business activities or transactions. KPIs are also interesting because they allow us to compare *actual* values to *budgeted* or *target* values. As we'll see, such transactions are typically stored as *line-of-business (LOB)* application data, and are refined through specific processes into meaningful KPIs. Building on our first sample objective, we may wish to establish KPIs for the following objectives:

- *"Number of Quarterly <Your Target Customer Segment> Repeat Sales at Store #1"*

- *"Number of Quarterly <Your Target Customer Segment> Repeat Sales at Store #2"*
- *"Number of Quarterly <Your Target Customer Segment> Repeat Sales at Store #3"*

It is important to note here that an objective can be supplemented by multiple KPIs, each with its own emphasis or *weight* within the objective itself. Using the three sample KPIs above, Store #1 may be twice as large as both Stores #2 and #3 combined—in this case, it may be best to acknowledge the emphasis of the Store #1 KPI on its overarching objective. We may also wish to set some boundaries for our KPIs. Our mysterious organization may choose to target 50 repeat customer visits within a given quarter for Store #1, 100 repeat customer visits for Store #2, and so on.

The road from mission statement to corporate strategy, supporting objectives, and KPIs is greatly simplified for the purposes of this book. Along the way, you may have noticed the shift from the qualitative to the quantitative—some of you at this point may be wondering how this all applies to the scientific method. It is at this point that the role of performance management begins to take shape.

Note:

Performance management goes by a number of different names and, unsurprisingly, acronyms—each more confusing than the last. Some people refer to it as BPM for *business performance management*, **while others reserve the acronym for** *business process management*, **which focuses more on automating business events and interactions between existing systems and applications. Others call it** *corporate performance management* **or CPM, but CPM also stands for** *certified property manager* **(see** `www.irem.org`**). How about EPM for** *enterprise performance management*, **or** *organizational performance management* **(OPM)? At the time of this writing, a quick search on** `http://en.wikipedia.org` **reveals many results for each acronym. You can see how confusing it can be. Performance management (without any acronyms) is probably the best term for clarity, and will be the term used throughout this book.**

The Performance Management Cycle

The goal of the scientific method is to prove or disprove a hypothesis through experimentation and make the results understandable. In business, a similar process takes place:

1. **Monitor** *what* is happening (or happened recently).

2. **Analyze** further to understand *why* something interesting is happening. Our hunches may turn out to be nothing important, or something we really need to address.

3. **Forecast** what we think *will* happen, based on what we have analyzed. Here we use our hunches to build one or more scenarios in order to help us predict certain outcomes. These outcomes help us to confirm or refute our hunches.

4. **Plan** what we would like to happen, setting expectations (or budgets) based on insights from analysis and forecasting.

5. **Execute**, by *making decisions and taking action*, based on the outcomes of planning activities. Here, our adjusted expectations or predictions from forecasting and planning may help us to arrive at new hunches.

6. **Monitor** the outcomes of our decisions and actions to determine whether our initial hunches (or indeed our adjusted ones) were correct, and if our decisions and actions had any impact on what was happening in the first place.

Figure 1.1 illustrates this process.

Figure 1.1: The Performance Management Cycle.

The scientific-method analogy should now be a bit clearer. Performance management involves monitoring KPIs, which serve to measure whether an organization is meeting its objectives and overarching strategy. A KPI in this sense is a measure defined by a business that allows for observation of actual values, as they may emerge from LOB applications and their comparison to established targets (or budgeted values). If a KPI reveals an actual value that deviates too far from (or in many cases, closely approaches) a pre-defined target, then further analysis is warranted. Discoveries made during analysis should help us plan our next steps, set new (or adjust existing) expectations, and predict what may happen based on our decisions. Corporate culture has changed significantly over the last decade, and themes of transparency, accountability, and empowerment have emerged. Performance management builds on these notions by making all steps in the cycle (illustrated in Figure 1.1) occur at executive, departmental, and operational layers of the modern organization.

If you've made it this far, then there should be more than a few questions in your mind right now. If actual values can be found in LOB transaction data, then where do the target values come from? How exactly do we analyze further when a KPI actual value is too far away from (or too close to) its corresponding target value? How do we actually know when a KPI stands out at all? Back in science

Note:

Although this book uses the Balanced Scorecard method as a way to introduce you to performance management, bear in mind that there are other methods. The Six Sigma Business Scorecard, for example, emphasizes seven business perspectives, namely: *Leadership and Profitability, Management and Improvement, Employees and Innovation, Purchasing and Supplier Management, Operational Execution, Sales and Distribution,* **and** *Service and Growth.* **Praveen Gupta writes extensively on this subject in** *Six Sigma Business Scorecard: Creating a Comprehensive Corporate Performance Measurement System; ISBN: 0071417303.*

class we used different tools like beakers to collect raw data, an HB-1 pencil and notepad to record our observations, and used calculators (and erasers) to apply more elaborate formulae throughout our experiments to communicate our results. It turns out that there is a suite of tools to help us on the road to performance management—these tools belong to a specific IT competency known as *business intelligence (BI)*.

The Business Intelligence Foundation

Earlier in this chapter, we positioned performance management as a first-class business discipline, like Finance, Marketing, and Operations. Performance management is indeed a broad undertaking, which begins with monitoring KPIs that reflect activities from multiple business areas. In modern organizations, there are typical investments in information technology to support each of these areas. For example, Marketing and Sales efforts are often supported by CRM (customer relationship management) technologies, while Finance may be managed by ERP (enterprise resource planning) or other Accounting systems. Although Marketing, Sales, Finance and other areas managed to function before the emergence of such LOB systems, the benefits of using such software and systems are typically realized in terms of time-saving productivity, accessibility, and secure storage of business activities or events as data. One of the challenges faced in supporting a performance management initiative involves the consolidation of raw business data, stored within LOB systems from these disparate business areas. In order to achieve a broad insight into the current state of a business, data consolidation into a single, centralized repository is an important step in preventing multiple, conflicting interpretations of said data. Delivering a "single version of the truth" is the primary goal of any BI initiative, since the quality of business decision making can only be maximized from a single and consistent view of the business. Consider our intentions to monitor the *"Number of Quarterly <Your Target Customer Segment> Repeat Sales at Store #1"* KPI. Instead of manually cross-referencing customer demographic information in a CRM system to specific sales transactions in a POS (point of sale) terminal, it would be far more productive to first centrally store business data, via *extracts* from the distinct systems. Also, in situations where business transactions are volatile, it is actually counterproductive to query LOB systems directly, because this can cause such systems to perform in a less-than-optimal fashion.

The second challenge in exposing additional information for our KPI is that the source LOB systems almost always have their own rules for storing raw data that can be cryptic by most human standards. The ability to *transform* SKUs and CustomerIDs into readable product and customer information becomes essential to support further analysis of information for our KPI. Finally, to make such in-depth investigation as fast as possible, we may need to *load* readable business information into a location dedicated to "speed of thought" analysis (for those of you familiar with using spreadsheet tools, such as Microsoft Office Excel PivotTables and PivotCharts to quickly manipulate numbers, this is also known as "slicing and dicing")—both within a specific domain (customers or products), or across domains (revealing how specific customer and product information intersect).

BI Infrastructure Layer

The process of extracting raw business data, transforming it into a model of readable business information, and loading it in such a way where access to it is both fast and flexible, is referred to as *Extract, Transform, Load (ETL)*, and is the basis for the *infrastructure layer* for a BI system (see Figure 1.2).

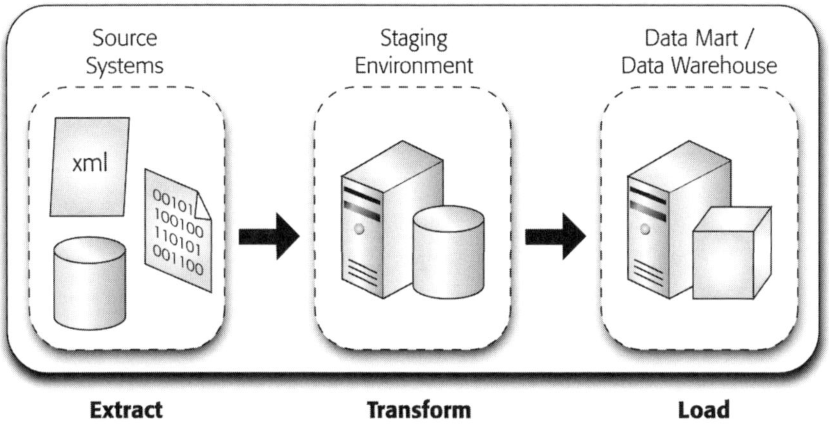

Figure 1.2: Basic ETL Process.

The other major facet to this layer is the actual storage mechanism, called a *data warehouse.* A data warehouse is an enterprise-wide database that stages LOB system data and stores human-ready business information. A data warehouse can be thought of as a collection of smaller *data marts* that store business information relevant to a specific domain or business area (like customer demographics or product sales, for example). Also, data marts and warehouses are typically modelled with end-user interaction in mind and store entities relevant to a business as *dimensions*. Data marts and data warehouses are able to deliver almost instant response times for large volumes of data because they store detailed historical records (*facts*) delineated by dimensions, with discrete *measures* (the dollar figures, percentages, and item counts a business is concerned with), as well as *aggregations* of those measures. Measures are of immense importance because they can be used to supply KPIs with *actual* and *target values.*

The storage of aggregations becomes increasingly important in enhancing query-response times because aggregations themselves reduce the effort in recalculating such rolled-up values. In most data marts and data warehouses, dimensions, measures, and their aggregations are stored in multi-dimensional structures known as *cubes*. In some cases, data marts and data warehouses store additional objects to support forecasting. These may include objects to calculate and store prediction data, generated by one or more algorithms that *mine* business information from the data mart/warehouse.

Note:

No discussion of data warehouses would be complete without mention of two major approaches to data warehouse design. Bill Inmon (*Building the Data Warehouse, 4th Edition; ISBN: 0764599445*) champions the approach of creating a normalized operational data store before flowing out into specific data marts for specific reporting needs. Ralph Kimball (*The Data Warehouse Toolkit: The Complete Guide to Dimensional Modeling, 2nd Edition; ISBN: 0471200247*) advocates an approach to denormalizing a data warehouse, building it in phases by integrating new business areas using pre-defined conformed dimensions. While there are several other emerging approaches that combine both schools of thought, the case study in this book uses a BI infrastructure based on the Kimball approach. Our choice for denormalization is taken solely because it suits the purposes of the case study—by no means are we suggesting that the Kimball method should *always* be endorsed over the Inmon approach.

BI Application Layer

Flexible and fast access to business information should offer a number of different ways to display it. A BI system often includes software for crafting production, analysis, or dashboard reports—such software can be considered the *application layer* of the BI platform. *Production reports* (Figure 1.3) display detailed, structured outputs (for example, work orders, sales summaries inventory counts, incident reports) for tactical decision making.

Analytical reports (Figure 1.4) allow us to interactively "slice and dice" business information, drill down to the structured details like those found in the production reports, and drill across business areas or domains.

Dashboard or management reports (Figure 1.5) are similar to the dashboard in a car or airplane. They serve as a heads-up display of KPIs for monitoring the state of the business.

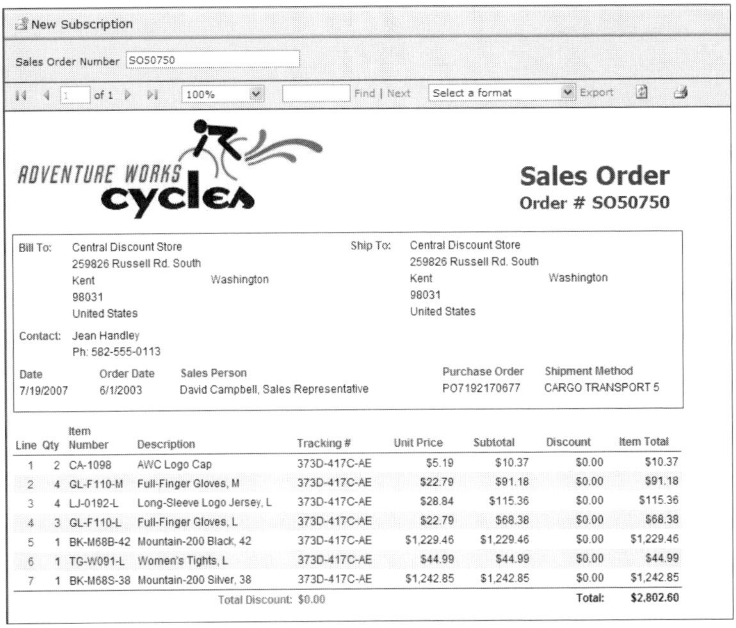

Figure 1.3: A Sample Production Report.

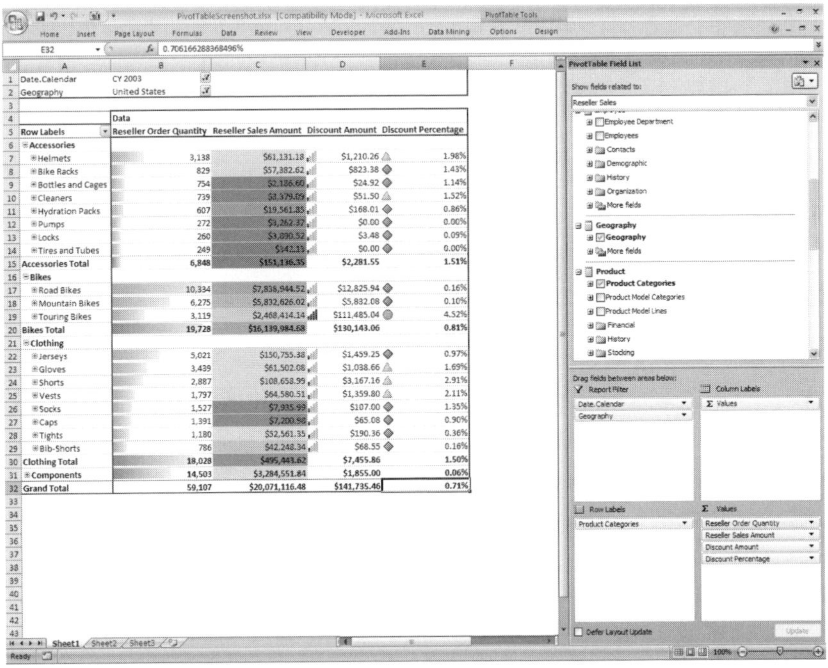

Figure 1.4: Sample Analytical Report.

Figure 1.5: Sample Dashboard Report.

The dashboard is an interesting interface because it can embed both analytical and production reports in a single place. Also, dashboards often expose another object, a *scorecard*, which exposes a hierarchy of perspectives, objectives, and KPIs. Furthermore, some dashboards use other data visualization tools such as *strategy maps* (showing how KPIs and objectives roll up into strategies and perspectives), *gauges* (which simulate the speedometer on the dashboard of a car), and other *charts and graphs*. Because of its flexible approach, a dashboard is a powerful and essential tool for performance management.

BI Delivery Layer

Modern organizations are increasingly using private intranets for sharing files and e-mail, and some extend their server and network assets by introducing a corporate portal. A *portal* is essentially an internal web site that allows its users to better collaborate and share knowledge on the documents that reflect their business processes. Portals are an excellent way to deliver the different types of reports from the BI application layer to the business users who need such reports to make decisions.

Key Terminology

Building on the scientific method analogy, BI could be considered the lab equipment for organizations. It follows that the dashboard itself becomes the key piece of lab equipment to monitor and analyze business conditions. The dashboard itself is central to the rest of this book; you will see in later chapters that PerformancePoint Server 2007 is used to create robust, interactive dashboard solutions. However, before moving on, it is important to become familiar with the terminology associated with dashboards. Although some of these terms have been already introduced earlier in this chapter, they are summarized in Table 1.1.

Term	Definition
Perspective	A major view of an organization. One or more business strategies may be aligned to a perspective. Kaplan and Norton's Balanced Scorecard method proposed four perspectives: financial, customer, internal business process, and learning and growth.
Strategy	Corporate strategies are often qualitative in nature, reflect the mission of the company, and are often subject to change as the business itself changes over time.
Objective	An objective supports a given corporate strategy, and expresses what a company would like to accomplish. Objectives, like strategies, may be adjusted over time.
Key Performance Indicator (KPI)	A measurement defined for a given objective, usually reflecting outcomes from specific business activities or transactions. KPIs are typically expressed in terms of *actual* values compared with *budgeted* or *target* values. With a BI Infrastructure in place, measures from a data warehouse/ data mart can be used to populate values in a corresponding KPI.
Scorecard	A dashboard element that exposes a hierarchy of perspectives, objectives, and KPIs, as part of a larger dashboard report or interface.
Dashboard	An interactive reporting interface that usually embeds a scorecard with other analytic or production reports, as well as other data visualization elements.

Table 1.1: Key Terminology.

Now that we have covered the basics of performance management and business intelligence, it is time to turn our attention PerformancePoint Server 2007 itself.

Overview of PerformancePoint Server 2007

PerformancePoint Server 2007 is a member of the Office 2007 system of products, and is positioned as a complete performance management application. Altogether, PPS 2007 enables users to:

- *monitor* progress of KPIs, articulated as key drivers or goals of their business
- *analyze* information behind the KPIs using a number of approaches
- *plan, budget,* and *forecast* in a dynamic fashion with business modelling tools

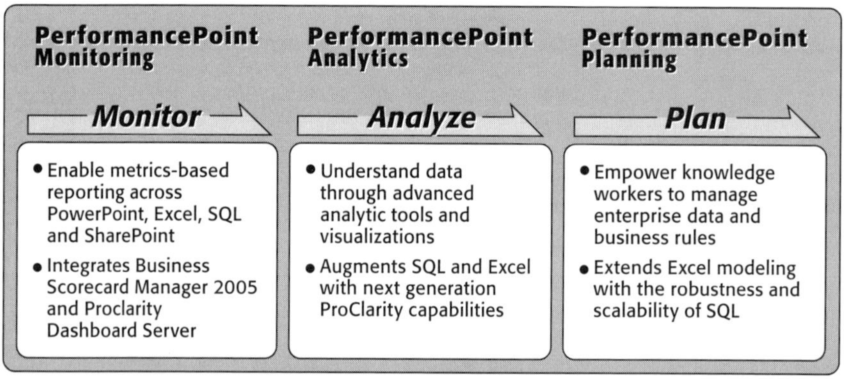

Figure 1.6: PerformancePoint Server 2007 Key Functions (Adapted with permission from Microsoft).

Figure 1.6 illustrates the *Monitoring, Analytics, and Planning* capabilities within PPS 2007. *Monitoring* builds on scorecard development and management tools found in Microsoft Office Business Scorecard Manager 2005, while the *Analytics* area integrates powerful data visualization and exploration technology from ProClarity, a company that Microsoft acquired in 2006 (`www.microsoft.com/bi/products/ProClarity`). *Planning* tools and technologies in PPS 2007 are entirely new, helping you to model scenarios to test business hypotheses and evaluate various outcomes as a part of typical financial processes during a budgeting cycle.

Moreover, new targets established with PPS 2007 Planning may be reintegrated into scorecard-centric dashboards, thereby closing the performance management cycle of continuous business improvement. Hopefully, the "scientific-method for business" analogy should be coming back to you right about now.

> **Note:**
>
> **This book is dedicated to bringing you up to speed on Monitoring and Analytics in PPS 2007. Although each of these functional areas is split in Figure 1.6, all references to Monitoring and Analytics will be simplified to** *Monitoring* **for the purposes of this book. For more information on PPS 2007 Planning, please refer to** *The Rational Guide to Planning with Microsoft® Office PerformancePoint Server 2007,* **available from** `www.rationalpress.com`.

PPS 2007 has a number of functional synergies with other Microsoft products. This is not by accident. Microsoft has a long history of ensuring that its products work well together, particularly within specific technical areas of depth. The next section of this chapter describes two other products in the Microsoft BI ecosystem, and illustrates how PPS 2007 fits in.

The Microsoft Business Intelligence Stack

In the case of BI-focused technologies, PPS 2007 can be considered an *Application* layer of an overall BI solution. PPS 2007 fits strategically between Microsoft SQL Server 2005 (the *Platform* or *Foundation* layer), and Microsoft SharePoint Products and Technologies (the *Delivery* layer), as shown in Figure 1.7.

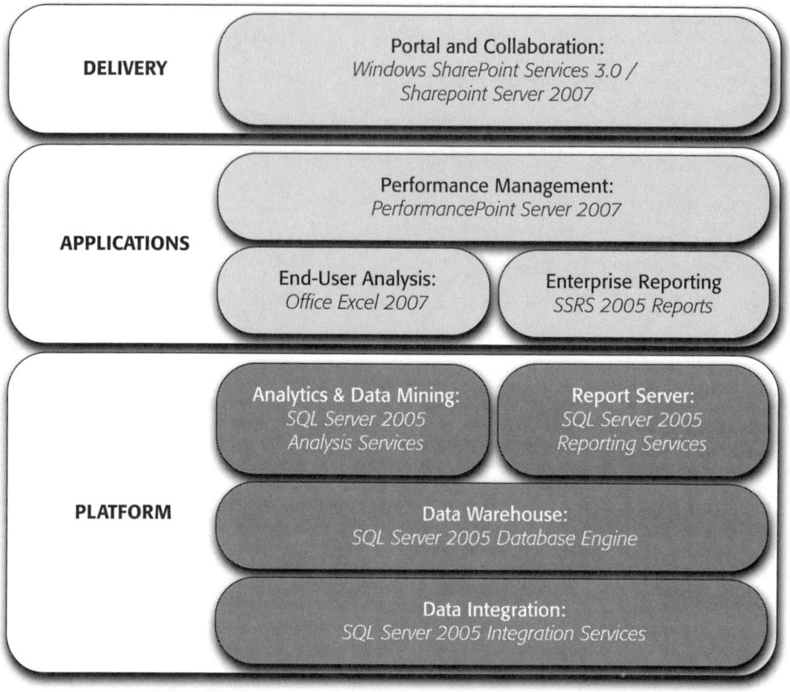

Figure 1.7: Current Microsoft BI Technology Stack.

Microsoft SQL Server 2005

SQL Server 2005 is an enterprise class database management system that bundles a number of BI-intensive services, specifically:

- SQL Server 2005 Integration Services (SSIS)
- SQL Server 2005 Analysis Services (SSAS)
- SQL Server 2005 Reporting Services (SSRS)

While an in-depth discussion of SQL Server 2005 is beyond the scope of this book, it is still important to understand the role it plays in the bigger picture. Table 1.2 describes the services in more detail.

Component	Description
SSIS	A powerful and robust tool set designed to integrate data from a variety of sources (databases, applications and web services). In the BI context, SSIS provides the data pipeline between Line-of-Business (LOB) systems and the OLAP database (data warehouse or data mart).
SSAS	SSAS serves prominently as the mechanism to make an OLAP database, which typically stores facts and dimensions in tables, highly accessible through cubes. SSAS also provides additional data mining algorithms and mining models that store results of predictive analyses against data stored in cubes and relational tables. Finally, SSAS exposes MDX, which is a special query language used to navigate cubes and define custom measurements based (typically) on time intervals.
SSRS	SSRS is the service that enables the creation of Web-accessible reports, which can be delivered to designated users either through a self-service approach or via data-driven subscriptions. In SQL Server 2005, SSRS introduces an additional tool named Report Builder, which empowers less-technically inclined users to craft reports visually against a predefined metadata abstraction called a Report Model.

Table 1.2: SQL Server 2005 Services.

The key point to note here is that SQL Server 2005 fulfills four roles in the BI stack:

- A raw LOB data refinery
- A reporting mechanism
- A centralized data source for dashboards created in PPS 2007
- A metadata store for PPS 2007

Microsoft SharePoint Products and Technologies

Microsoft SharePoint Products and Technologies are web portal technologies used to retrieve and display information critical to collaborative performance management.

Microsoft SharePoint Products and Technologies include:

- **Windows SharePoint Services Version 3.0 (WSS 3.0)** — WSS is a free add-on for Windows Server 2003 that serves as a platform for creating web pages geared for content management and collaboration. Using an assemble-and-configure paradigm, WSS exposes a variety of ASP.NET-based web parts that act as building blocks for creating both corporate intranets as well as Internet-accessible web sites.

- **Microsoft Office SharePoint Server 2007 (MOSS 2007)** — MOSS 2007 builds on WSS with additional functionality for user-personalization, content classifications, searches, and audience targeting.

PPS 2007 Monitoring ships with custom web parts to deliver the final product to users.

> *Note:*
>
> **In keeping with the ongoing theme of simplicity, this book focuses on WSS only for delivery of the dashboard that we will begin to develop in Part III. Registered Web Parts apply both to WSS 3.0 and MOSS 2007. All mention of *SharePoint* in this book, unless otherwise stated, refers to WSS 3.0.**

Excel 2007

"Most BI data eventually ends up in Excel" is not just something people say, it's true. One of the first questions people ask when evaluating a product is "can I export this to Excel?" Microsoft has acknowledged the community's use of Excel by creating a very BI-focused version of the product. Among the many improvements are a redesigned charting engine, enhanced pivot tables, and advanced visualization capabilities. An Analysis Services data mining add-in further underscores Microsoft's strategy of "BI for the masses." Because of its expanded capabilities and power, Excel is the thick-client delivery platform for Microsoft BI and BPM data.

From the smallest garage-based business to multinational corporations, Excel is the de facto standard application for creating and managing budget and forecast data; it is for these reasons that PPS 2007 Planning uses Excel as a key end-user application.

Summary

The first part of this chapter introduced performance management as a business discipline that sets out to establish and execute business strategy by defining objectives, monitoring KPIs, analyzing business information, and making decisions. A number of performance management approaches are used in organizations today, such as the Balanced Scorecard and Six Sigma Business Scorecard methods. A business intelligence platform is a solid way to set the foundations for performance management, by centralizing and consolidating raw line-of-business data, and expressing important measures as KPI actual values. Dashboards, an output of a BI platform, are often displayed on corporate portals and are used to help all levels of an organization to interactively view current performance, as well as collaborate and act on certain areas in exception. The second part of this chapter briefly introduced you to PPS 2007, its high-level purpose, and how it fits in with SQL Server 2005 and SharePoint Products and Technologies.

The journey continues in Chapter 2 with a closer look at PPS 2007 Monitoring.

Did you know?

The art and science of performance management has many incarnations, spanning well over 100 years of industrialization and automation—arguably starting with the formal positioning of Scientific Management (1911), which reflects the ideas and concepts of Frederick Taylor (1856 - 1915). Taylor built on earlier companies-as-machines metaphors, and introduced time-and-motion studies that attempt to uncover optimal performance in work processes (both human and early machines).

Chapter 2

Introducing PerformancePoint Server Monitoring

Everyone wants dashboards! PPS 2007 Monitoring makes designing, publishing, and managing dashboards simple and the resultant solution very powerful. From this chapter onwards, we will look at all aspects of the Monitor and Analyze (M&A) part of the Monitor, Analyze, Plan paradigm introduced Chapter 1. We will simply refer to it as *Monitoring* throughout the remainder of the book. Don't worry, though, we will cover both the Monitor and Analyze parts in plenty of detail.

This chapter briefly looks at the history of applications that have contributed to where we currently find ourselves in the Microsoft performance management roadmap. We also take a high-level look at the Monitoring architecture and just what pieces are necessary to produce the dashboard solutions end users really want.

PerformancePoint Planning

The Planning component of PerformancePoint Server 2007 is not covered in this book. Originally, we were going to write a single Rational Guide covering the Monitor, Analyze, and Plan paradigm in one publication, but there was simply too much to cram into one guide. So we wrote a companion book, *The Rational Guide to Planning with Microsoft® Office PerformancePoint Server 2007*, available from `www.rationalpress.com`. Each book provides specific details about its particular aspect of the PPS product. Wherever possible, we'll note how the two halves of the product can interact.

Monitoring History

The Monitoring part of PerformancePoint is very definitely *not* a v1 product, as many would think. The software discussed in this Rational Guide is the end product of quite a few years of evolution, integration, and development.

While there were certainly many smaller steps along the way, the major punctuation marks in the lead up to the product we are writing about are summarized in Figure 2.1.

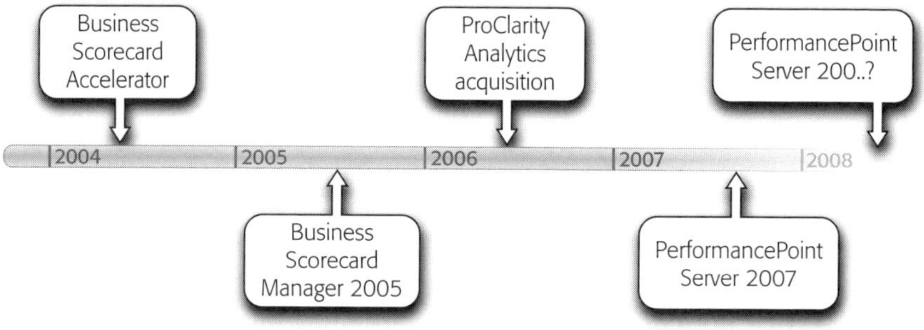

Figure 2.1: Microsoft Office Performance Management Software Timeline.

In 2004, Microsoft released the *Business Scorecard Accelerator*. This was a completely SharePoint Portal-based solution for creating KPIs and grouping them underneath specifically defined objectives and perspectives in a scorecard.

In the second half of 2005, *Business Scorecard Manager 2005* (originally codenamed Maestro) was released. BSM provided much enhanced functionality in creating scorecard-centric dashboards, complete with interactive reports. BSM used the base SharePoint product included with Windows Server 2003 licenses as the delivery mechanism; reliance on the SharePoint Portal Server product was removed. BSM shipped with a development and management application named BSM Builder to create KPIs and scorecards and manage the central web service.

In April 2006, Microsoft acquired *ProClarity*, one of the world leaders in analytic and visualization technologies, an area where Microsoft found itself a bit behind. The BSM team in Redmond were already hard at work on the next version of BSM, codenamed Concerto. The dashboarding and analytical technology acquired from ProClarity was to be merged with this new version. At the same time, another team was working on a completely new budgeting and forecasting tool codenamed Biz# (pronounced Biz Sharp). There was some speculation as to just how many specific products would result from all this. In mid-2006, it was announced that the next version of BSM (Monitor), the acquired technology from ProClarity (Analyze), and the fruits of the Biz# team's labor (Plan) would become *PerformancePoint Server 2007*.

Note:

The integration of the next version of BSM and ProClarity technology was a prime objective of the two teams: Microsoft in Redmond and ProClarity in Boise, Idaho. The current functionality of Monitoring does not yet encompass the full breadth of the ProClarity toolset. However, a PerformancePoint license does extend to the full ProClarity suite, so while they may not be an integrated part of the product itself, decomposition trees, performance maps, or perspective views can still be surfaced in dashboards using the ProClarity server products. Subsequent versions of PerformancePoint will incorporate more of the ProClarity features into the base product, along with a few new ones.

Architecture

The architecture of Monitoring is really quite simple. It is centered around the Monitoring server web service as seen in the simplified architecture diagram in Figure 2.2. Dashboard Designer (DD) is the primary design tool and management interface to the Monitoring server web service. DD is used to build and publish XML definitions of elements to the web service; these XML definitions are stored in a SQL database managed by the Monitoring server. When users interact with published dashboards, SharePoint 2007 retrieves element definition and security information from the Monitoring system database, queries data from configured business data sources, and then exposes the finished product to users using custom Dashboard web parts.

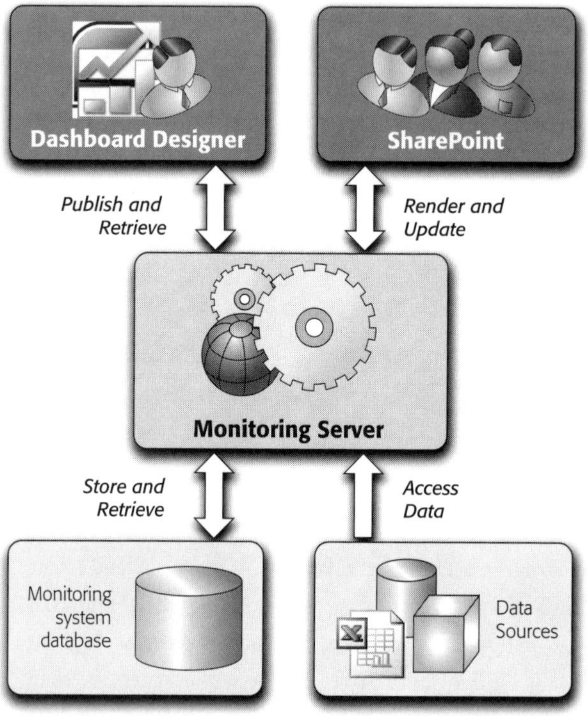

Figure 2.2: Simplified Monitoring Architecture.

Components

A number of different components make up the Monitoring server installation. Depending on the desired architecture, these components can be installed on any machine that meets the minimum requirements. We will go through the installation process and hardware and software requirements in the next chapter. In the meantime, the more fleshed out architecture diagram in Figure 2.3 shows more detail on where each component fits within a complete Monitoring server.

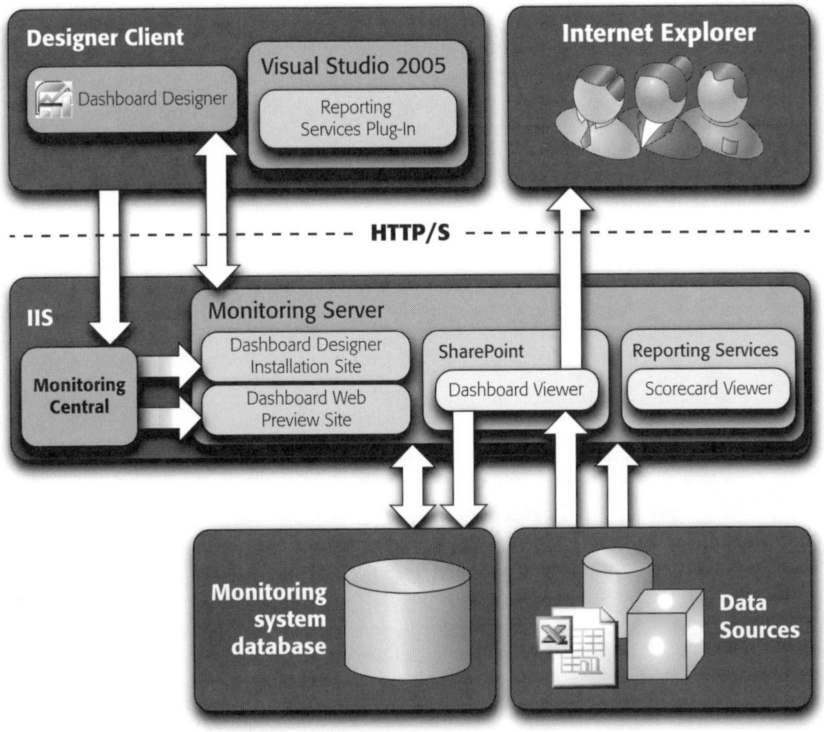

Figure 2.3: Monitoring Component Architecture.

Let's review the components.

- **Dashboard Designer** — Primary application for building out element definitions and management interface to the Monitoring server.

- **Monitoring Server** — The central engine that controls all Monitoring processes; manages element definitions published through Dashboard Designer in the Monitoring Database, surfaces dashboards through SharePoint web parts.

- **Monitoring System Database** — A SQL Server 2005 relational database used to store and manage element definitions.

- **Dashboard Viewer for SharePoint Services** — Facilitates deployment and viewing of completed dashboard content through SharePoint. Custom web parts render individual items contained in published dashboard pages.

- **Monitoring Central** — A launch pad site that is created on any machine is running a Monitoring server web service. The site contains links to the local Dashboard Designer installation site as well as the Dashboard Designer preview site (see Figure 2.4).

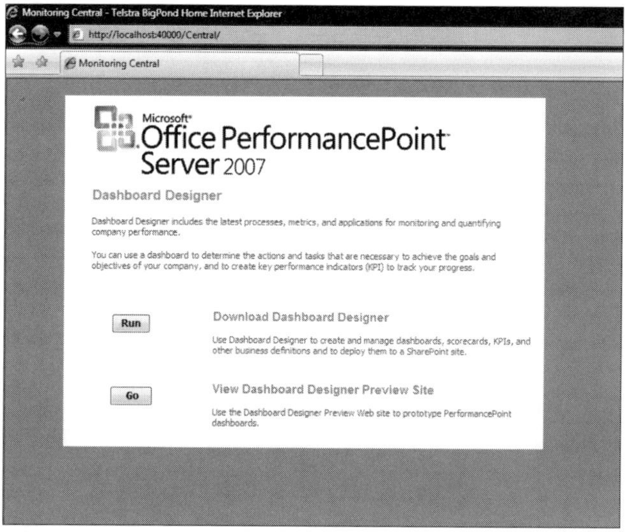

Figure 2.4: Monitoring Central Site.

- **Dashboard Designer Installation Site** — Site from which Dashboard Designer can be installed using ClickOnce technology.

- **Dashboard Web Preview Site** — ASP.NET preview site used to emulate the dashboard viewer functionality. This site enables designers to test the functionality of their dashboards without the need for a complete SharePoint installation.

- **Scorecard Viewer for Reporting Services** — Data extension that enables Reporting Services to generate and render Report Definition Language (.rdl) files based on the definition of a scorecard.

- **Reporting Services Plug-in (VS2005)** — Data extension that allows developers to view generated scorecard .rdl files in Visual Studio 2005 using the Report Designer plug-in.

Elements

Elements are the essential building blocks of Monitoring. They are created using Dashboard Designer and subsequently published to the Monitoring server. Each element plays an important role in a complete performance management solution. There are six elements in total: *indicators, data sources, KPIs, scorecards, reports,* and *dashboards*. Many of the six elements depend on definitions of another element type in order to be complete. These relationships form a simple hierarchy that can be seen in Figure 2.5.

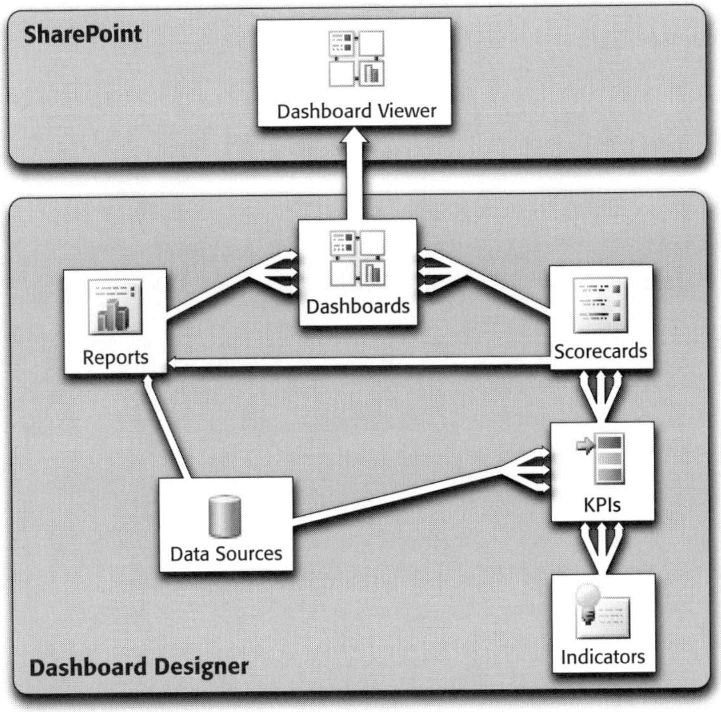

Figure 2.5: Element Hierarchy.

Let's look at each of the elements.

- **Data Sources** — Contain connection settings that are used to gain access to various types of structured data. KPIs and reports utilize this element to access the data they require.
- **Indicators** — Provide visual prompts pertaining to the status of a particular KPI. They use differing graphics, background colors, or text settings to convey their message.
- **KPIs (Key Performance Indicators)** — Bring metrics together from one or more data sources in order for comparisons or calculations to be made. These elements utilize more than one data source element and more than one indicator element as part of their definition.
- **Scorecards** — Collections of one or more KPIs organized hierarchically under a series of zero or more objectives or grouped by members of a dimension. Scorecards provide the mechanism for both grouping and rolling up the values contained in their constituent KPIs.
- **Reports** — Expose business data in a number of different formats in order to suit requirements. There are many report type options available, ranging from Analytic Grids or Charts to SQL Reporting Services reports. Some report types connect to data using a data source element; others use data from a scorecard or a connection defined within the report itself.
- **Dashboards** — Bring all the elements together by exposing the data contained in scorecard and report elements. They are the delivery mechanism to the end user in SharePoint via the Dashboard Item web part. Dashboards contain all the logic used to control what the user sees, and how they can interact with the elements contained therein.

Multidimensional is Best

Those who have been working in the BI industry for some time do not need convincing that multidimensional analysis of data is by far the fastest, most powerful, and flexible method. The ability to query numeric facts aggregated across many dimensions has been the backbone of many of the world's best BI implementations. PPS Monitoring thrives on multidimensional data through its support of Microsoft Analysis Services databases. It should come as no surprise that PerformancePoint Planning also puts the Analysis Services engine to good use. The examples in this book are primarily focused on multidimensional data sourced from Analysis Services 2005 cubes.

As we will see in the coming chapters, Monitoring also supports access of information from many other structured data sources, it even enables tabular data to be converted on the fly into pseudo multidimensional structures. The ability to dynamically convert 'flat' data into a cube, while powerful and convenient, serves as an enticement of what is possible in the multidimensional world. Tabular sources are great for prototyping and capturing data from an unstructured system, but they have limitations that AS doesn't have (such as scale issues). If data in your enterprise is to be effective in driving a PM solution, then as much of it as possible should be contained in fully-fledged multidimensional databases instead of relying PerformancePoint to do it for you. While it may not be possible for *everything* to end up in a cube, enterprises should strive to get as much of the data as they can into multidimensional structures.

A working knowledge of Analysis Services 2005 is assumed throughout the course of this book. Deep knowledge and experience with Multidimensional eXpressions (MDX) is certainly a bonus but is not absolutely necessary. Some people are a little apprehensive when it comes to MDX and may not wish to spend time getting to know its potential. We hope that once you have completed this book, there will be little doubt as to the power and extra functionality MDX can bring to the table.

Summary

In this chapter we have learned a bit of the history behind PerformancePoint Server. Monitoring combines the strengths of what could otherwise be considered the next versions of Business Scorecard Manager and ProClarity analytics into one product. We saw a high level view of the various components that make up a complete Monitoring installation. Six elements form the building blocks of Monitoring solutions: data sources, indicators, KPIs, scorecards, reports, and dashboards. These elements are built, published, and managed using the PerformancePoint Dashboard Designer application. Dashboard Designer is also used to perform Dashboard Server administration.

Part II

Installation and Configuration

RATIONAL PRESS™

Chapter 3

Installation and Configuration

Monitoring configuration and installation has been designed so that all its constituent components can be installed on a single server or alternately to a number of different machines in a scale out scenario. For the purposes of this book, we will simply install all components on one machine.

There are two parts to a Monitoring installation:

1. Installing the Monitoring server.
2. Running the Monitoring Server Configuration Manager to configure the required Monitoring server components.

The Monitoring Server Configuration Manager enables the setup of two different kinds of installation: standalone and custom. Let's discuss both of these options briefly.

Standalone Installation

If you are planning to follow all the examples in this book, you will want a standalone setup. As the name suggests, all the constituent components are installed on one server that already meets the prerequisite SQL Server, SharePoint, and IIS requirements detailed in the next couple of pages.

Standalone Designer

If the Monitoring Server Configuration Manager is run on a Windows XP or Vista machine, it will set up a standalone design environment that encompasses all the functionality of a standalone server installation. This is the most useful configuration from a pure design and test perspective. Once set up, you can then build out, preview, and test a complete data-bound dashboard solution without the need to be connected to any other server. This kind of disconnected development environment was simply not possible with Business Scorecard Manager and is a very welcome feature. The only functionality that is not available in this configuration is the deployment of dashboards to a local SharePoint server. As we all know, SharePoint cannot be loaded on XP or Vista. As we will learn in the coming chapters, the Dashboard Designer application has built-in functionality to preview scorecards. Coupled with the existence of the ASP.NET preview web site for dashboards, this negates the need to have a connected SharePoint server available to test the fruits of your labor; it can all be done locally.

Distributed Installation

The different components that make up a complete installation can be installed on different servers to suit a scale out scenario. For example, the Monitoring server database would be installed on a dedicated SQL Server machine, the Monitoring web service and Dashboard Designer installation site on a dedicated web server and so forth.

Prerequisites

As usual there are several hardware and software prerequisites that need to be covered.

Hardware

The hardware requirements are pretty standard, as detailed in Table 3.1

Hardware	Description
CPU	Intel Pentium 4, 2.5Ghz
RAM	1GB
Disk Space	2GB

Table 3.1: Monitoring Server Minimum Hardware Requirements.

Software

Depending on whether you are performing a server install or a standalone on XP or Vista, you will need one of these three operating systems:

- Windows Server® 2003 with Service Pack 1 (SP1), Standard Edition
- Microsoft Windows® XP Professional with Service Pack 2 (SP2)
- Microsoft Windows® Vista

Table 3.2 details the software requirements of each part of the Monitoring server. The items listed in the table can look a little daunting. Don't worry, though—if your machine already has the SQL Server 2005 suite and SharePoint installed and running, you can pretty much cross off all the items listed. The only item that may need to be installed manually is the ASP.NET 2.0 AJAX Extensions 1.0, which can be downloaded from Microsoft's official AJAX site: `http://asp.net/ajax/`. Either way, the Monitoring configuration wizard will figure out what you don't have and promptly let you know.

Prerequisite	Required for installing
• SQL Server 2005 Standard or Enterprise Edition (SP2)	• Monitoring Server System Database
• Windows SharePoint Services 3.0 (WSS) or Microsoft Office SharePoint Server 2007 (MOSS)	• Dashboard Viewer Web Part
• Internet Information Services 6.0 • Microsoft ASP.NET 2.0 • Microsoft .NET Framework 2.0.50727 • IIS 6.0 Isolation Mode • Microsoft ASP.NET 2.0 Registration with IIS • ASP.NET 2.0 Web Service Extension in IIS	• Monitoring Server • Dashboard Designer Installation site • Dashboard Web Preview Site
• SQL Server Native Client 9.0 • ADOMD.NET	• Monitoring Server System • Database Monitoring Server • Dashboard Web Preview site

Table 3.2: Monitoring Server Software Requirements.

Prerequisite	Required for installing
• ASP.NET 2.0 AJAX Extensions1.0	• Monitoring Server • Dashboard Web Preview • Dashboard Viewer Web Part
• Microsoft SQL Server 2005 Reporting Services	• Monitoring Plug-in for Reporting Services
• Visual Studio 2005	• Monitoring Plug-in for Report Designer

Table 3.2: Monitoring Server Software Requirements (continued).

Tech Tip:

Monitoring only requires SQL Server 2005 Standard Edition. If you are going to install PPS Planning, you *will* need SQL Server 2005 Enterprise Edition. Planning uses cube writeback functionality, which is a feature of Analysis Services 2005 Enterprise Edition.

Note:

If you wish to follow every single example in this book, a configured SharePoint server installation is essential. However, a great deal of this book's content is centered around using DD to build, publish, and manage Monitoring elements. If you set up a Standalone Designer environment on your XP or Vista machine, you will be able to follow the majority of the book's step-by-step exercises; only the few that specifically require SharePoint will be unavailable to you. For some people, this may be a much more convenient option.

Other Requirements for this Book

To successfully complete all examples in this book, please ensure that you have also installed the following components:

- Microsoft Office Excel 2007
- Microsoft Office PowerPoint 2007
- Microsoft Office Visio 2007
- SQL Server Analysis Services 2005 (SP2)
- Office 2003 Web Components (OWC)

Installing the Monitoring Server

Now that we have a little more perspective on the overall architecture and requirements of Monitoring, we'll go ahead and install and configure it. The initial setup process installs the Monitoring Server Configuration Manager and copies the required files to the machine. Once this initial setup is complete, the configuration manager is run in accordance with the role in the performance management architecture that a particular machine is to play. In this case, we will perform a standalone server install.

Follow these steps to install the Monitoring Server Configuration Manager software on your machine:

1. Double-click the **Setup.hta** file, which will launch the PerformancePoint Server 2007 splash screen.
2. Under the **Monitoring** heading, click the **Install Monitoring Server** link (shown in Figure 3.1).
3. Accept the EULA. Click **Next**.
4. Accept the default installation directory. Click **Next**.
5. Click **Install**.
6. Make sure the **Run the Monitoring Server Configuration Manager Wizard** check box is checked and click **Finish**.

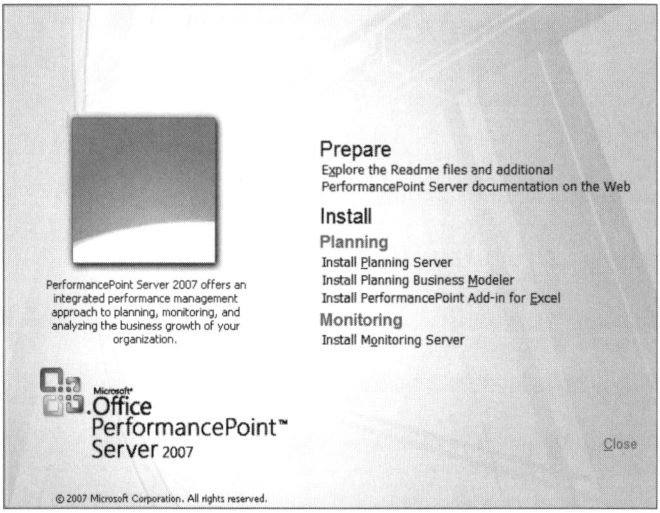

Figure 3.1: Installation Splash Screen.

Configuring the Monitoring Server

With the Monitoring server now installed, we can now run configuration manager to set up our Monitoring server. If you forgot to select the check box in the last installation step of the exercise, don't worry—you can launch the configuration manager by clicking **Start ⇨ All Programs ⇨ Microsoft Office PerformancePoint Server 2007 ⇨ Monitoring Server Configuration Manager**.

Follow these steps to complete the setup of the Monitoring server:

1. On the **Welcome** screen, click **Next**.

2. On the **Prerequisites** screen, ensure all is green; if so, click **Next**. You may see a yellow warning next to the ASP.NET AJAX extensions item if you have not installed them. If this is the case, exit the configuration manager and make sure you download and install the required bits. When you're done, run this exercise again.

Note:

If you wish to install a Standalone Designer environment on your XP or Vista machine, the MOSS/WSS prerequisite will be flagged with a yellow warning. Not to worry, though. As mentioned earlier, SharePoint is not required for an install of this kind.

3. On the **Installation Options** step, select the **Standalone configuration** radio button (Figure 3.2). Click **Next**.

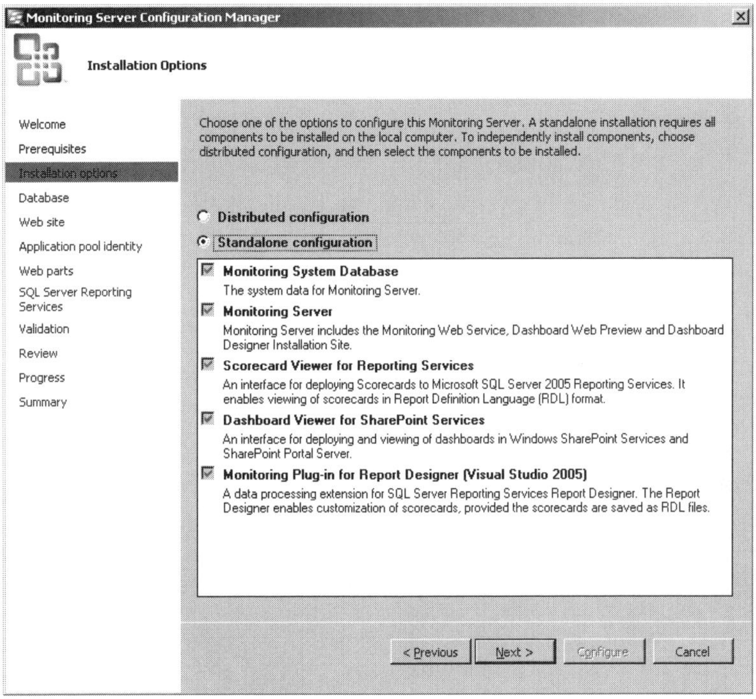

Figure 3.2: Installation Options Step.

4. In the SQL Server location combo box, type in (or select) the name of the SQL Server instance where the Monitoring system database will be created. Leave the default database name of PPSMonitoring. Click **Next**.

5. Uncheck the **Require SSL Connections to Monitoring Web Site** option. Accept the default **TCP Port** and **IP Address** settings. Click **Next**.

6. On the **Application Pool Identity** step, accept the **Predefined (NETWORK SERVICE)** option. Click **Next**.

> *Caution:*
>
> **It is strongly recommended to use a domain account for the Service Account as well as SSL connections to the Monitoring site. For simplicity, we are using the default NETWORK SERVICE account and bypassing SSL.**

7. On the **Web Parts** step, enter the URL to the SharePoint site collection that you wish to install to. Naturally, this URL will depend on the way SharePoint was set up. On a vanilla WSS installation this would be `http://<servername>/`. Click **Next**.

8. Select the SQL Reporting Services Reporting Server instance on which the Monitoring plug-in will be installed. On a default installation this will be MSSQLSERVER. Click **Next**.

9. Ensure that all checks on the **Validation** screen are green (see Figure 3.3). Click **Next**.

10. On the **Review** step, click **Configure** to install.

11. When all is complete, click **Close**.

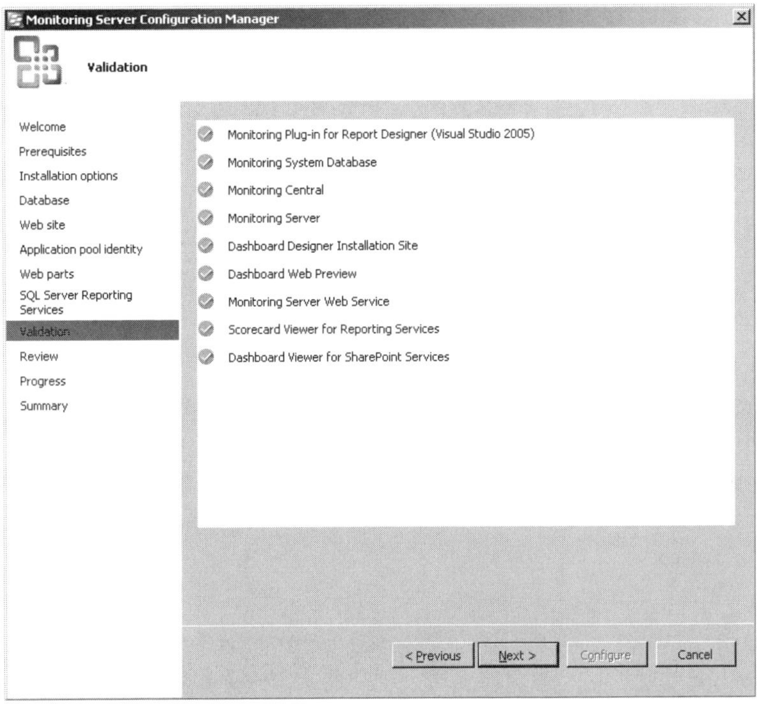

Figure 3.3: Final Validation Checks.

Note:

Aside from setting up the usual help documentation, the Monitoring installation and configuration process creates links to the home pages of MSDN, Office Online, and Technet sites. The links are found under Start ⇨ All Programs ⇨ Microsoft Office PerformancePoint Server 2007. These will be the sites where product documentation updates, whitepapers, and other valuable information will be made available. Both the PerformancePoint Server 2007 Planning and Architecture Guide and the PerformancePoint Server 2007 Deployment Guide can be found on the Technet site. Please refer to both guides for more detailed information on Monitoring (and Planning) deployments of varying kinds.

Sample Database

The majority of demonstration material in this book is based on multidimensional (OLAP) data. As discussed in the previous chapter, multidimensional data is the way to go when it comes to really making use of Monitoring's feature set.

The sample database used for the examples in this book is a customized version of the AdventureWorksDW multidimensional database named AdventureWorksPPS. The Analysis Services project for AdventureWorksPPS can be downloaded with the book's bonus material.

Naturally, you will need to have access to a copy of the AdventureWorksDW relational database in order to successfully process the AdventureWorksPPS OLAP database. If you have not already installed the AdventureWorksDW relational database, this can be achieved by using the SQL Server 2005 setup application.

> **Tech Tip:**
> **All SQL Server 2005 sample databases and applications can be downloaded from** `http://www.codeplex.com`.

Summary

This chapter covered the installation details for a Monitoring server. The hardware and software requirements were detailed, along with information on the different ways in which a Monitoring server (or parts thereof) can be installed. We installed and configured a Monitoring server instance using the Monitoring Server Configuration Manager.

Now that we have gone through the necessary steps for installing and configuring a Monitoring server and ensured that we have all other prerequisite bits, it is time to step into the wide blue yonder of PerformancePoint Server Monitoring. Onward!

Chapter 4

Introducing Dashboard Designer

In order to provide dashboards, reports, and scorecards to end users, these elements and the elements that make them up must be built. Then they need to be published to a Monitoring server, which may also need attention from time to time. Virtually all design and management tasks for Monitoring are performed using a Windows Forms application named *Microsoft Office PerformancePoint Dashboard Designer* (DD). Using DD, we are able to:

- Create new elements from scratch
- Publish to or delete elements from a Monitoring server
- Alter elements already published to a Monitoring server
- Manage element security, versions and metadata
- Manage Monitoring server settings and security

Technically, DD is a member of the Office 2007 family, but it is not an application you will see on a great many desktops around the enterprise alongside Office stalwarts like Excel, Word, and PowerPoint. Nonetheless, DD should not be viewed as a tool reserved only for use by developers—quite the opposite, in fact. Other BI tools in the Microsoft stack such as Integration, Analysis, and Reporting Services have their primary development environment integrated into Visual Studio by means of customized snap-ins. While the more technically-savvy power users will use DD, this application has no ties to Visual Studio. DD's place in the Office family has a purpose: to provide a familiar, unintimidating environment to those who are not hardcore developers in which to design and manage the components that make up a performance management solution.

Installing and Launching

DD is a ClickOnce application, which enables it to be installed and run from a web page. The Monitoring Central web page that was created as part of the installation contains a link to the *Dashboard Designer Installation Site*. Like all ClickOnce applications, after DD has been installed on a machine, subsequent initialization of the application triggers a call to the server to check for newer versions. If updates are available, they will be downloaded and applied.

> **Tech Tip:**
> **There are a number of configuration options available to administrators for controlling the specific behavior of ClickOnce applications. For more information, refer to** `http://msdn2.microsoft.com/en-us/vbasic/ms789088.aspx`.

Follow these steps to launch DD for the first time from the Monitoring Central site:

1. Open Internet Explorer and browse to `http://<servername>:40000/Central/`. This will be the link that can be sent to DD users in order to get set up initially.

2. Click the **Run** button or click the **Download Dashboard Designer** link. The ClickOnce technology will check to see whether the application is already installed.

3. Click **Run** when prompted by the **Security Warning** dialog. The necessary files will be downloaded and DD will launch.

The first time the installation is run, a **Start** menu item is added on the user's machine at **Start ⇨ All Programs ⇨ Microsoft Office PerformancePoint**

Server 2007 ⇨ **Dashboard Designer** for subsequent use. Regardless of whether DD is launched from the browser or the **Start** menu, a check for the latest updates will be made to the server from which DD was last launched.

Tech Tip:

Because it is a ClickOnce application, DD allows users to add or remove file associations and Start menu items associated with the program. This setting can be adjusted in the DD options dialog by clicking either the Add File Associations or Reset File Associations buttons.

User Interface

DD has a three-paned user interface as shown in Figure 4.1. The three panes from left to right are the *workspace browser*, *workspace pane* and the *details browser*. All the functionality provided by the application is within easy reach, thanks to the new Office 2007 *ribbon* interface.

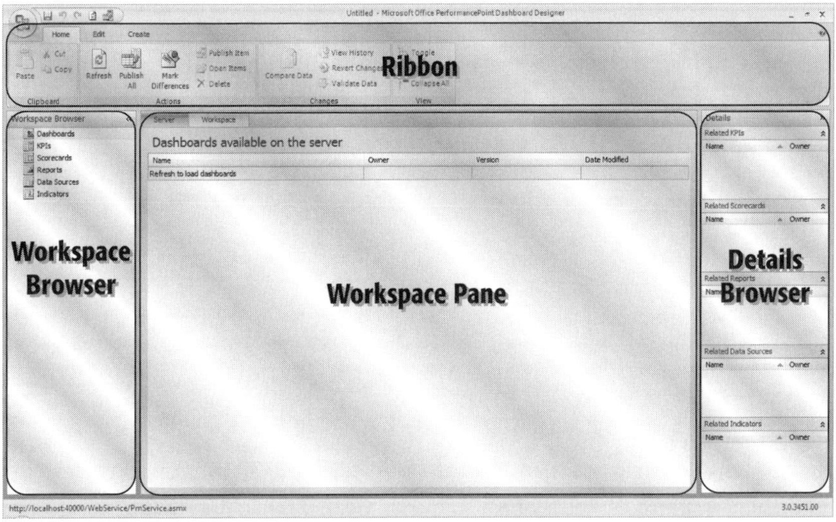

Figure 4.1: Three-paned User Interface.

Workspace Browser

The workspace browser displays a hierarchically organized list of the six element types defined in an open workspace under correspondingly named parent nodes. The elements can be further grouped into folders underneath these parent nodes. Selecting a parent node, folder, or individual element in the workspace browser hierarchy will expose specific user interfaces and metadata in both the workspace pane and details pane.

Workspace Pane

A different user interface is displayed in the workspace pane depending on the level or the element type selected in the workspace browser hierarchy. Selecting an individual element at the bottom (leaf) of the hierarchy will bring up the design UI in the workspace pane, allowing creation and configuration of properties for that element. Figure 4.2 shows a selected KPI element in the workspace browser and the corresponding user interface in the workspace pane.

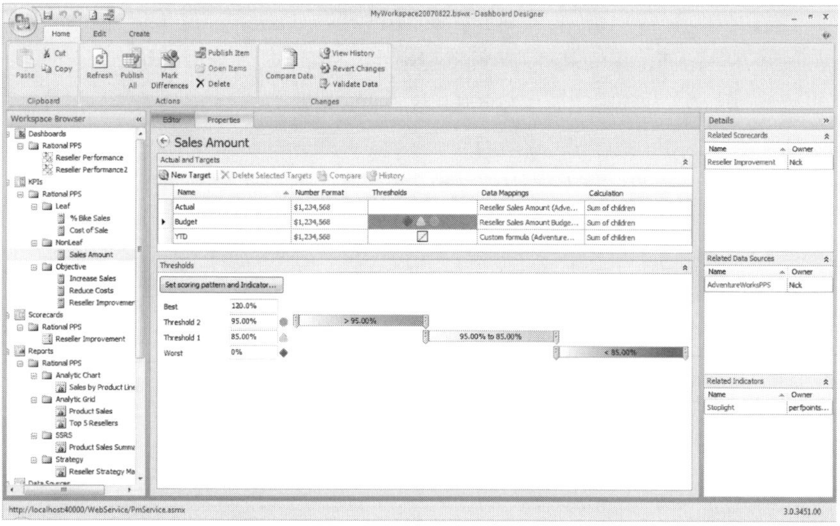

Figure 4.2: A KPI Workspace Pane User Interface.

Selecting any folder or element root node in the workspace browser hierarchy will display a summary view of all elements located beneath it in the workspace pane. In summary view for an element root node, the workspace pane is tabbed so the view can be switched from either the elements in the open workspace or those published to the server to which DD is currently connected by selecting the corresponding **Workspace** or **Server** tab (see Figure 4.3). This shows how DD facilitates easy interaction with both elements in the open workspace or published to the server within one simple interface.

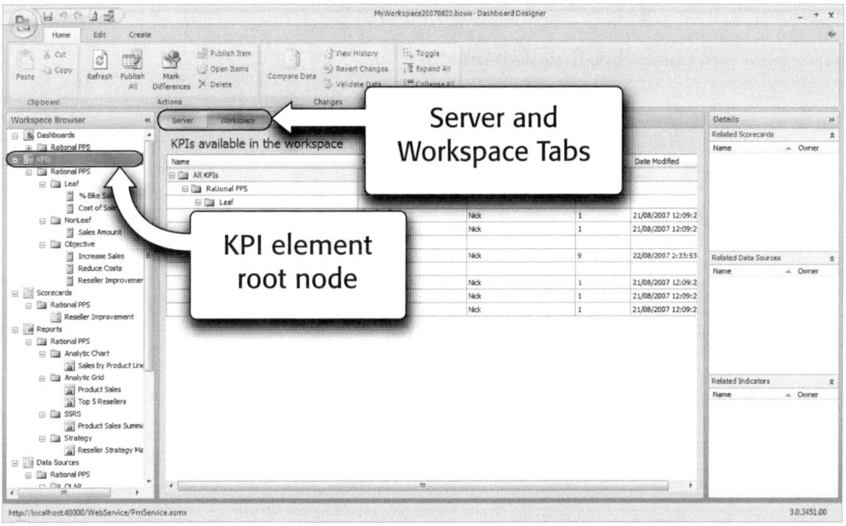

Figure 4.3: KPI Summary View with Workspace and Server Tabs.

Details Pane

The details pane plays different roles depending on the element selected in the workspace browser or workspace pane. In certain situations, this pane displays links to elements used by (or required by) the currently selected element. In other cases, the details pane provides access to items required to build out scorecard, report, and dashboard definitions. The many uses of the details pane will become much clearer in subsequent chapters.

The Ribbon

As member of the Office 2007 family, DD's user experience is improved by the incorporation of the new *ribbon* interface. The DD ribbon is divided into three different tabs: *Home*, *Edit*, and *Create*. Within each of these tabs, the buttons for related functions are organized into *chunks*. The organization of the ribbon, along with intuitive icons and tooltips, means that all the functionality that DD provides is visible and within easy reach.

Home

The tools on the **Home** tab (Figure 4.4) are those that are common to all elements.

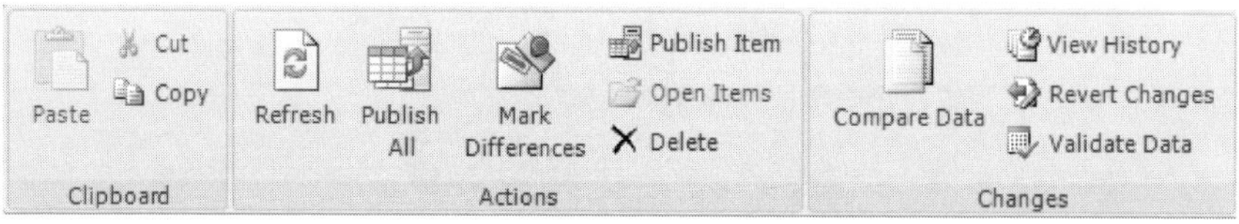

Figure 4.4: The Home Tab.

Edit

The ribbon is a dynamic user interface that automatically adjusts the contents of certain tabs depending on the actions being performed by the user. Of the three DD ribbon tabs, the most dynamic by far is the **Edit** tab. Depending on the element selected in the workspace browser, the **Edit** tab will display chunks containing tools specific to that element. Because of its dynamic nature, it is not worth including screenshots showing the many different chunks hosted by the **Edit** tab. Instead, the varied contents of the **Edit** tab will feature in the chapters that cover each element.

Create

The **Create** tab (Figure 4.5) is home to buttons used to create each element type. Because the report element supports a number of different types, a separate **Reports** chunk has been created.

Figure 4.5: The Create Tab.

For a complete breakdown of the contents of each ribbon tab and chunk, refer to the product documentation.

Workspaces

Work is done in DD using files called *workspaces* that have a file extension of .bswx. DD provides a simple Graphical User Interface (GUI) that allows designers to create definitions for each of the six elements. Within a workspace file, DD creates detailed XML definitions of elements as a result of user interaction with its GUI. Designers need not have any working knowledge of XML; DD ensures that well-formed, PPS schema-compliant XML is created as a result of designers' efforts. Each individual element (e.g., KPIs) created in DD is represented as an XML node that exists inside the workspace file. Using DD's ability to connect directly to a Monitoring server, these XML definitions can be easily published to the Monitoring server one-by-one or en masse. Because a single workspace can contain the definitions of elements that make up a complete dashboard solution, it is a useful container and deployment mechanism—especially when it comes to moving through the development cycle (e.g., Development > Test > QA > Production). For example, once development is complete, migration of elements to the test server is done by simply connecting to the Monitoring server on the appropriate machine and publishing.

Workspace files should be treated the same as any other piece of source code. They should be managed through some form of source control, such as Microsoft Visual Source Safe. When the contents of a workspace are published to the Monitoring server, the XML element definitions are stored and managed in the Monitoring server database. Ensuring that this database is regularly backed up is essential, in addition to the .bswx files in which the elements were originally defined.

Note:

It is important to understand that the eventual end users do not interact with the workspaces themselves. The elements developed in workspaces must first be published to the Monitoring server in order for users to access and interact with them through SharePoint.

Tech Tip:

A workspace is actually nothing more than a well-formed XML document. Changing the .bswx file extension to .xml and then opening the file with Internet Explorer will allow a clear view of the element definitions created by DD. Naturally, before making any change to a file extension, make a backup of the original file.

Creating a Workspace

Follow these steps to create and save a workspace. If you already have DD open as a result of the previous exercise, you can skip Step 1.

1. Click **Start** ⇨ **All Programs** ⇨ **Microsoft Office PerformancePoint Server 2007** ⇨ **Dashboard Designer**. A window pops up to inform you that it is checking back with the server to see if there are any new updates to the application.

2. When DD opens, a blank workspace is created by default; this is the same behavior as other Office applications like Word or Excel. Click the **Office** button in the top left corner of the screen and select **Save As**.

3. Save the .bswx with the name **MyWorkspace** to a directory of your choice.

Workspace Configuration

When DD launches, it connects to the Monitoring server it was originally installed from, and it also creates a blank workspace. Each individual workspace file can be configured to connect to a specific Monitoring server if required. By default, the connection for new workspaces is set to the Monitoring server that DD was initialized from. The *Server URL* property can be changed on the **Server** tab of the DD Options dialog while the workspace is open by clicking the **Office** button and then clicking the **Options** button in the bottom right of the menu (next to the **Exit** button). The address of the Monitoring server web service to which DD is currently connected is displayed in the status bar in the bottom left of the application.

Element Synchronization

DD provides an environment in which elements can be created and managed both in a local workspace file and on the connected Monitoring server. Because of this, it is possible to have two differing versions of the same element—one in the workspace and one on the server. It is important to be able to determine quickly which workspace element definitions differ from those on the server.

Clicking the **Refresh** button on the **Home** tab of the ribbon will "pull down" the latest versions of all elements published to the currently connected Monitoring server. If an element exists in the workspace but hasn't been modified by a user, clicking the **Refresh** button will prompt the user to overwrite the current workspace definitions with the version from the server, if there are any differences. Once the refresh process has finished, clicking the **Mark Differences** button will compare element definitions in the open workspace to their published version (if they have been published). If the workspace definition of an element differs in any way from the server version since the last refresh (or is simply not published), a pencil is superimposed on that element's icon to indicate a difference between the workspace and server versions. Figure 4.6 shows that the Gross Margin % KPI's definition is not the same as that on the server (or may not have been published).

Figure 4.6: Gross Margin % KPI Out of Sync with the Server.

The pencil icon will also appear whenever an element definition is altered in any way or initially created. Publishing the element to the Monitoring server will remove the pencil.

Element Metadata

Metadata is a vital part of any business intelligence project and should not be overlooked. All elements have the same framework to ensure that appropriate metadata is captured and maintained consistently. Good metadata management will only serve to improve any business intelligence implementation. Element metadata can be accessed and configured in each element's **Properties** tab (see Figure 4.7).

Table 4.1 details the common metadata properties that can be accessed via the **Properties** tab.

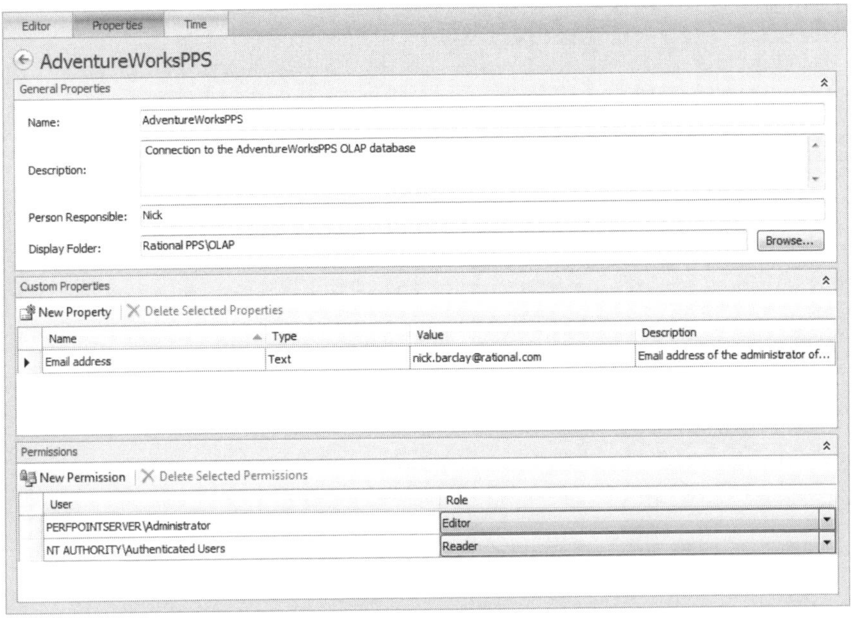

Figure 4.7: Element Properties Tab.

Property	Description
Description	Textual description of the element.
Person Responsible	This field is auto-populated with DomainName\UserName of the user currently logged in when the element is created. The value can be changed to whatever is desired.
Display Folder	Used to organize elements within the workspace and those published to the Monitoring server. Display folder settings exist as a property on an element rather than as an independent object. The hierarchy UI for specifying a display folder is generated on the fly, based on the properties of other elements in the workspace or on the server. To exist on the server, a display folder must contain at least one published element.
Custom Properties	A simple user interface for adding custom element metadata. Each custom property is made up of a name, description, data type, and value. Custom properties can then be exposed using a scorecard to add further context to the data contained within it.

Table 4.1: Element Metadata Properties.

Server Administration

DD provides simple administrative capability over the Monitoring server. The Monitoring server web service itself is actually quite simple and does not require too much work to administer and maintain. Server administration options can be accessed on the **Server** tab of the DD **Options** dialog. To configure global settings for a particular Monitoring server, the server name and port number of the corresponding Monitoring server instance should be entered into, or selected from, the available list in the **Server name** dropdown list.

Once the server has been selected, clicking the **Connect** button (see Figure 4.8) will bring the grayed out **Server Options** and **Permissions** buttons to life, enabling access to these areas.

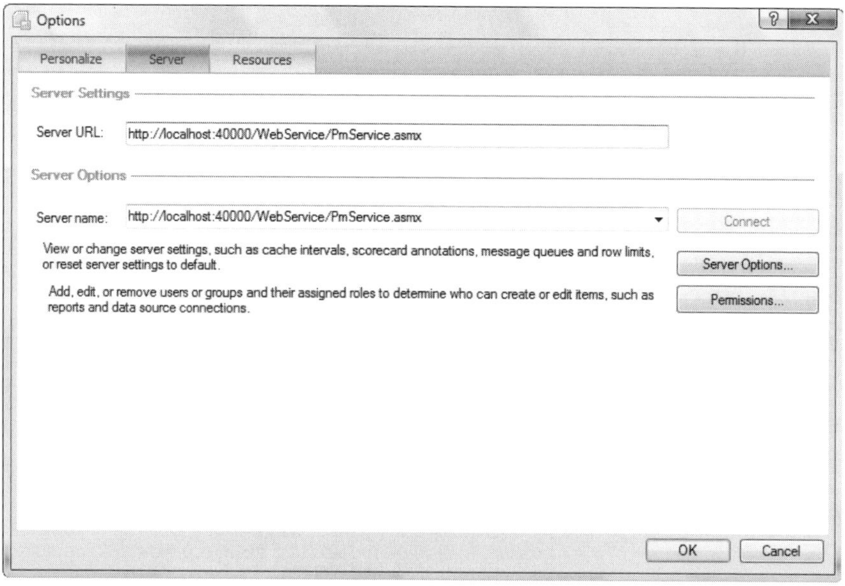

Figure 4.8: Server Tab of Dashboard Designer Options.

By default, the Monitoring server web service listens on port 40000. If a standard Monitoring install has been performed, the path to connect to a Monitoring server will be http://<servername>:40000/WebService/PmService.asmx. Naturally, if the Monitoring server is located on the same machine as DD, this path can be http://localhost:40000/WebService/PmService.asmx.

Tech Tip:

There is a simple trick to finding the path to a particular Monitoring server web service if you are unable to find or remember it. Simply browse to the monitoring central web page on that server `http://<servername>:40000/Central`. Launch DD using the link provided. DD will be automatically be configured to connect to *that* particular Monitoring server. Check the Server URL property in the Personalize tab and the Server Name property in the Server tab of the Options dialog in the default workspace. Remember that on subsequent initializations of DD from the Start menu, it will automatically connect to the Monitoring instance on the server it was last launched from.

Server Options

Once connected to the server, clicking the **Server Options** button brings up a grid that lists the configurable server options. These fit into five broad categories:

- **Comments** allow users to add comments to scorecards from within SharePoint. Before this functionality can be enabled for individual scorecards, it must first be configured at the server level.
- **Cache settings** determine the amount of time that an element is kept in the web server cache.
- **Microsoft Message Queue** enables the Monitoring server to send messages to a stipulated MSMQ.
- **Analysis Services** server name information facilitates data mining functionality used by Trend Analysis reports.
- **Row Limit** sets the threshold for OLAP "Show Detail" functionality.

The **Server Options** dialog can be seen in Figure 4.9. Each item can be configured by double-clicking it.

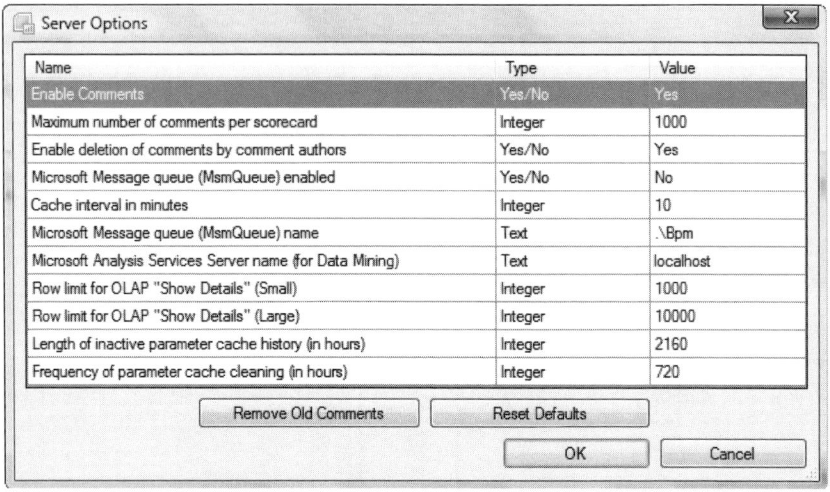

Figure 4.9: Server Options Dialog.

Note:

Alerts are not currently supported in this version of PPS. In BSM 2005, alerts were dependant on the SQL Server 2000 notification framework. This framework has been superseded by SQL Server 2005 Notification Services. An alerting mechanism is currently a candidate feature for a future version or service pack.

Permissions

Global security settings for the currently connected Monitoring server can be configured by clicking the **Permissions** button. Domain users or Windows groups can be assigned one of four different Roles: Admin, Creator, Power Reader, or Data Source Manager. Chapter 12 provides in-depth coverage of these roles and their application.

Migrating from BSM

As mentioned in Chapter 2, a significant portion of Monitoring functionality could otherwise be referred to as the next version of Business Scorecard Manager (BSM). Many businesses have already invested significant time and money in setting up BSM environments (creating KPIs, scorecards, etc.). Naturally, there is a migration path from BSM to PPS. It is not, however, an in-place upgrade of a BSM installation; it would be more aptly called a workspace migration.

The *Performance Point Server 2007 Scorecard Migration Tool* converts a BSM workspace (.bsw) schema to the new schema required by PerformancePoint workspaces (.bswx). Once the .bsw workspace has been converted to a .bswx workspace, the contents can be published to the newly configured Monitoring server. The upgraded elements are now available to be incorporated into dashboard elements, which did not exist in BSM. A detailed breakdown of which BSM items can or cannot be migrated to corresponding PPS elements is contained in the product help files. The Scorecard Migration Tool can be downloaded from `www.microsoft.com/downloads`.

Extensibility

The Monitoring server and DD are both built on rich, well-documented APIs. These APIs provide a plug-in architecture that has been used by the PPS team to build the product itself. The plug-in architecture supports the creation of custom wizards, reports, and data source providers.

DD is an application for interacting with the Monitoring server via a web service. There is no functionality provided by DD that a developer can't replicate and extend using the Monitoring web service and Monitoring Software Development Kit (SDK). This provides a great opportunity for customers and Independent Software Vendors (ISVs) alike to create customized functionality.

The ribbon is also a highly extensible interface. Aside from its usability, the ribbon interface places great emphasis on extensibility. Adding custom buttons and dynamic chunk functionality in DD is made very simple when leveraging the flexibility inherent in the ribbon interface.

Tech Tip:

Keep a close eye on the official PPS team blog (`http://blogs.msdn.com/performancepoint/default.aspx`) for posts detailing extensibility features and techniques.

Summary

In this chapter, we looked at PerformancePoint Dashboard Designer and the part it plays in building and publishing elements as well as server administration. DD is a ClickOnce application that uses files called workspaces to store and manage completed work. At any one time, DD can be connected to a single Monitoring server and have one workspace file open. The workspace pane's tabbed interface enables a user to easily work with element definitions located in either area. As a member of the Office family, DD provides usability benefits in the form of the ribbon interface.

In this chapter, we launched Dashboard Designer for the first time and created a workspace that we will build out throughout the remainder of this book.

Part III

The Elements

Chapter 5

Data Sources

It goes without saying that data sources are paramount to any data driven application. Data sources are simple elements whose sole purpose is to store connection information required to access data that will eventually be exposed via other elements such as KPIs and reports. This is illustrated well in the element hierarchy diagram in Chapter 2, which shows data sources at the very bottom of the stack. The only elements that do not have any dependency on data sources are indicator elements. The other four elements (KPIs, scorecards, reports and dashboards) are all directly or indirectly reliant on the connection information held in a data source.

Data Source Types

Data sources can be configured to connect to three different kinds of structured data store:

- Multidimensional
- Tabular Lists
- Standard Queries

Multidimensional

As we have already mentioned, multidimensional is the storage format to aim for because of the functionality and flexibility it provides. Monitoring supports connectivity to SQL Server Analysis Services 2005 and SQL Server Analysis Services 2000 multidimensional databases.

The best bang for your analytical PerformancePoint buck will come from having data stored in Analysis Services cubes, particularly when it comes to the use of MDX.

> **Tech Tip:**
> **Any performance management implementation plan should involve some form of data consolidation—preferably into a dimensional data warehouse, which then leads nicely into the creation of an OLAP (On Line Analytical Processing) database using SQL Server Analysis Services 2005.**

> **Tech Tip:**
> **PPS Planning uses Analysis Services (SSAS) cubes to store and manage budget and forecast data. These cubes are no different than any other cube managed by SSAS.**

Creating an OLAP Data Source

Follow these steps to create a multidimensional data source:

1. Open MyWorkspace.bswx in DD.

2. Select the **Create** tab on the ribbon and click the **Data Source** button.

3. In the **Category** pane, select **Multidimensional**, and select **Analysis Services** in the **Template** pane. Click **OK**.

4. Fill in the properties in the **Create New Data Source** window as shown in Table 5.1, then click **Finish**.

Property	Value
Name	AdventureWorksPPS
Default display folder location	Rational PPS\OLAP
Grand Read Permission to all users...	Checked ✓

Table 5.1: OLAP Data Source Properties.

5. Now that the element has been created, DD will display the **Editor** tab in the workspace where the data source configurations are to be made (see Figure 5.1). In the **Server** text box, enter the server name on which the **AdventureWorksPPS** OLAP database is located. If the Analysis Server is located on the same machine, `localhost` can be used.

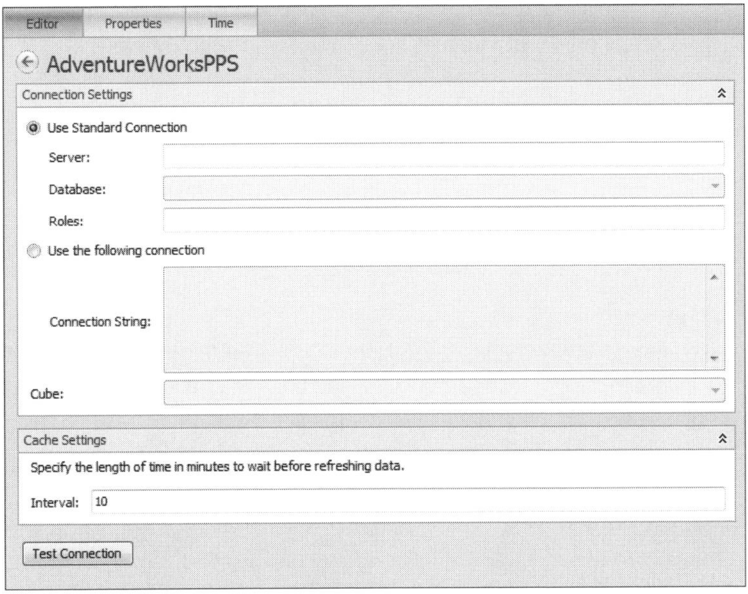

Figure 5.1: Analysis Services Data Source Editor Tab.

6. Select **AdventureWorksPPS** in the **Database** dropdown list.

7. Type `AllUsers` in the **Roles** text box.

8. Select **AdventureWorksPPS** in the **Cube** dropdown list.

9. Click the **Test Connection** button to confirm a successful connection. Click **Close** on the **Test Connection** dialog.

10. On the ribbon, select the **Home** tab and click the **Publish Item** button on the **Actions** chunk.

Refreshing Published Elements

Now that we have published an element to the Monitoring server, we can refresh the connection to view that item as it exists on both the server and in the workspace.

1. On the **Home** tab of the ribbon, click the **Refresh** button. This will go out to the connected Monitoring server and retrieve metadata about all published elements.

2. Select the **Data Sources** node in the workspace browser.

3. Select the **Server** tab in the workspace pane. Observe that the **AdventureWorksPPS** data source is now listed as a published data source available on the server.

> **Note:**
> **Server metadata does not need to be refreshed each time an element is published; this was just for demonstration purposes. Nonetheless, the Refresh button can be clicked at any time.**

Tabular List

A table is the most common format in which to organize information. Data is arranged in contiguous columns and rows, enabling simple, intuitive access to the information it contains. Monitoring introduces the *Tabular Data Source Provider* (TDSP), which facilitates the transformation of tabular data into a multidimensional structure on the fly. This functionality is quite similar to that performed by Excel when creating a PivotTable using data contained within a spreadsheet. The TDSP transforms flat, tabular data into a cube-like structure, complete with basic dimensions and aggregated facts. The data produced from the TDSP appears in DD interfaces in much the same format as data sourced directly from an actual OLAP cube.

A Tabular List data source can be created from the following sources:

- Excel Services
- Import from Excel 2007 Workbook
- SharePoint Lists
- SQL Server Table

Tech Tip:

The only tabular data source listed above that is static is the Import from Excel 2007 Workbook. This option allows the manual entry of data into an Excel spreadsheet from within the DD interface. This data remains static unless it is altered via DD; the data is stored as part of the data source and hence the workspace, not a separate Excel file. The other three options are not static in nature—i.e., a connection is made to the SQL Server table or SharePoint list and the latest data contained therein is retrieved.

The workspace pane UI for each of the tabular data source types is the same. In order to create a multidimensional structure out of the tabular data, we need to configure which columns are facts and which are dimensions. DD does some of the work for us automatically by marking non-numeric columns as dimensions and numeric columns as facts and setting the default aggregation property to *sum*. The columns containing dates are considered time dimensions and also need to be configured as such. The **View** tab provides a window into the data stored in the source table. To configure a column, select the header and use the dropdowns which appear in the details browser (see Figure 5.2).

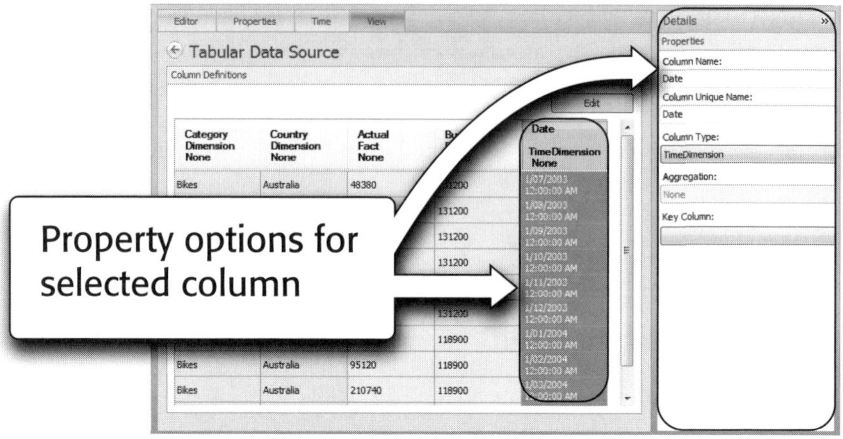

Figure 5.2: Configuration of Tabular Columns.

Five different properties can be configured to determine the role of each column:

- **Column Name** — The display name for the column.
- **Column Unique Name** — Unique identifier for the column, used internally. This feature can enable more advanced scenarios, such as lining tabular data up with that in a cube. For example, the column could contain text that uniquely identifies a member of an OLAP dimension attribute, such as `[Geography].[Country].[Australia]`.
- **Column Type** — Either *Dimension, Fact, Ignore, Key*, or *TimeDimension*.
- **Aggregation** — Active only for column types of *Fact*. There are a number of aggregation types to choose from, including the usual *Sum*, *Minimum*, and *Average*, along with several more advanced options like *Statistical Standard Deviation* and *Statistical Variance*.

- **Key Column** — Will contain the names of columns with a column type of *Key*. This property can be used in much the same way as **Column Unique Name**—to provide identifying attributes in order to line up with OLAP data or other tabular data sets.

The functionality provided by the TDSP is very useful in a number of contexts, but it is certainly not something that should be taken for granted. Dynamically converting tabular data into a multidimensional object is a costly exercise; the more data there is, the longer the conversion will take. As a general guide, tabular data source record sets should be kept under 10,000 records. Our testing revealed that performance began to slow when record sets began to creep over 5,000 records. Naturally, the number of columns that make up a tabular data set and their data types can influence the speed of conversion too. If your data is organized well enough to be parsed into a multidimensional structure on the fly, you should be asking yourself why you have not loaded it into an SSAS cube already. Doing so can potentially reduce the load on the network and server infrastructure and can only increase the value of your stock with IT administrators.

Standard Queries

There is currently only one option available under standard queries: ODBC. While it is certainly recommended to use data from a multidimensional data source whenever possible, ODBC data sources allow data to be gathered from just about any other structured data source, such as Access, DB2, or Oracle.

ODBC data sources require an explicit connection string in order to connect. Table 5.2 lists some sample connection strings for some common ODBC sources.

Source	Connection String
Access	`Driver={Microsoft Access Driver (*.mdb)}; dbq=C:\databasename.mdb; uid=userid;pwd=password;`
Oracle	`Driver={Microsoft ODBC for Oracle};Server=ServerAddress;Uid=Username;Pwd=Password;`
Excel	`Driver={Microsoft Excel Driver (*.xls)}; dbq=C:\workbookname.xls; ReadOnly=True;`

Table 5.2: Sample Connection Strings.

Tech Tip:

A great reference site for just about any kind of connection string to any kind of data source is `www.connectionstrings.com`**.**

Astute readers will have noticed that we have included Excel as an option for ODBC data sources when it is listed as a tabular data source option. The tabular option for connecting to Excel data is perfect when the aggregation of tabular data is required. As mentioned above, the TDSP creates a multidimensional structure on the fly, which can then be interacted with as if it were a cube. When using ODBC to connect to an Excel spreadsheet (or any other ODBC data source), our aim is to return a single scalar value as the result of a query. Using Excel spreadsheets with an ODBC data source can be very handy for prototyping, especially as it enables simple manipulation of values within the source spreadsheet, which are then reflected in the dashboard.

Time Intelligence

One of the most common requirements of any BI application is the ability to slice data by time relative to the current date. Monitoring has a sophisticated Time Intelligence (TI) framework to support this functionality. The real details of TI functionality will come later when we cover dashboards in Chapter 10. In order for TI functionality to be available when designing dashboards, we need to provide some time configuration information on the data source itself. Both the Tabular and Multidimensional data sources have a **Time** tab where this metadata must be configured.

Multidimensional

The multidimensional data source **Time** tab requires us to provide data about the primary time dimension we wish to use with TI (see Figure 5.3).

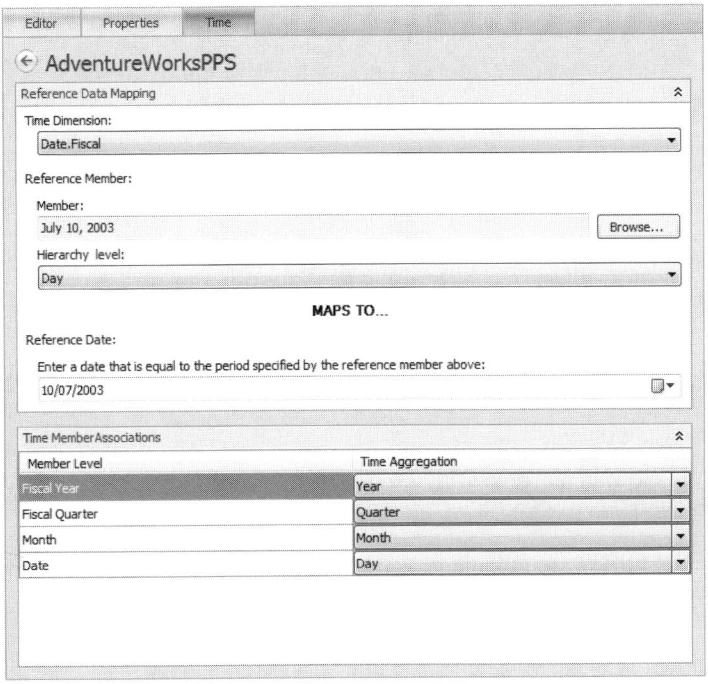

Figure 5.3: Time Tab of a Multidimensional Data Source.

In the **Reference Data Mapping** section, the name of the required **Time Dimension** is selected. Specific information about one member of the time dimension is configured in the **Reference Member** and **Reference Date** sections. By doing this we tell TI: "...in my time dimension, *this* member is considered the 10th day of July 2003." The reference member and date give TI a known place in the calendar to start from. Based on this one reference member, TI can now figure out all other members of the time dimension relative to it, provided the date dimension members are contiguous (no gaps).

In the **Time Member Associations** section, we tell TI about the makeup of the time dimension levels (*Year* > *Quarter* > *Month* > *Day* or *Year* > *Week* > *Day*, etc.), so that TI knows, for example, that the level above days is months, above that is quarters, and so on.

Configure OLAP Data Source Time Metadata

Follow these steps to configure the time settings on the AdventureWorksPPS data source:

1. Select the **AdventureWorksPPS** data source in the workspace browser. In the workspace pane, select the **Time** tab.

2. Select **Date.Fiscal** in the **Time Dimension** dropdown.

3. Click the **Browse** button to the right of the **Member** text box, drill down the date hierarchy and select **July 10, 2003** (there is no pertinent reason for this particular date; you can use another if you wish). Click **OK**.

4. In the **Hierarchy level** dropdown, select **Day**.

5. In the **MAPS TO** section, use the date picker on the **Reference Date** dropdown to select **July 10, 2003** (if you used another date in Step 3, make sure this date matches it).

6. The **Time Member Associations** will already be populated with the level names in the Date.Fiscal hierarchy. Use the dropdowns on the right-hand side of each level to associate the time aggregation with each level. Fiscal Year = Year, Fiscal Quarter = Quarter, Month = Month, Day = Day.

7. Right-click the **AdventureWorksPPS** data source in the workspace browser and click **Publish**.

Tabular

The tabular data source **Time** tab is a little simpler. We are not working with dimensions here, simply a column in the tabular source that contains a well-formed datetime value and has been configured as type **TimeDimension**. The tabular data source **Time** tab has two sections: **Time Dimensions** and **Time Period Levels** (see Figure 5.4).

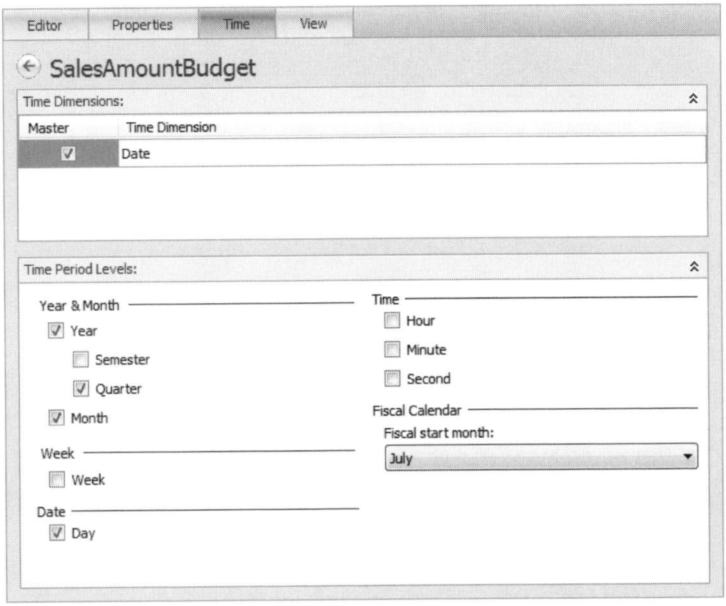

Figure 5.4: Tabular Data Source Time Tab.

In **Time Dimensions**, we stipulate which of the datetime columns (if there is more than one) in the data source we wish to use for TI by selecting the **Master** check box next to it.

Checking the appropriate boxes in the **Time Period Levels** area communicates which levels we wish to use, such as Year, Quarter, and Month. Because we use a well-formed datetime column, the TDSP simply derives the year, month, day etc. from each value and creates individual dimensions from them. We can also configure a fiscal start month if necessary by making a selection in the **Fiscal start month** dropdown.

Data Source Security

While the topic of security will be covered in Chapter 12, it is important to call out a particular security concept here. When connecting to data sources, the credentials of the user operating DD are *not* used at all to make data connections. By default, the account defined in the **PPSMonitoringWebService** IIS Application Pool is used. You'll recall from Chapter 2 that we configured the

Monitoring application pool to run under the NETWORK SERVICE account. The identity configured in this application pool *must* have at least read access to the data for which a data source has been defined. Even if the user building the workspace is a "master of all" in the domain they are working in, it is still the Application Pool account that must have the right database access privileges. Figure 5.5 shows an all too common error message when trying to connect to a data source where the Application Pool account does not have access.

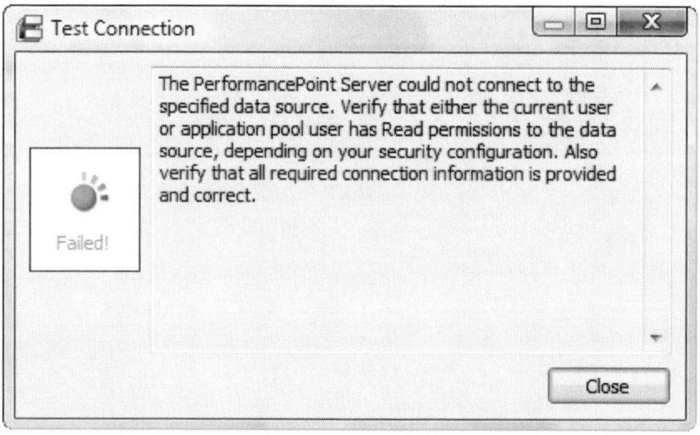

Figure 5.5: Data Source Connection Failure.

The default account we used in the installation chapter was the NETWORK SERVICE account. The sample AdventureWorksPPS OLAP database has an `AllUsers` role that includes the NT AUTHORITY\Authenticated Users as a read-only member of the AdventureWorksPPS cube. It is this configuration that enables a successful connection to be made.

Another very common cause of connection failures is that the open workspace is not appropriately configured to point towards the correct Monitoring server (see Figure 5.6). Check the Server URL value in the workspace options (**Office button** ⇨ **Options** ⇨ **Server** tab) to ensure that it contains the correct URL.

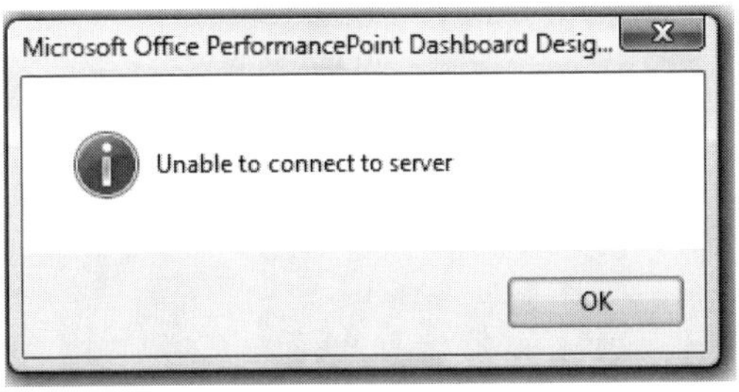

Figure 5.6: Monitoring Server Connection Failure Message.

Summary

This chapter covered the data source element. Monitoring supports connections to three different types of data source: multidimensional, tabular lists, or standard queries. We created and published a multidimensional data source which will be used to access data in subsequent chapters. Time dimension metadata must be configured in multidimensional and tabular data sources in order to take advantage of time intelligence functionality in dashboards. Data source security is an important topic to understand early on; by default, data source connections are made using the PPSMonitoringWebService application pool identity, not a user's domain account.

Did you know?

An excellent resource on PerformancePoint from both the Monitoring and Planning aspects is the official team blog: `http://blogs.msdn.com/performancepoint`. At the time of this writing, there are already many posts about a great range of topics, including best practices and step-by-step instructions for various topics. This blog is the official channel for PPS team communication. It is worth a click on the Subscribe button in your favorite feed aggregator.

The free bonus material for this book includes details on books, blogs, and web sites to help round out your knowledge. See the last page in this book for more information.

Chapter 6

Indicators

Scorecards and the KPIs that make them up would be just a collection of numbers if it weren't for *indicators*. One of the key concepts of scorecarding is the ability to visually represent how your business is tracking. Visual representation helps identify problem areas in the business.

Many scorecarding products on the market come with their own set of indicators, ranging from gauges to traffic lights or even smiley faces. Monitoring provides an extensive range of pre-configured, commonly used scorecard indicators, along with the ability to "roll your own." Monitoring goes a long way to provide flexibility in creating indicators to cover any scorecarding scenario.

Indicators of two types can be configured: *standard* or *centered.* Each indicator is comprised of two to ten levels, each of which can be configured with an image and other display-related properties to indicate the status of the KPI(s) that the indicator will eventually be used in.

Standard Indicators

People and businesses usually set goals. More often than not, these goals are expressed as a number representing a level of goodness that is desired. If that goal is reached or exceeded, this indicates success. Standard-type indicators are the most common and encompass this kind of KPI well. KPIs using standard indicators can be best classified as either *Increasing is Better* or *Decreasing is Better.*

For example, the sales budget for the North East region is $100,000. Adventure Works wishes to sell as much product as possible, so reaching or exceeding this budgeted figure is good for the business, and the indicator is *Increasing is Better*. On the other hand, the return of defective products is to be kept to a minimum of 0.5% of all products sold. Getting close to this goal number (or even zero) for the return count percentage is highly desirable for the business, so the indicator is *Decreasing is Better*.

Centered Indicators

In some cases, a goal is defined as a value above *or* below that which is undesirable. Centered indicators are suited for these *Closer to target is better* type KPIs. The reason why indicators are separated into two categories is to support the asymmetric banding requirements of *Closer to target is better*.

For example, a help desk aims to have an 80% utilization rate for its technicians. "Over-utilization" could mean that they may be dropping requests, while "under-utilization" means that resources are being wasted. The best indicator to use for this KPI would be centered, because any deviation above or below the goal is undesirable. While both under and over-utilization are undesirable and while both situations may produce the same score, they are distinctly different. The centered indicator was created to support this kind of scenario.

Indicator Levels

Indicators support from two up to ten levels. The visual detail an indicator is required to display will determine the number of levels to use. One-level indicators don't exist, because there would only be one state for the KPI—it would never change! Indicators with two levels serve KPIs with a True/False, Good/Bad type outcome. For indicators with three to ten levels, an odd number of levels is often desirable because of the availability of a specific "middle level." Naturally, level numbers will depend on the specific requirements of the KPIs that an indicator is designed for.

Every indicator contains a **No Data** level as well as the other levels between two and ten. For certain kinds of KPIs, defining meaningful (sometimes conspicuous) visual indicators for the **No Data** level can assist in pinpointing precisely that problem (i.e., there is no data available).

Level Properties

For each indicator level, a collection of settings can be configured for the display name, text color, background color, and most importantly, image. Figure 6.1 shows the property screen for a three-level, standard indicator using stoplight images. Note the **No Data** level that has been configured with an easily distinguishable image. Aside from the **Level** property on the left, the settings for the **Display Name**, **Image**, **Text Color**, and **Background Color** properties can be altered by simply double-clicking the appropriate cell. A grey square with a red slash running diagonally through it signifies that a property has not been set, as can be seen in the **Text Color** and **Background Color** attributes of the **No Data** level in Figure 6.1.

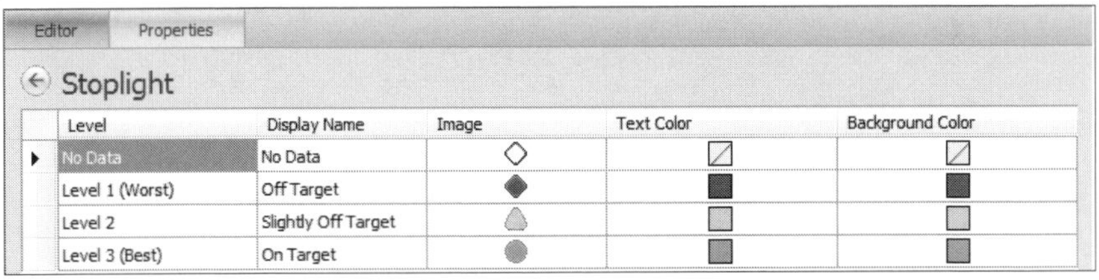

Level	Display Name	Image	Text Color	Background Color
No Data	No Data			
Level 1 (Worst)	Off Target			
Level 2	Slightly Off Target			
Level 3 (Best)	On Target			

Figure 6.1: Three-level Standard Indicator Level Properties.

Not every property in an indicator *has* to be configured with values for Background Color, Text Color, and Image, but defining at least an indicator image and background color for each level is certainly good practice. Having a library of rich, well-defined indicator elements will encourage reuse and avoid duplication of common indicator types.

It is entirely up to the designer to decide how each indicator level is configured to visually represent good, bad, and everything in between. Far and away the most popular form of indicator is an image of some sort. The image used can be anything—a picture of the smiling boss to represent a good outcome, or a picture of her frowning to show that you missed budget...again! Supported image types are. jpg, .gif, .bmp, and .png. Animated .gifs are also supported, so if displaying a smiley face with tears streaming down its cheeks helps to show just how bad the customer satisfaction ratings are, then go for it. A quick visit to your favorite search engine will turn up a number of graphics sites where the desired indicator images can be freely downloaded and used (be sure to check the copyright restrictions, though).

Built-in Indicators

Before you rush out to the nearest web browser to search for the perfect set of images for your first indicator, have a look at the myriad of preconfigured indicators that can be created within DD in a couple of clicks. Sample standard and centered indicators of many differing variations are available, including gauges, progress bars, smiley faces, and stoplights—to name but a few. Figure 6.2 shows just some of the pre-configured indicators available.

Figure 6.2: Selection of Available Indicator Images.

Creating an Indicator

Follow these steps to create and publish an indicator using a pre-built template:

1. Choose the **Start ⇨ All Programs ⇨ Microsoft Office PerformancePoint Server 2007 ⇨ Dashboard Designer** menu item.

2. Click the **Office** button, select **Open** and browse to where you have saved MyWorkspace.bswx, then click **Open**.

3. In the workspace browser, right-click the **Indicators** icon and choose **New Indicator**.

4. In the **Category** pane under **Centered**, select **Smiley Faces**. In the **Template** pane, select **Smiley B – Medium (Centered)**. Note that the indicators in the **Category** pane are grouped under Centered and Standard headings. Click **OK**.

5. In the workspace pane, select the **Properties** tab. In the **Permissions** area at the bottom of the screen, click the **New Permission** button and enter `NT Authority\Authenticated Users` in the **User** box. Ensure the **Role** is set to **Reader**.

6. In the workspace browser, right-click the newly created **Smiley B – Medium (Centered)** indicator and select **Publish** from the contextual menu.

Figure 6.3 shows the summary view of the new indicator.

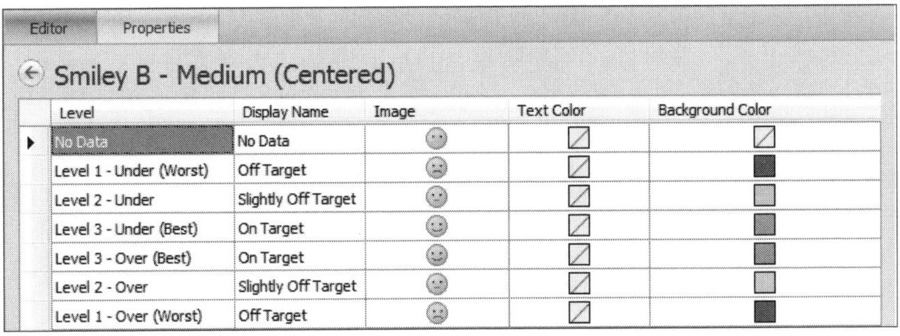

Figure 6.3: Configured Smiley Indicator.

In preparation for some of the exercises to come, follow the steps in the preceding walkthrough again (from Step 3 onwards) to create a second indicator. In Step 4, use **Standard ⇨ Miscellaneous** in the **Category** pane and **Check – A Medium** in the **Template** pane.

Pre-built indicators should cover a great many of your needs. When creating template indicators, much of the metadata we need (including display folder settings) was configured automatically. All properties (image, background color, etc.) of an indicator created from a template can be completely changed to suit your needs.

Tech Tip:

As noted above, display folder settings are automatically configured for template KPIs. In the case of the Smiley B – Medium (Centered) indicator, the value is *Centered\Smiley Faces*. **While the display folder value can easily be changed, it may be a good idea to leave it as is. Because indicators are quite a generic element, there is great potential for reuse and a generic, descriptive display folder hierarchy helps maintain a central area in which to find common (and already published) indicators.**

Edit Tab Tools

This is the first example where the ribbon shows its functionality (Data Sources do not have any specific **Edit** tab tools). When working on an indicator, an **Indicator** chunk appears in the **Edit** tab of the ribbon (Figure 6.4).

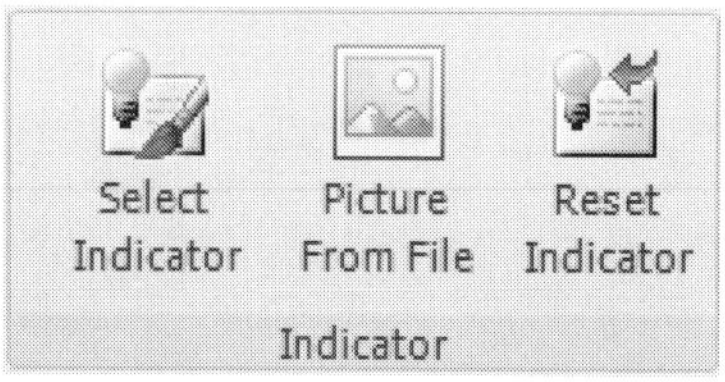

Figure 6.4: Indicator Chunk.

Building Your Own

The only properties that cannot be changed once an indicator is created are the *indicator type* (standard or centered) and the *number of levels*. If you wish to build an indicator from scratch, simply follow the same route as the above example, but choose the **Blank Indicator** option in the **Select an Indicator Template** dialog. After filling out the *Name*, *Display Folder*, and *Security* settings (these options are identical when creating any element from scratch), you will be asked to select an indicator type and number of levels for the new indicator (see Figure 6.5).

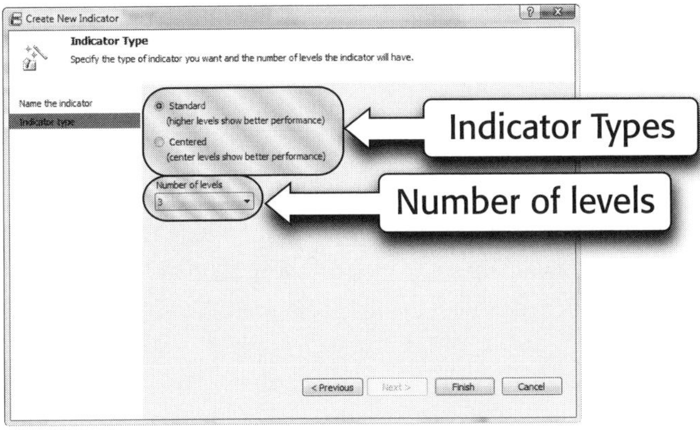

Figure 6.5: Indicator Type Step of Create New Indicator Wizard.

Once you click the **Finish** button on that dialog, you will be confronted with a blank indicator canvas as seen in Figure 6.6. All that is left to do is configure each individual part of the indicator to suit your requirements.

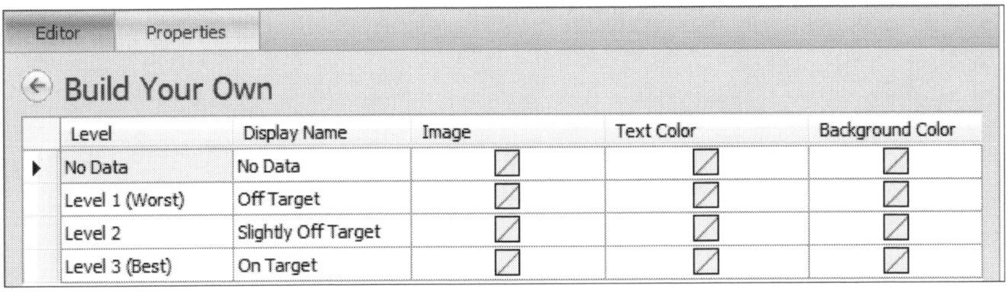

Figure 6.6: Custom Indicator Awaiting Configuration.

The gray square with a red diagonal slash indicates that particular property has not been set. Double-clicking the cell corresponding to a specific level's **Image**, **Text Color**, or **Background Color** will bring up the appropriate dialog to configure a color image for that property. The **Display Name** property can also be changed as desired.

Summary

This chapter detailed the functionality of the indicator element. Indicators can be comprised of two to ten levels and can be either standard (increasing / decreasing is better) or centered (closer to target is better). Each indicator level can be configured to use text, color, or images to convey its message visually.

Indicators are a simple element, but that simplicity does not diminish their importance. A big part of what a user wants when they ask "Can we see that in a scorecard?" are the visual cues delivered by well-designed indicators. Like all of the other elements, indicators are of no use by themselves. They are destined for use in KPIs, which will in turn make up a scorecard. Those scorecards will then make up the definition of dashboards, but let's not get ahead of ourselves.

Chapter 7

KPIs

Key Performance Indicators (KPIs) are the workhorse element of PPS Monitoring and the cornerstone of any serious PM initiative. An individual KPI represents a particular facet of the business that we wish to measure and keep track of in order to drive improvement. Even before a single piece of PM software is installed (or even purchased), serious consideration should be given as to precisely *what* the KPIs actually are that will drive the business onward and upward. While a discussion of KPI definition is beyond the scope of this book, it should be noted that far too few companies really spend the time they should aligning KPIs with business strategy.

Like data source and indicator elements, KPIs are of little use by themselves. They are the building blocks from which we will create scorecards; without KPIs there can be no scorecards. KPI elements can play the role of *leaf*, *non-leaf*, and *objective* KPIs. Their role is determined by their individual configuration and placement within a particular scorecard.

KPIs connect to data using data sources. They display visual representations of their status using indicators. As we will see shortly, a lot of information can be packed into an individual KPI definition. Just as the actual KPI definitions should be well thought out, so should the design of KPI elements themselves. A rich, multi-faceted KPI available on our Monitoring server will encourage reuse across more than one scorecard. Like all other published elements, we should strive for as much reuse of our published elements as possible.

Actual and Target Metrics

Each individual KPI element is a collection of at least one or many *metrics* that are classified either as *Actual* or *Target*. Each KPI is comprised of exactly one Actual and zero or more Target metrics. The precise number of Targets is determined by the requirements of the KPI. Each of these Actual or Target metrics can each utilize information from different data sources if required.

KPIs come by default with one Actual named "Actual" and one Target metric named "Target" (see Figure 7.1). The default Target metric can be deleted, or as many Target metrics can be added to the KPI as required. The Actual, however, cannot be deleted, nor can its position be moved from the top line of the KPI interface. The names of each metric (both Actual and Target) can be changed as required.

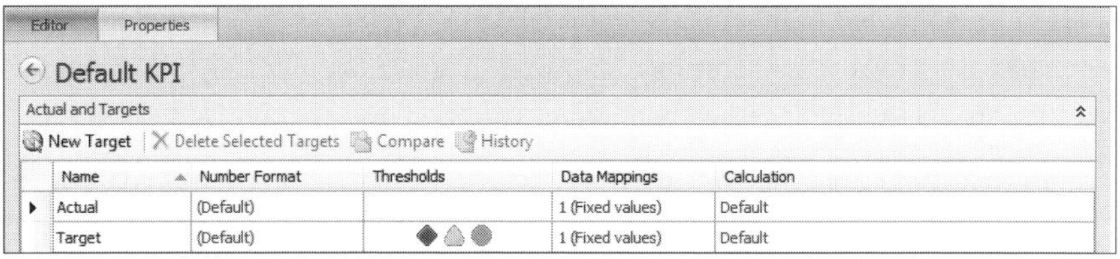

Figure 7.1: Default KPI Metrics.

The default concept of an Actual value compared to one or more Target values may not apply in all instances. Targets could, in a way, be renamed "non-Actuals." The name *Target* naturally implies that any Target metric created in a KPI is something to be "aimed at" and hence be compared with the Actual value. This is not always the case. The data in a Target metric does *not* need to be comparable to the Actual value of the KPI. The ability to add more than one Target (non-Actual) metric to a KPI is provided so that other relevant data can be contained by the KPI that adds context to the value contained in the Actual, but does not necessarily need to be compared to it.

For example, the KPI metrics in Figure 7.2 are made up of the compulsory Actual and two Targets named **Budget** and **Year to Date**.

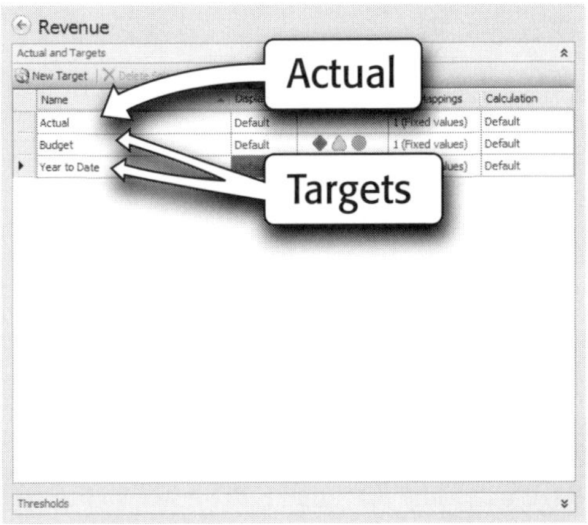

Figure 7.2: KPI Metrics.

The data linked to the Actual metric is revenue, which is measured monthly. The first Target metric is Budget, which also references monthly values. Comparison of the Actual and Budget attributes is desired in order to drive an indicator to visually represent the relationship between the two. The Actual value for, say, May 2007 is $10,000; the Budget for the same month is $9,000. Comparison of these numbers will show that the company has made budget for this month. The associated indicator for this KPI, depending on how it is set up, should show something positive (maybe something green?) as a result of this comparison.

The second Target, Year to Date, has a value of $47,000 and has no place being compared to the Actual for this particular KPI. However, the data contained in it *does* provide added context to the Actual and Budget data. Using extra Targets (non-Actuals) to provide context to an Actual adds further meaning to a KPI. Figure 7.3 shows what this KPI configuration could look like when contained in a scorecard.

	Actual	Budget	Year to Date
⊟ **Sales**			
Revenue	$10,000	$9,000	$47,000

Figure 7.3: Year to Date Target Adding Context.

Note in Figure 7.3 that there is no visual indication of a direct comparison between **Year to Date** and **Actual**. The **Year to Date** Target figure simply adds value to the KPI overall.

Metric Names

To facilitate design efforts, try to ensure that the Actual and Target metrics that make up a KPI are named in a consistent way. The Revenue KPI shown in Figure 7.3 could eventually be one of many KPIs in a particular scorecard. Note the generic names that were given to the Actual and each Target—**Actual**, **Budget**, **Year to Date**, rather than **Revenue Actual**, **Revenue Budget**, or **Revenue Year to Date**. These names are not KPI-specific. The benefits of consistent naming of the Actual and Targets will become evident in the next chapter when we set up our first scorecard. For now, remember that consistency between KPIs is useful.

Configuring Actual and Targets

The configuration options for the Actual and Targets that make up an individual KPI are almost exactly the same. The exception is that targets can optionally have *threshold* settings configured. Thresholds and their configuration will be covered later in this chapter, but for now we will look at the configurable properties shared by both: *Number Format*, *Data Mappings*, and *Calculation.*

Figure 7.4 shows the KPI metric user interface. To configure a specific property, simply click the link in the appropriate cell.

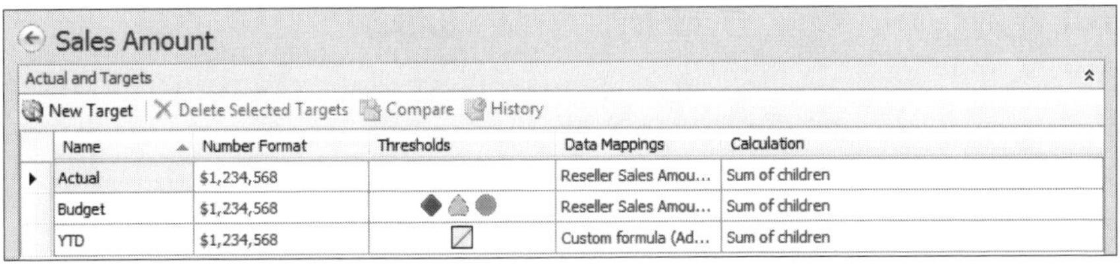

Figure 7.4: KPI Metric Workspace Pane User Interface.

Number Format

By default, the format of a number will be brought through from the data source that each metric is configured to use. If the format of the number is not appropriate, this can be overridden by using the **Format Number** dialog. Format masks can be applied to the numbers displayed for each metric. The **Edit** tab of the ribbon contains only one chunk when working on KPI metrics, the **Number** chunk can be seen in Figure 7.5. Simple numeric formats can be configured using the options located on this chunk.

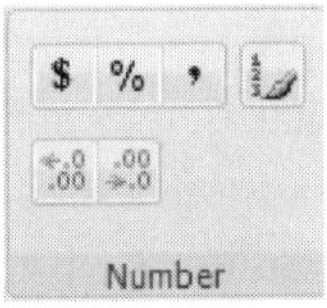

Figure 7.5: Number Chunk.

For more advanced configuration, the **Format Numbers** dialog (see Figure 7.6) can be used.

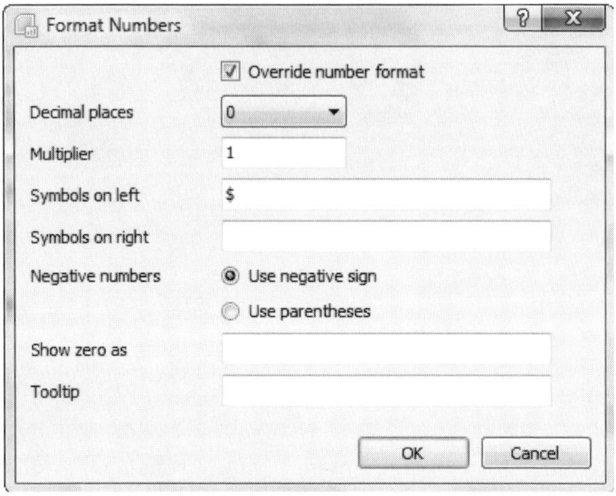

Figure 7.6: Format Numbers Dialog.

Data Mappings

Each KPI metric can be configured to either display fixed values or connect to data via a data source. This configuration is done with the **Data Mappings** dialog. The user interface displayed depends on the data source type that is selected for use. The **Change Source** button brings up the **Select a Data Source** dialog (Figure 7.7), which contains **Server** and **Workspace** tabs, each containing a list of available data sources.

Fixed Values

By default, all KPIs are created with an Actual and Target that each contain a fixed value of 1. Although not dynamic in nature, fixed values provide the simple ability to populate proof-of-concept KPIs manually with realistic numbers or maintain static values that do not change.

Standard Queries

Choosing an ODBC data source presents designers with a simple text box where they can enter the query text to be executed against the data source. Queries to any ODBC data source should be formulated to return a scalar value—a single field in a single row result set (as shown in Figure 7.8).

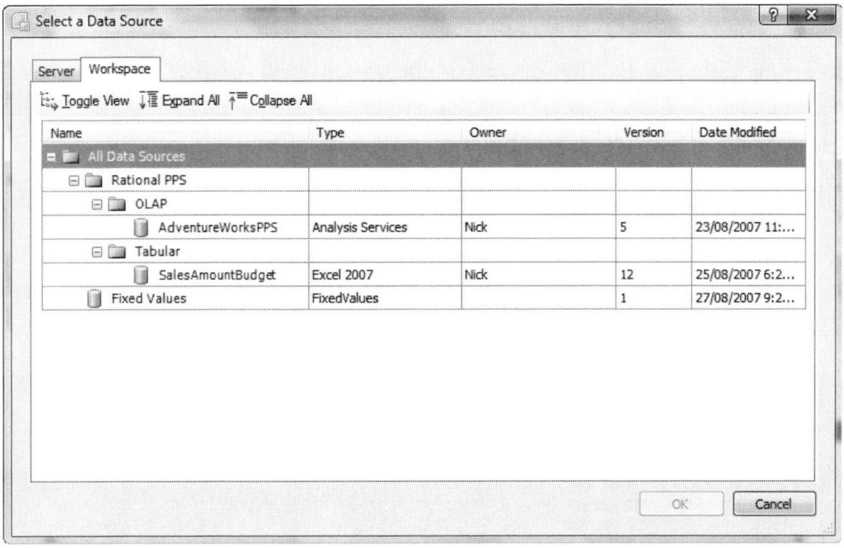

Figure 7.7: Select a Data Source Dialog.

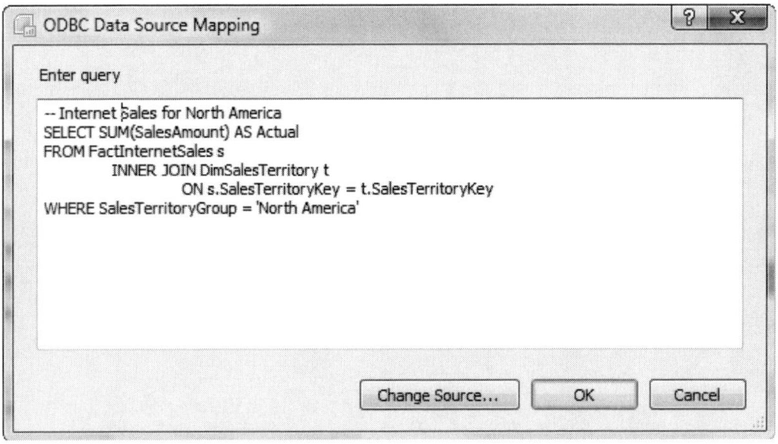

Figure 7.8: Scalar T-SQL query.

Tabular or Multidimensional

Selecting either a tabular or multidimensional data source brings up the dimensional data source mapping dialog (see Figure 7.9). A measure can be selected in the dropdown list at the top of the dialog and optional dimensional data filters can be applied to the measure. The ability to apply dimension filters is useful when a KPI Actual or Target is derived from a specific combination of members of one or several dimensions. For example, a company may have a requirement for country-based KPIs on Reseller Gross Profit (one KPI per country). We would use the filter functionality to slice the measure by USA, Canada, Australia, etc. for each individual KPI; the data contained in that KPI would always refer to only that region.

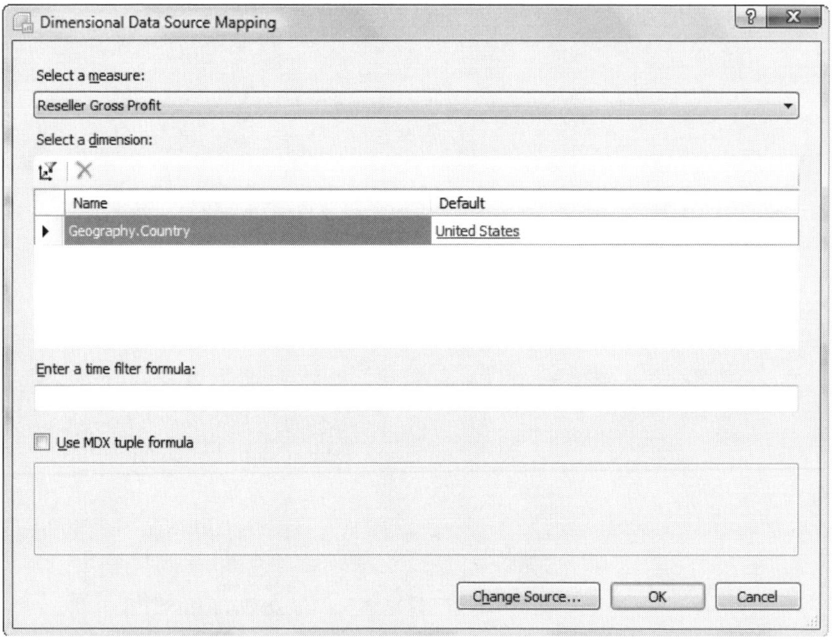

Figure 7.9: Dimensional Data Source Mapping Dialog.

This dialog also supports the configuration of a time filter formula. This functionality involves the use of a Time Intelligence (TI) formula, which will be covered in Chapter 10 when we look at dashboards.

> **Note:**
> **When speaking of *dimensions*, the term is being used broadly. In Analysis Services we would be slicing members of an attribute or attribute hierarchy; however, with Tabular Data Source Provider output, the more generic term *dimension* is better suited.**

Checking the **Use MDX tuple formula** option will disable the measure dropdown and dimensional filter grid in lieu of a tuple formula typed into the available text box. The full power of the MDX (MultiDimensional eXpression) language is at the disposal of the designer through this option, so long as the stipulated formula returns a tuple. Using MDX, anything from simple to very complex calculations can be defined here. The ability to use the MDX tuple formula option is only available for Analysis Services multidimensional data sources.

A detailed explanation of a tuple or in-depth coverage of MDX is beyond the scope of this book. The most powerful and flexible implementations of PPS (both Monitoring and Planning) will involve multidimensional databases. MDX is what we use to make the data from OLAP databases sing and dance. References to books, sites, and blogs on MDX can be found in the downloadable bonus material for this book.

Calculation

KPIs are destined to be contained in scorecards; they cannot be exposed to users any other way. We have several options when it comes to determining precisely what role a particular KPI will play in a scorecard. This is where the calculation settings come in. The calculation settings of a particular metric, coupled with the placement of the KPI within a scorecard hierarchy, will classify a KPI as one of three types: leaf, non-leaf, or objective. Note that these are just names that we have given them—in the end they're all just KPIs with different settings.

Figure 7.10 shows the calculation options available. Typically, **Default** and **Source data** calculations are used for leaf KPIs, **Average**, **Sum**, **Min**, and **Max of children** are used for non-leaf KPIs, and **No value** for objective KPIs.

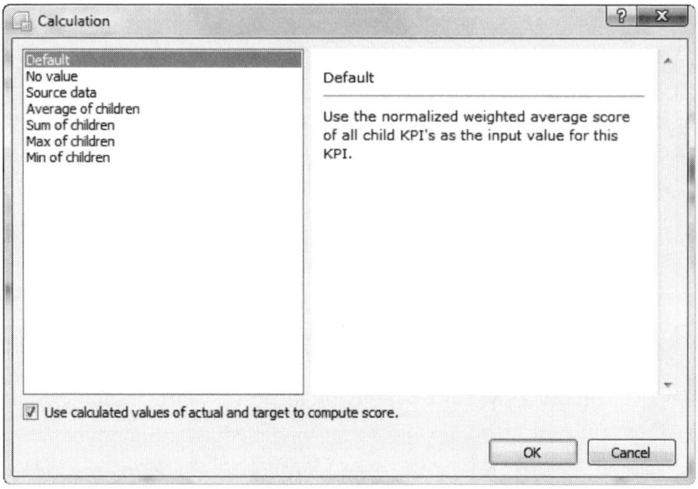

Figure 7.10: KPI Metric Calculation Options.

Let's take a closer look at each type of KPI.

Leaf KPIs are used at the bottom-most point of the scorecard hierarchy (the leaf level) and simply display their Actual and Target numbers as configured. In Figure 7.11, both the **Bike Sale %** and **Cost of Sale %** KPIs are located at the leaf level of the scorecard hierarchy. Targets in leaf KPIs must have the **Use calculated values of actual and target to compute score** option *checked* as seen at the bottom of Figure 7.10. It is the Actual and Target calculation that provides the value to drive the configured indicator.

Non-leaf KPIs must be placed somewhere other than the leaf level of the scorecard hierarchy. As a result, the items located below a non-leaf KPI in the hierarchy are aggregated in line with the chosen calculation option. The non-leaf KPI metrics display the result of the aggregation. For example, the **Sales Amount** KPI in Figure 7.11 has been configured with the **Sum of Children** calculation for both Actual and Budget metrics, which adds up the dollar figures for the children items beneath it. Using a calculation such as Sum, Min, or Max (of children) will only be of use if the numbers in the KPIs beneath it are all the same type; adding a percentage to a dollar figure will give you an answer, but it's not going to be of much use.

Objective KPIs are precisely what is required when we wish to roll up KPIs that contain completely different and unrelated numbers. The difference between "rolling up" and "aggregating" is worth noting. Non-leaf KPIs can aggregate, but objective KPIs roll up. The purpose of the **Reseller Improvement**, **Increase Sales**, and **Reduce Costs** objectives in Figure 7.11 are to roll up the score of all items beneath them in the scorecard hierarchy to drive the configured indicator. Note that these objective KPIs have no totals.

Target metrics in objective KPIs have the **Use calculated values of actual and target to compute score** option *unchecked* and have **No Value** configured as their calculation in order to do their job.

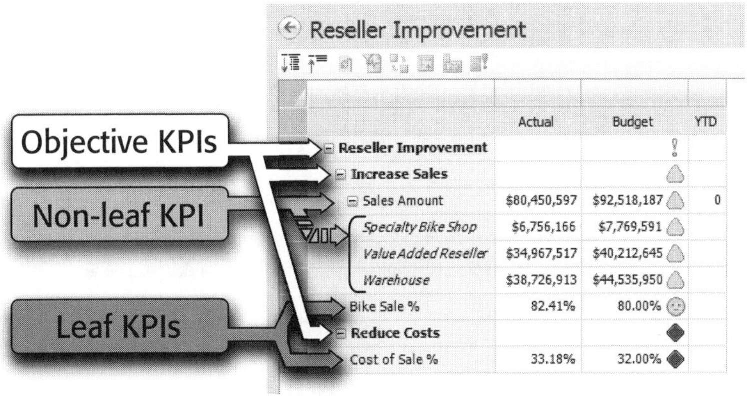

Figure 7.11: Different KPI Types in a Scorecard.

Creating Leaf and Non-Leaf KPIs

Now we're going to create and configure three KPIs: two leaf and one non-leaf. The KPIs share many similarities. For the sake of efficiency, we will reuse some of the steps taken to build the initial Sales Amount KPI.

Creating a KPI

Follow these steps to create the **Sales Amount** KPI.

1. Open MyWorkspace.bswx in DD.

2. On the **Home** tab, click the **Refresh** button to bring published element information into the application.

3. In the **Create** tab, click the **KPI** button in the **Objects** chunk.

4. Select **Blank KPI** in the **Select a KPI Template** dialog and click **OK**.

5. Fill in the appropriate element details as detailed in Table 7.1 and click **Finish**.

Property	Value
Name	Sales Amount
Default display folder location	Rational PPS\NonLeaf
Grand Read permission to all users...	Checked ✓

Table 7.1: Sales Amount KPI Properties.

6. On the **Home** tab, click the **Publish All** button.

Now repeat Steps 3 through 6 to create the **Bike Sale %** and **Cost of Sale %** KPIs using the values in Tables 7.2 and 7.3. Don't forget to publish them too.

Property	Value
Name	Bike Sale %
Default display folder location	Rational PPS\Leaf
Grand Read permission to all users...	Checked ✓

Table 7.2: Bike Sale % KPI Properties.

Property	Value
Name	Cost of Sale %
Default display folder location	Rational PPS\Leaf
Grand Read permission to all users...	Checked ✓

Table 7.3: Cost of Sale % KPI Properties.

KPI Default Indicators

When a KPI is created, it is assigned an indicator by default. If the default indicator does not exist, DD automatically adds it to the workspace. Take a look under **Indicators** in the workspace browser, and notice that an indicator called

Stoplight has been added. You can tell it's new because the pencil icon appears next to it. Follow these steps to ensure appropriate security permissions are assigned to the Stoplight indicator:

1. Under **Indicators** in the workspace browser, select the newly created **Stoplight** indicator that has been placed in the **Standard > Stoplights** folder.

2. Select the **Properties** tab in the workspace pane.

3. Click the **New Permission** button in the **Permissions** area and type `NT AUTHORITY\Authenticated Users` in the user box. Select **Reader** role in the **Role** dropdown.

4. Click **Publish All**.

There is also a **Publish All** and **Refresh** button on the **Quick Access** toolbar located above the ribbon next to the **Office** button.

Bulk Editing Elements

We want our three new KPIs to have a common Actual and Target metric structure. Using DD's bulk editing capability, we can make changes to all three KPIs at once. Follow these steps:

1. Select the **Rational PPS** folder underneath the **KPIs** folder in the workspace browser to display a summarized list of the three new KPIs in the workspace pane.

2. Hold down the CTRL key and select all three KPIs in the workspace pane.

3. On the **Edit** tab, click the **Bulk Edit** button. Click **Next** on the first screen.

4. Click the **New Target** button.

5. Change the name of **Target** to `Budget`, and change the name of **Target (1)** to `YTD`.

6. Click the **Select to Change** link in the **Calculation** property of the now renamed YTD Target. In the **Calculation** dialog, select **Default**. Click **OK**.

7. Click **Finish**, then click **Close**. Click **Publish All**.

> **Caution:**
> In the RTM build of DD, extra Target metrics added to a KPI will be created with a calculation property of No Value. This calculation value for new targets should be Default. As stated above, No Value calculations are suited to objective KPIs but not leaf or non-leaf KPIs. Until this is fixed, simply remember to manually change the calculation property on those Target metrics.

Configure Number Format

Follow these steps to configure the display settings for the Actual and Budget metrics in the **Sales Amount** KPI.

1. Select the **Sales Amount** KPI in the workspace browser and make sure the **Editor** tab is selected in the workspace pane.

2. Click the gray box to the left of **Actual** metric's **Name** box to select the metric row.

3. Select the **Edit** tab on the ribbon and click the **$** button on the **Number** chunk.

4. Perform Steps 1-3 again for the **Budget** and **YTD** metrics for the **Sales Amount** KPI.

5. Click **Publish All**.

> **Tech Tip:**
> Bulk editing functionality is not only limited to KPIs. Reports, scorecards, data sources and indicators all have bulk edit capabilities.

The **Budget** metric **Number Format** property needs to be changed from the default for both the **Bike Sale %** and **Cost of Sale %** KPIs to a two decimal place percentage. Set the Number Format for both KPIs by following these steps:

1. Select the **Bike Sale %** KPI in the workspace browser and make sure the **Editor** tab is selected in the workspace pane.

2. Click the gray box to the left of **Budget** metric's **Name** text box to select the metric row.

3. Select the **Edit** tab on the ribbon and click the **%** button on the **Number** chunk.

4. At the bottom left corner of the **Number** chunk, click the **Increase Decimal Places** button once.

5. Perform Steps 1-4 again for the **Budget** metric on the **Cost of Sale %** KPI.

6. Click **Publish All**.

Configure Data Mapping

Now we can connect our KPIs to some data. Each KPI is a little different in its requirements but we will endeavor to reuse as many steps as possible. The sample KPIs attempt to cover a good many of the data mapping options available.

Configure Measures

Here we are simply connecting directly to measures that are directly defined in the source cube. Follow these steps:

1. Select the **Sales Amount** KPI in the workspace browser and click the **1 (Fixed values)** link for the **Actual** metric **Data Mappings**. Click the **Change Source…** button.

2. Select the **AdventureWorksPPS** data source. Click **OK**.

3. In the **Select a measure** dropdown, select **Reseller Sales Amount**. Click **OK**.

4. Click **Publish All**.

There are several other KPI metrics that are sourced directly from measures in the AdventureWorksPPS cube. Repeat the steps above to configure them using the values in Table 7.4.

KPI	Metric	Measure
Sales Amount	Budget	Reseller Sales Amount Budget
Bike Sale %	Actual	Reseller Ratio to All Products
Bike Sale %	YTD	Reseller Ratio to All Products YTD
Cost of Sale %	Actual	Reseller Standard Cost of Sale
Cost of Sale %	YTD	Reseller Standard Cost of Sale YTD

Table 7.4: KPI Data Mappings.

Configure Data Filters

The **Bike Sale %** KPI Actual and YTD metrics both need a dimension filter configured so that they display bike sales only. Follow these steps to accomplish this:

1. Open the **Data Mappings** dialog for the **Actual** metric on the **Bike Sale %** KPI.

2. Click the **Select Members** button just underneath the **Select a dimension** label (the one with the filter on it).

3. Select **Product.Product Categories** in the **Dimension Selector** dialog. Click **OK**.

4. Click the **(Default)** link on the new line that has appeared in the dimension grid for **Product.Product Categories**.

5. Expand the **All** level in the member selector and select the **Bikes** member. Click **OK** twice.

6. Now repeat Steps 1-5 for the **YTD** metric in the **Bike Sale %** KPI.

7. Click **Publish All**.

Configure Fixed Values

Fixed values are very simple to take care of. All that needs to be done is to alter the value from the default value of 1. Follow these steps:

1. Open the **Data Mappings** dialog for the **Budget** metric in the **Bike Sale %** KPI.

2. Change the value in the **Value** text box to 0.8. Click **OK**.

3. Follow Steps 1-2 for the **Budget** metric in the **Cost of Sale %** KPI, but this time set the value to 0.32.

4. Click **Publish All** (This time, try the shortcut key for Publish All: CTRL + F4)

Configure MDX Tuple Formulas

All that is left to do is configure an MDX formula for the **Sales Amount** KPI's **YTD** metric. Follow these steps:

1. Open the **Data Mapping** dialog for the **YTD** metric in the **Sales Amount** KPI.

2. Click the **Change Source** button and select the **AdventureWorksPPS** data source. Click **OK**.

3. Check the **Use MDX tuple formula** check box .

4. Enter the following MDX in the text box and then click **OK**.

```
AGGREGATE(YTD([Date].[Fiscal].CURRENTMEMBER),[Measures].
➲[Reseller Sales Amount])
```

5. On the **Quick Access** toolbar, click **Publish All**, then click the **Save** button.

Configure Calculation

As mentioned earlier, calculation settings make leaf, non-leaf, or objective KPIs what they are. A change in metric calculation settings can change the role a KPI performs.

Configure Non-Leaf Calculation

As it currently stands, the **Sales Amount** KPI's **Calculation** settings for all three metrics still contain default settings. We will enable this KPI into perform the role of a non-leaf by following these steps:

1. Select the **Sales Amount** KPI in the workspace browser.

2. Click the **Default** link to display the **Calculation** property of the **Actual** metric.

3. Select **Sum of Children** in the **Calculation** dialog. Note the absence of the **Use calculated values of actual and target** option at the bottom of the dialog. Remember, this option is *not* available for Actual metrics. Click **OK**.

4. Perform Steps 2 - 3 again for both the **Budget** and **YTD** targets on the Sales Amount KPI, this time noting that the **Use calculated values of actual and target** option is indeed there and is checked. Don't forget to click **Publish All**.

Creating Objective KPIs

When creating the KPIs earlier, you may have noticed that there is an **Objectives** option available in the wizard. The KPIs created with this option are structurally no different than the KPIs we have already built. The only differences in KPIs created using the **Objective** option is that the default Target metric has its **Use calculated values of actual and target to compute score** option unchecked and the calculation value on both default Actual and Target metrics is set to **No Value**.

Use the property details in Tables 7.5, 7.6, and 7.7 to create three KPIs using the **Objective** option.

Property	Value
Name	Increase Sales
Default display folder location	Rational PPS\Objective
Grand Read permission to all users...	Checked ✓

Table 7.5: Increase Sales Objective Properties.

Property	Value
Name	Reduce Costs
Default display folder location	Rational PPS\Objective
Grand Read permission to all users...	Checked ✓

Table 7.6: Reduce Costs Objective Properties.

Property	Value
Name	Reseller Improvement
Default display folder location	Rational PPS\Objective
Grand Read permission to all users...	Checked ✓

Table 7.7: Reseller Improvement Objective Properties.

Bulk Edit Target Name

As we will see in the next chapter, the name given to the metrics that make up KPIs destined for the same scorecard is very important. To that end we have just created three vanilla objective KPIs, each of them containing two metrics named Actual and Target. The name of Actual is fine because it matches the other three KPIs created earlier. The name of Target will not do and should be changed to Budget. Once more we will take advantage of **Bulk Edit** to do this all in one hit. Follow the same steps performed earlier on the original three KPIs under "Bulk Editing Elements" to ensure that the structure of the objective KPI metrics is Actual, Budget, YTD.

Thresholds

What makes Target metrics different from the Actual in a KPI is the **Thresholds** option. Configuring thresholds for a Target signifies the designer's wish to use an indicator element to convey visual meaning for that particular number based on a number of different settings. The opposite is also true. In the Year To Date Target example earlier in this chapter, no thresholds needed to be configured on that Target because there was no need to compare that number to the Actual. These decisions are up to the discretion of the KPI designer.

Clicking the **Thresholds** cell of a Target displays the **Thresholds** window in the bottom half of the workspace pane (Figure 7.12).

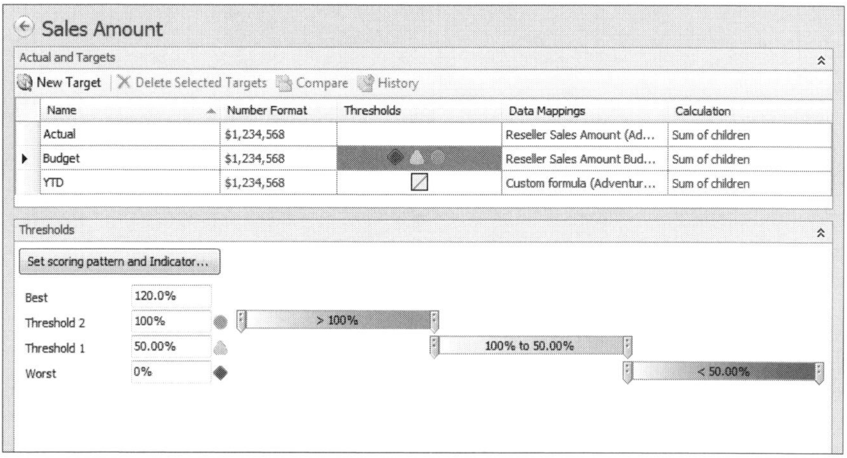

Figure 7.12: Thresholds User Interface.

Scoring Pattern and Banding Method

Clicking the **Set scoring pattern and Indicator** button will bring up the **Edit Banding Settings** wizard. Choosing different combinations of **Scoring pattern** and **Banding method** in the first step of the wizard will change the graphics in the pane below them to reflect precisely how values that drive indicators will be calculated (Figure 7.13).

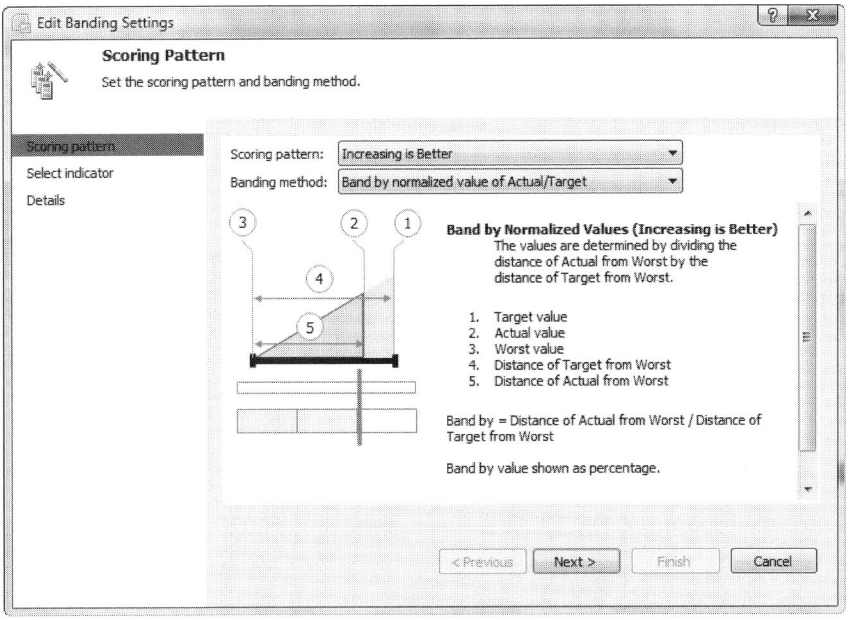

Figure 7.13: Scoring Pattern Pane.

These graphics explain *precisely* what calculations are to be made with which metrics of the KPI in question. It is highly recommended that designers pay close attention to these images when questions are raised as to how a specific threshold calculation is made. When broken down, the calculations are quite simple, so an Excel spreadsheet or even the traditional pen and paper are great ways of double-checking the math.

The **Scoring pattern** dropdown list contains three options that should remind you of the chapter on indicators:

- **Increasing is Better**
- **Decreasing is Better**
- **Closer to Target is better**

Choosing either of the first two options will enable the use of standard indicators; the third will enable the use of centered indicators defined in the current workspace.

The **Banding method** list box also contains three options:

1. **Band by normalized value of Actual/Target** — The most commonly used banding method. Returns a percentage value by comparing the value of the Actual to that of the Target.

2. **Band by numeric value of Actual** — Does not require a specific Target value. No actual calculation is made, only a comparison of where the Actual fits in relation to boundaries set between Best and Worst values. This banding method is well suited for Actuals that need to be compared against fixed scales, such as a score out of ten.

3. **Band by stated score (advanced)** — Does not actually reference values from either the Actual or Target but instead uses a value directly from a configured data source to drive the indicator. This banding method can also be used to bring in an arbitrary data value on which to band. For example, a KPI like "Number of products with serious defects" may have an explicit goal of "0" (i.e., the value to which the Target value is mapped for display) and yet have a status that is mapped to the percentage of products with serious defects, rather than to the absolute number displayed in the scorecard.

Selecting an Indicator

Once the scoring pattern and banding method have been configured, an indicator can be selected. Only indicators defined in the open workspace will be available for selection. Remember that the choice made in the **Scoring pattern** dropdown will determine if standard or centered indicators are available for selection (see Figure 7.14).

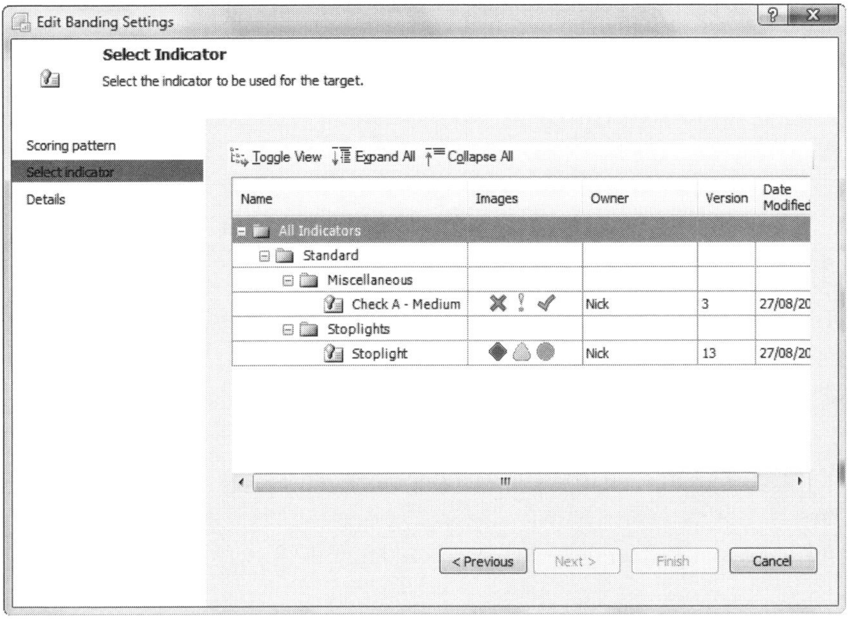

Figure 7.14: Select Indicator Pane.

Tech Tip:

If you wish to work with any element that is published to the Monitoring server but is not part of the active workspace, simply select the element(s) in the Server tab of the workspace pane and click the Open Items button on the Actions chunk of the Home tab. This will bring the definition into the workspace. Be careful: changing and republishing that element will affect all other elements that reference it. Make good use of the details browser to see which other elements rely on it before making any drastic changes.

Best/Worst Value

Different banding methods require different combinations of **Best** and **Worst** values to achieve their end. This is really an effort to put a limit on "Just how *bad* is terrible?", "Just how *good* is great?" For example, if the server room temperature needs to be as close to 21 degrees Celsius as possible, what is the temperature below which it simply *cannot* drop? Is it freezing point? 15 degrees? How high is too high? 30 degrees? Boiling point?

For banding methods such as **Band by Numeric Value of Actual**, the required **Best** and **Worst** values are an integral part of the calculation. On the other hand, the **Band by normalized value of Actual/Target** needs only a **Worst** value.

Threshold Boundaries

Once the indicator has been configured, we are left with the simple task of adjusting the threshold boundary numbers using the interface shown in Figure 7.15.

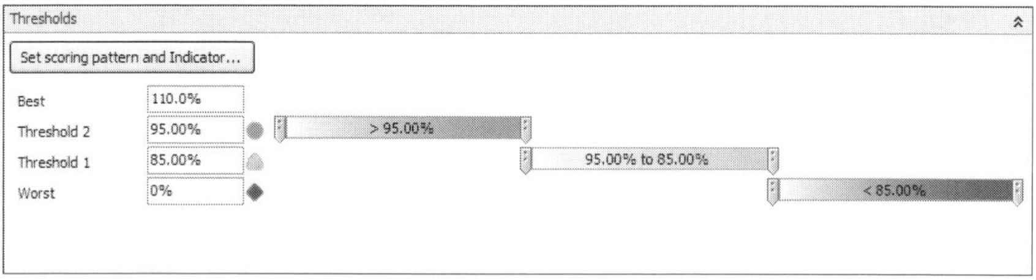

Figure 7.15: Threshold Boundaries Interface.

The number of bands displayed here (along with the images and level colors) is driven directly from the properties of the associated indicator. The threshold boundary values can be adjusted either by dragging the slider controls from left to right or typing the desired values into the corresponding threshold text box. The user interface gives a good visual representation of which indicator level settings will be displayed as a result of the calculation determined by the Banding method and Scoring pattern (remember to refer to the diagram in the wizard!). For example, a KPI Target using the **Band by Normalized value of Actual/Target** method has an Actual value of 867 and a Target value of 1000 and a Worst value of 0. Therefore, (867 – 0)/(1000 – 0) = 86.7%, which falls in the yellow (95% to 85%) threshold boundary defined in Figure 7.15.

Tech Tip:

Don't get the Best and Worst threshold boundaries confused with Best Value and Worst Value configured in the Edit Banding Settings wizard. In Figure 7.15, the Best and Worst threshold boundaries could otherwise be referenced as Boundary 3 and Boundary 0 respectively.

In post match interviews, football players are infamous for saying they "gave 110%." There is always someone in the room who will annoyingly remind all within earshot that it's impossible to give more than 100%. KPIs are different. When it comes to certain kinds of KPIs, values greater than 100% are terrific! Would a manager prefer to achieve 100% of their sales budget or 120%? For this reason, best and worst threshold values can be configured above or below 0% and 100% if required.

Non-Leaf and Objective KPI Thresholds

Thresholds can be configured on non-leaf and objective KPIs too. Don't forget that these are simply KPIs with a different job; the threshold configuration process does not differ at all. Objective KPIs will not use threshold settings like Scoring pattern and Banding method when rolling up values in a scorecard; the internal scoring engine takes care of this. When it comes to thresholds for objective KPIs, all we have control over is the indicator element and the threshold boundaries.

Keep in mind that the behavior of threshold indicators (for all KPI types) will also be influenced by the score type that is configured on the Target metric. Scoring and rollups in scorecards are covered in detail in the Scoring chapter in this book's bonus material. See the last page in this book for information on how to register your book and download bonus material.

> *Note:*
>
> **For those with experience in BSM, the ability to define specific indicators for these higher level scorecard objects will come as good news. BSM did not support the concept of non-leaf and objective KPIs. In fact, BSM scorecards could not aggregate data and objectives were simply a part of the definition of the scorecard itself, not separate objects unto themselves.**

Configuring Thresholds

All that is left to do now is configure indicator settings. In the KPIs just created there is no need to compare the YTD Target with the Actual, because the comparison is meaningless. Therefore, we won't be configuring any threshold properties there. We do, however, want to compare the Budget Target with the Actual.

Because non-leaf and objective KPIs are KPI elements unto themselves, we have even more flexibility in terms of the indicators used. Each of these can be configured with its own specific indicator.

The **Bike Sale %** KPI exists to keep AdventureWorks on track. They know from research that sticking their bike sales as close to 80% of their sales mix as possible optimizes cross-selling of other products. Follow these steps to configure threshold settings to accommodate this.

1. Select the **Bike Sale %** KPI in the workspace browser.

2. Click the **Thresholds** cell for the **Budget** metric to activate the **Thresholds** interface in the workspace pane.

4. Click the **Set scoring pattern and Indicator** button.

5. Select **Closer to Target is Better** in the **Scoring pattern** dropdown (note the change in the calculation graphic that is displayed as a result). Ensure the **Banding method** is set to **Band by normalized value of Actual/Target**. Click **Next**.

6. Because we chose **Closer to Target is better**, the **Select Indicator** step will only list centered indicators that exist in the open workspace. Select **Smiley B – Medium (Centered)**. Click **Next**.

7. AdventureWorks considers 60% to be as bad as this KPI can get, so enter 0.6 as the **Worst** value. Click **Finish**.

8. Using either the slider bars or by typing into the appropriate text boxes, set the threshold boundary values to the following. Worst(High) = 200%, Threshold 5 = 125%, Threshold 4 = 105%, Threshold 3 = 100%, Threshold 2 = 95%, Threshold 1 = 75%, Worst(Low) = 0%.

9. Click **Publish All** and save the workspace.

Repeat the steps above for the **Sales Amount** and **Cost of Sale %** KPIs, using the values in Tables 7.8 and 7.9. Remember to publish and save as you go.

Property	Value
KPI	Sales Amount
Scoring Pattern	Increasing is Better
Banding Method	Band by normalized value of Actual / Target
Indicator	Stoplight
Best / Worst Value	0
Threshold Boundaries	Best = 120%, Threshold 2 = 95%, Threshold 1 = 85%, Worst = 0%

Table 7.8: Sales Amount KPI Threshold Settings.

Property	Value
KPI	Cost of Sale %
Scoring Pattern	Decreasing is better
Banding Method	Band by numeric value of actual
Indicator	Stoplight
Best / Worst Value	N/A
Threshold Boundaries	Best = 0.25, Threshold 2 = 0.31, Threshold 1 = 0.32, Worst = 0.35

Table 7.9: Cost of Sale % KPI Threshold Settings.

Configuring Objective Thresholds

Objective KPIs ignore the threshold settings except for the chosen indicator. With that in mind, we will adjust the **Reseller Improvement** objective KPI to use a different indicator than the default. All other properties of the threshold can be left at the default value.

Follow the same steps as you have with the previous KPI threshold settings. Set the indicator used by the **Reseller Improvement** KPI to **Check A – Medium**. Don't forget to **Publish All**, then save and close MyWorkspace.bswx.

Summary

There is a lot of flexibility in defining KPI elements. Careful thought and planning when it comes to KPI design and definition will pay dividends in the end. KPI elements are comprised of one Actual and zero-to-many Target metrics. Each metric within a KPI can have a number of different properties configured. The settings on these metrics determine the role a KPI will play in a scorecard (leaf, non-leaf, or objective) and the data it will convey. Consistent naming of metrics across KPIs assists greatly when it comes to creating scorecards, as we will see in the next chapter. With our KPIs built and published, it is time to put them to work in a scorecard.

Chapter 8

Scorecards

All buildings require a solid foundation in order for further construction to take place. Once the building has been completed, the foundation structure itself is not directly used by its occupants, but the levels built atop the foundation are. The *scorecard* element can be viewed in a similar fashion. KPIs (and their related data sources and indicators) are the foundation on which scorecards are built.

The scorecard element provides great flexibility in presenting the data contained in one or more KPIs. What would be considered a traditional, run-of-the-mill scorecard can be created with ease. Figure 8.1 shows a simple scorecard designed around the Balanced Scorecard methodology.

Dynamic, interactive, complex scorecards are not much harder to build. Dashboard Designer provides a feature-rich, drag & drop user interface for both laying out and previewing scorecards. This WYSIWYG ("what you see is what you get") environment makes scorecard development quick and intuitive.

Available scorecard items are laid out across column and row axes. Multiple KPIs that reference data from one or many sources can be used on the same scorecard. Conversely, a scorecard may only contain one KPI, whose data can then be broken down across different dimensions. Figure 8.2 shows a scorecard made up of multiple KPIs hierarchically arranged down the row axis. The data contained in these KPIs is then broken out into quarters across the column axis.

	Actual	Target
Overall Performance		
Financial Performance		
Increase Revenue		
Maintain Overall Margins		
Net Profit	10.00%	
Net Profit Margin %	6.00%	
YOY Revenue Growth	22.00%	
New Product Revenue	$2,463,887	
Control Spend		
Customer Satisfaction		
Count of Complaints	127	
Market Share	22.00%	
Unique Repeat Customer Count	785	
Avg Customer Survey Rating	7	
Acquire New Customers		
Operational Excellence		
Improve Service Quality/Responsiveness		
Average Call Wait	57.00 minutes	
Service Error Rate	3.00%	
Fulfillment Percentage	55.00%	
Understand Customer Segments		
Build Quality Products		
Time to Market on New Products	33.00 weeks	
Number of Defects Reported	978	
Industry Quality Rating	44	
People Commitment	**5**	
Keep Quality Employees		
Turn Over Ratio	3.00%	
OHI	66.00%	
Attract Top Talent		

Figure 8.1: Balanced Scorecard Layout.

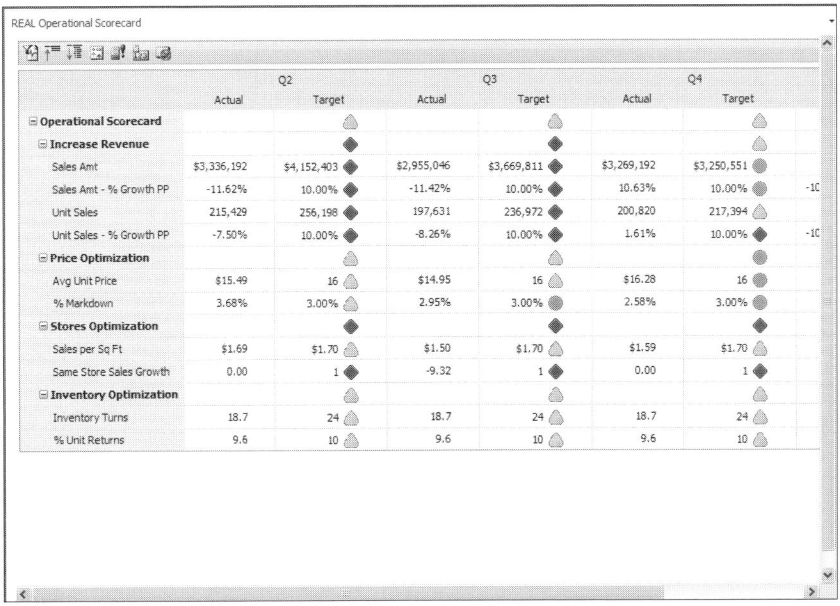

REAL Operational Scorecard

	Q2		Q3		Q4		
	Actual	Target	Actual	Target	Actual	Target	
⊟ Operational Scorecard							
⊟ Increase Revenue							
Sales Amt	$3,336,192	$4,152,403	$2,955,046	$3,669,811	$3,269,192	$3,250,551	
Sales Amt - % Growth PP	-11.62%	10.00%	-11.42%	10.00%	10.63%	10.00%	-1C
Unit Sales	215,429	256,198	197,631	236,972	200,820	217,394	
Unit Sales - % Growth PP	-7.50%	10.00%	-8.26%	10.00%	1.61%	10.00%	-1C
⊟ Price Optimization							
Avg Unit Price	$15.49	16	$14.95	16	$16.28	16	
% Markdown	3.68%	3.00%	2.95%	3.00%	2.58%	3.00%	
⊟ Stores Optimization							
Sales per Sq Ft	$1.69	$1.70	$1.50	$1.70	$1.59	$1.70	
Same Store Sales Growth	0.00	1	-9.32	1	0.00	1	
⊟ Inventory Optimization							
Inventory Turns	18.7	24	18.7	24	18.7	24	
% Unit Returns	9.6	10	9.6	10	9.6	10	

Figure 8.2: KPI Data Broken Down by Quarter.

Things become even more interesting from this point on. We're going to see the fruits of our labor in creating the foundational elements in the previous three chapters.

Details Browser

When building scorecards, the details browser becomes relevant to the design process. Up until now, this part of the UI usually contained interrelated element links for the currently open element, which have so far been KPIs, indicators, and data sources. The other function of the details browser is to provide access to the components available for building out a scorecard. Available items are dragged from the details browser onto the row or column axes in the workspace pane to build out the element. Figure 8.3 shows a blank scorecard canvas in the workspace pane and the details browser. The details browser will contain a number of different items available to work with: **KPIs**, **Metrics**, **Aggregations**, **Dimensions**, **Properties**, **Named Sets** and **Set Formulas**.

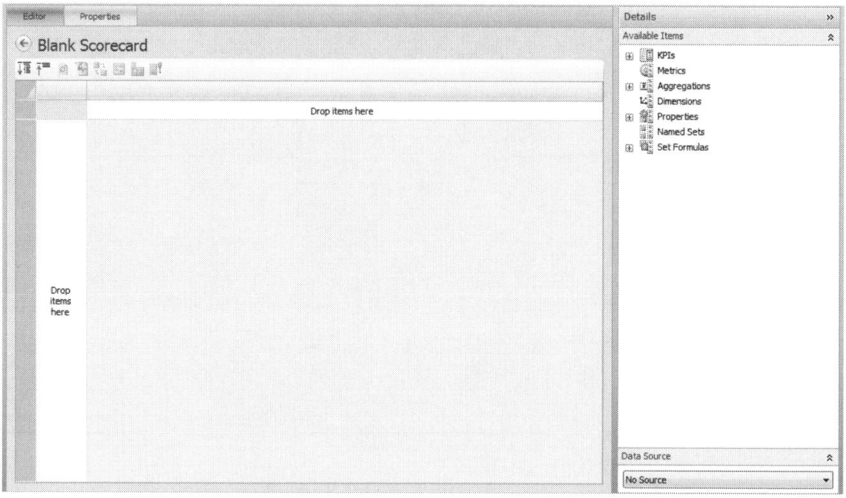

Figure 8.3: Scorecard User Interface.

The details browser is used in this same capacity for scorecards, reports, and dashboards, as we will see in subsequent chapters. Rest assured that element interdependency metadata is still available for these three elements. When the **Editor** tab is active, the details browser will display available items. Selecting the **Properties** tab will display element dependency details.

Drag and Drop Guides

The layout of scorecards is somewhat similar to that of a PivotTable (i.e., there are row and column axes on which to place items). Items can be nested along each axis as well as above and below each other. The scorecard user interface provides simple drop indicators to assist in correct placement along the axis (see Figure 8.4).

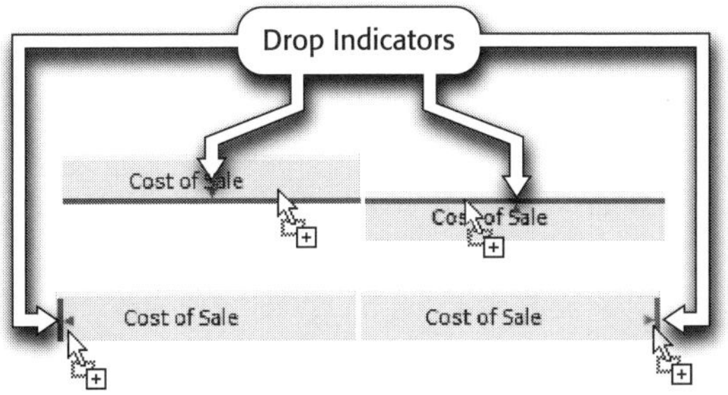

Figure 8.4: Place Above, Place Below, Nest Right, Nest Left (on Row Axis).

Commonly, it is the row axis that is used to build out a hierarchy of KPIs. On the rows axis, dropping an item to the left or right of another will nest that item accordingly. Dropping above or below will place that item at the same level of the axis hierarchy. This behavior is reversed when performed on the columns axis.

Although likened to a PivotTable style layout, scorecards have far greater flexibility when it comes to placing or moving individual items (or groups of items) on each axis. Scorecards are not bound by the same dimensional constraints as PivotTables. Once items have been placed on an axis cell by cell, adjustments can be made by using the buttons in the **Format** chunk of the **Edit** tab to either increase or decrease the items' location in the levels of the hierarchy, or move them up or down one place (Figure 8.5).

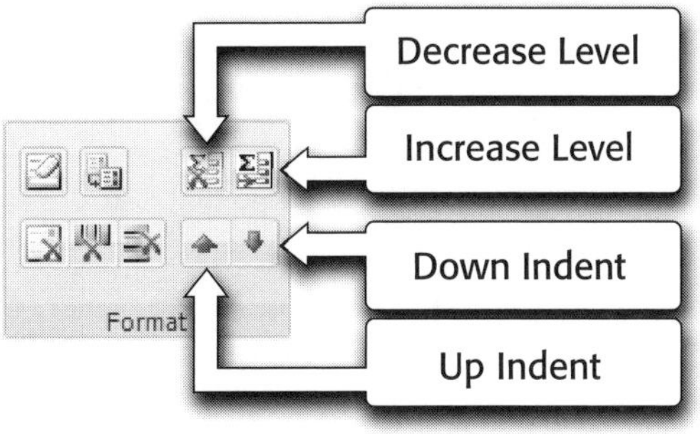

Figure 8.5: Format Chunk on Edit Tab.

Let's have a closer look at each item group available in the workspace browser.

KPIs

Without KPIs there are no scorecards. The construction of a scorecard will always begin with at least one KPI. The KPIs to be used within a scorecard must exist within the currently open workspace. Figure 8.6 shows the KPIs available for use in the workspace browser as a result of the work done in the previous chapter.

Data Source Dropdown

The **Data Source** dropdown (at the bottom of Figure 8.6) will contain the names of all the data sources used by KPIs that have been dropped onto the row or column axes of a scorecard. When the scorecard is first created, the **Data Source** dropdown will remain empty until at least one KPI has been dropped onto either the row or column axis.

Selecting a particular data source will populate the details browser with the scorecard items that are available for use. The availability of some items will depend on the data source type. For example, both tabular and multi-dimensional data sources will contain dimensions and named sets while ODBC data sources will not. Only Analysis Services data sources will enable the use of set formulas, because they are MDX based.

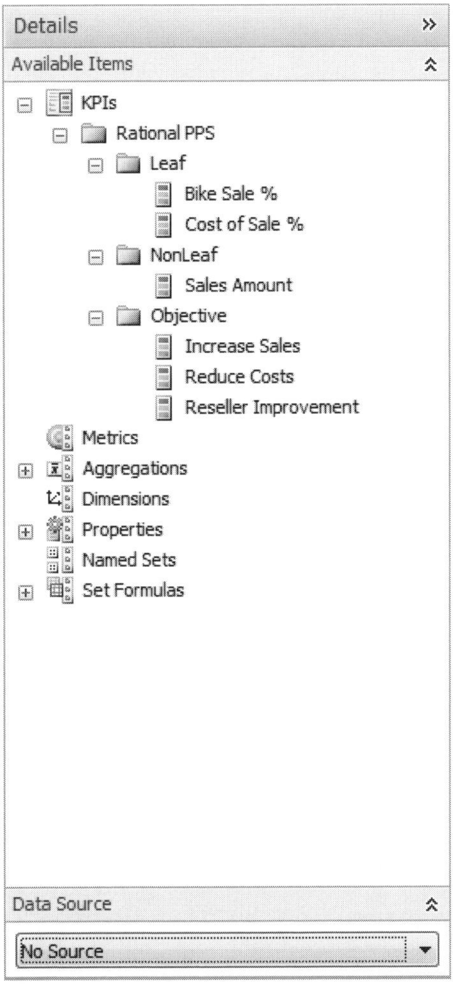

Figure 8.6: Workspace KPIs in the Details Browser.

Metrics

This is where the effort put into naming metrics within a KPI consistently pays off. Expanding this item will display the unique metric names contained in all the KPIs that are being used in the scorecard. If each KPI used in the scorecard contains consistently named metrics, this list will be short and simple to work with. The opposite is also true.

The list on the left of Figure 8.7 contains three unique metric names, while the list on the right contains nine. Both lists reference three KPIs: Revenue, Sales, and Cost. The list on the left references KPIs with consistently named metrics. In the list on the right, no care was taken to ensure the same names were used. Chaos ensues.

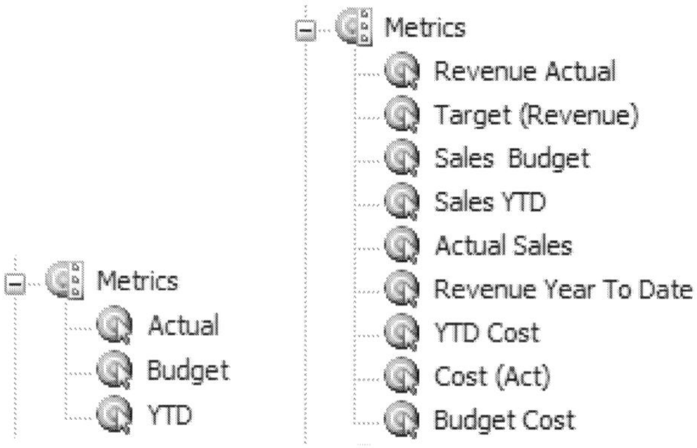

Figure 8.7: Well-named and Inconsistently-named Metrics.

Tech Tip:

Remember the time-saving benefits of the element Bulk Edit feature, which makes creating KPIs with consistent metric names and structure much easier.

Aggregations

In the past, the job of aggregating business data was left to reports, while scorecards simply rolled up KPI figures. Aggregations begin to the blur the line between what could be considered a traditional scorecard and a report.

Expanding the **Aggregations** item in the details browser reveals that this feature supports the creation of sum, minimum, maximum, average, and trend aggregations. Typically, aggregations can be configured on scorecard columns or rows. Remember that aggregation functionality can also be performed by non-leaf KPIs thanks to their calculation settings. Aggregations on the scorecard row axis are typically handled well by the use of non-leaf KPIs, whereas scorecard aggregations are best configured across the columns axis. Simply drag and drop the aggregation item of choice and use the drop guides to place them appropriately.

Figure 8.8 shows a scorecard that includes one of each type of scorecard aggregation. The **Sum**, **Minimum**, **Maximum**, and **Average** aggregations perform their functions across the four quarters of FY 2004. The **Trend** aggregation compares the last two non-aggregate columns and uses an indicator (that is created automatically) to display the result of the comparison.

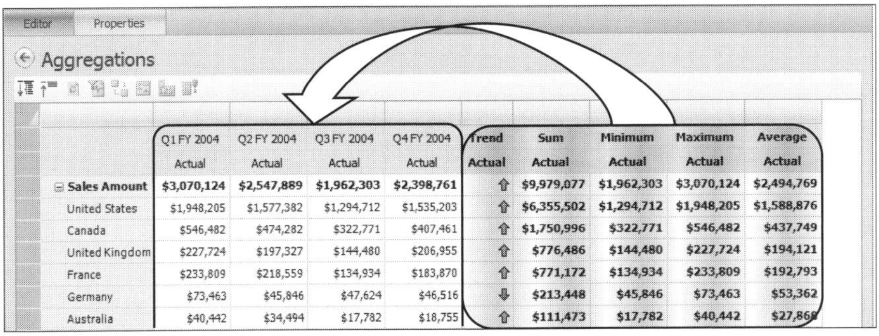

	Q1 FY 2004	Q2 FY 2004	Q3 FY 2004	Q4 FY 2004	Trend	Sum	Minimum	Maximum	Average
	Actual	Actual	Actual	Actual	Actual	Actual	Actual	Actual	Actual
Sales Amount	$3,070,124	$2,547,889	$1,962,303	$2,398,761	⇧	$9,979,077	$1,962,303	$3,070,124	$2,494,769
United States	$1,948,205	$1,577,382	$1,294,712	$1,535,203	⇧	$6,355,502	$1,294,712	$1,948,205	$1,588,876
Canada	$546,482	$474,282	$322,771	$407,461	⇧	$1,750,996	$322,771	$546,482	$437,749
United Kingdom	$227,724	$197,327	$144,480	$206,955	⇧	$776,486	$144,480	$227,724	$194,121
France	$233,809	$218,559	$134,934	$183,870	⇧	$771,172	$134,934	$233,809	$192,793
Germany	$73,463	$45,846	$47,624	$46,516	⇩	$213,448	$45,846	$73,463	$53,362
Australia	$40,442	$34,494	$17,782	$18,755	⇧	$111,473	$17,782	$40,442	$27,868

Figure 8.8: Scorecard with Aggregations.

Tech Tip:

The trend calculation performed by trend aggregations in scorecards is quite rudimentary. More advanced trend calculations can be created using MDX tuple formulas within a Target. For example, you could determine the trend based on the average of the last *n* periods compared to the period in question.

Dimensions

When a multidimensional or tabular data source is selected in the details browser **data source** dropdown, all the dimensions configured in that structure will be made available for use. The drag and drop functionality for dimensions (or attributes and attribute hierarchies in Analysis Services 2005) is very flexible. Any members of any dimension can be placed anywhere on a scorecard axis; this provides enormous potential to the way a scorecard can be laid out.

When a dimension is dropped into an axis, the **Member Selector** dialog appears, filled with the members of the dimension. Individual members can be selected manually using the check boxes. Alternately, right-clicking members produces a contextual menu containing several time saving options, such as **Check Children** and **Check Visible** (see Figure 8.9).

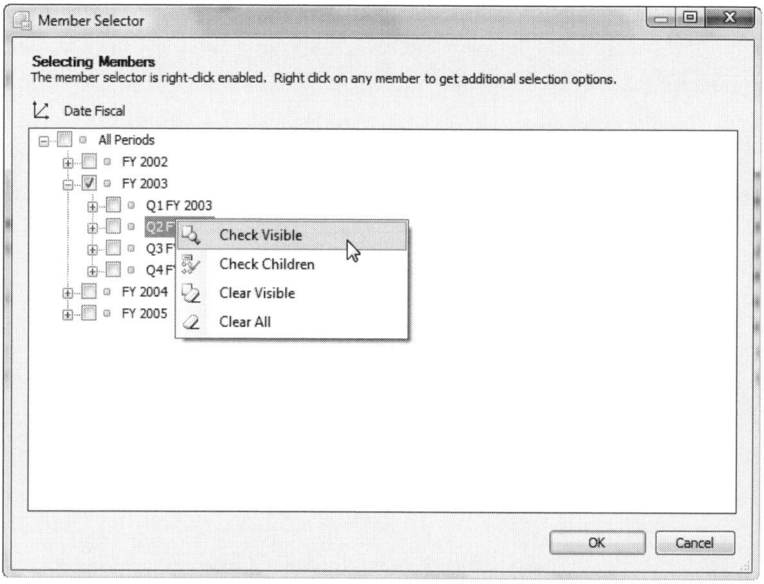

Figure 8.9: Member Selector Dialog.

Properties

Alongside the ever present Name, Description, and Person Responsible properties, each element can have Custom Properties defined (these were referenced in Chapter 4 when covering element metadata). The data configured in both the common and custom properties for each KPI contained in the scorecard will be available under the properties item. The creation of Custom Properties on a KPI (or any other element for that matter) should be named consistently, just like we saw with metrics.

Tech Tip:

Properties present a simple way to add extra metadata to a scorecard. Information such as the e-mail address of the KPI owner or the last date that the KPI definition was changed are useful additions to KPI metadata. Element custom properties support text, decimal, date, and hyperlink data types. Use them liberally and consistently.

Named Sets

The **Named Sets** node in the details browser will only contain items for use in a scorecard if the data source type selected is a multidimensional or tabular data source. If it's an Analysis Services data source, then named sets must be defined within the cube. For tabular data sources, a collection of named sets is created on the fly by the tabular data source provider (TDSP) using the metadata configured on the data source itself.

Named sets are added to a scorecard by dropping them onto one of the axes. When the **Update** button is pressed, the tuples that make up the set will be added to the scorecard. The AdventureWorksPPS cube contains several named sets that can be experimented with. For example, the *Large Resellers* named set contains the members of the Reseller dimension attribute that have 81-100 employees.

Set Formulas

Set formulas do a very similar job to named sets with one major difference: these sets do not need to be defined in the source cube first. Instead, any MDX statement that returns a set can be used in a set formula at scorecard design time. The members of the set are added to the axis on which the set formula was defined.

Dragging the **Custom** item under the **Set Formula** node from the details browser onto a scorecard axis will bring up the **Set Formula Editor**, where you can enter an MDX expression that returns a set (see Figure 8.10).

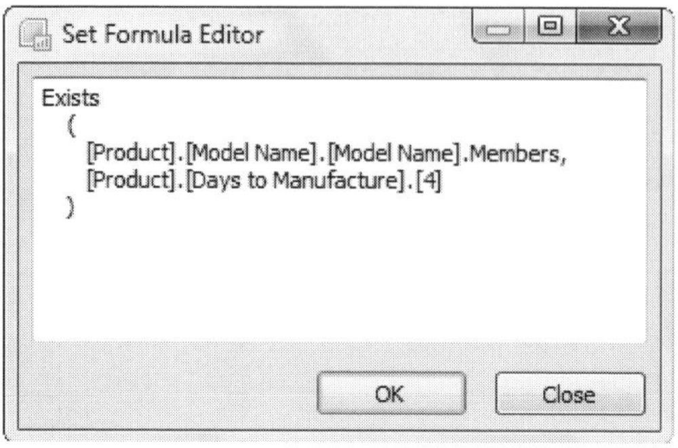

Figure 8.10: Set Formula Editor with MDX Set Expression.

Tech Tip:

When configuring named sets and set formulas, the corresponding members do not appear on the scorecard immediately. Clicking the Update button on the Scorecard Editor chunk of the Edit tab will populate the axis with the appropriate set members.

Creating the Reseller Improvement Scorecard

Now that we know a bit more about the tools we have to work with, it is time to build out a scorecard. Follow these steps to create the Reseller Improvement scorecard:

1. Make sure MyWorkspace.bswx is open in DD.
2. On the **Objects** chunk of the **Create** tab, click **Scorecard**.
3. In the **Category** pane, select **Standard** and select **Blank Scorecard** in the **Template** pane. Click **OK**.
4. Fill in the standard element metadata as per Table 8.1 and click **Finish**.

Property	Value
Name	Reseller Improvement
Default display folder location	Rational PPS
Grand Read permission to all users...	Checked ✓

Table 8.1: Reseller Improvement Scorecard Properties.

Populating the Scorecard

Follow these steps to populate the scorecard with KPIs:

1. In the details browser, expand the **KPIs** node down to **Rational PPS \ NonLeaf**. Drag and drop the **Sales Amount** KPI onto the row axis. Note how the three metrics contained in this KPI were automatically added to the scorecard.

2. Select the **Edit** ribbon tab and click the **Update** button on the **Scorecard Editor** chunk to populate the metrics with data from the data source.

3. In the details browser, expand the **Dimensions** node. Drag and drop the **Reseller Type** dimension to the right of the **Sales Amount** KPI to nest members beneath it in the hierarchy. Remember to use the drop guides.

4. In the **Member Selector**, right-click **All Resellers** and select **Check Children**. Click **OK**.

5. Click **Update** again. Note how the **Reseller Type** figures are being aggregated by the **Sales Amount** KPI.

6. Expand the **KPIs** node to **Rational PPS\Leaf**. Drag the **Bike Sale %** KPI onto the row axis and drop it beneath the **Warehouse Reseller Type** item. This is not exactly where we want this KPI in the hierarchy; it needs to be out-dented one level so that it is a sibling of the **Sales Amount** KPI. To do this, select the **Bike Sale %** item and click the **Increase Level** button on the **Format** chunk of the **Edit** tab.

7. Expand the **KPIs** node to **Rational PPS\Objective** and drop the **Increase Sales** KPI to the left of the **Sales Amount** KPI. Because the **Sales Amount** and **Bike Sale %** KPIs are on the same level, the drop guides appear to the left of both (see Figure 8.11)

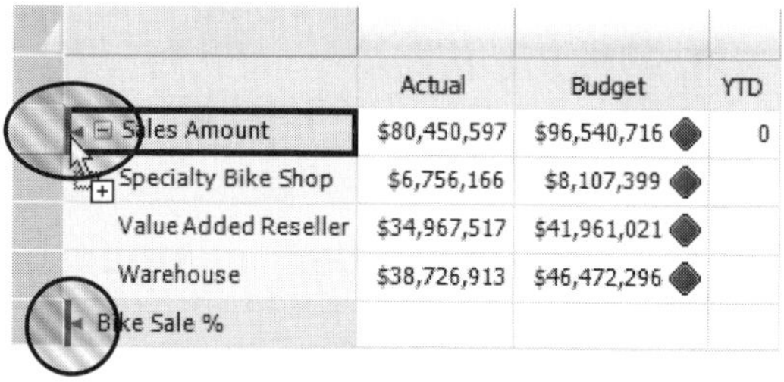

Figure 8.11: Drop Guides for KPIs on Same Level.

8. Drop the **Reduce Costs** objective KPI (Rational PPS\Objective) directly underneath the **Bike Sale %** KPI. Select the **Reduce Costs** item in the hierarchy and click **Increase Level** to nest it at the same level as the **Increase Sales** objective KPI.

9. Drop the **Cost of Sale %** leaf KPI (Rational PPS\Leaf) to the right of the **Reduce Costs** KPI. Click **Update**.

10. Drop the **Reseller Improvement** objective KPI (Rational PPS\Objective) to the left of the **Increase Sales** KPI. Note once again that the drop guides indicate that this objective will be a parent for the **Increase Sales** and **Reduce Costs** hierarchy items.

11. Click **Update**. Your scorecard should look similar to Figure 8.12. It is worth calling out the fact that the YTD column does not show any data in the scorecard preview. This behavior is correct; we are not yet slicing the scorecard data by a time dimension. Year-to-date calculations, naturally, require a year value. This will be configured in Chapter 10.

12. Click **Publish All** and save the workspace.

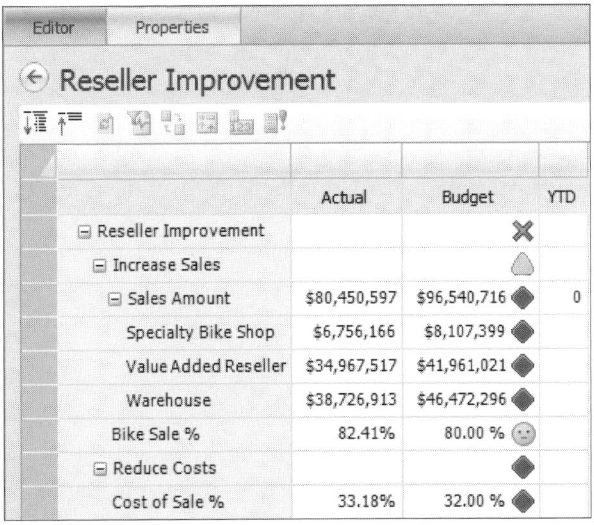

Editor | Properties

Reseller Improvement

	Actual	Budget	YTD
Reseller Improvement			
Increase Sales			
Sales Amount	$80,450,597	$96,540,716	0
Specialty Bike Shop	$6,756,166	$8,107,399	
Value Added Reseller	$34,967,517	$41,961,021	
Warehouse	$38,726,913	$46,472,296	
Bike Sale %	82.41%	80.00 %	
Reduce Costs			
Cost of Sale %	33.18%	32.00 %	

Figure 8.12: Scorecard Preview.

Tech Tip:

Scorecards have great capabilities when it comes to creating complex, useful layouts. Take the time to experiment by adding multiple nested hierarchies along axes, as well as using increase/decrease level and up/down buttons to further customize the layout. Holding down the SHIFT key when adding nested dimension members changes the drop guide options available, facilitating the creation of more asymmetric scorecard hierarchies.

Scorecard Wizards

While creating the scorecard, you will have noticed the multitude of scorecard wizards that are available. Each of these wizards is made up of a very similar framework—they facilitate not only the creation of a scorecard, but optionally the creation of the KPIs that are contained in that scorecard. At first glance, many would wonder why we have gone to all the trouble to craft KPIs and a scorecard by hand when the one of the many scorecard wizards can do it for us in several easy steps. The KPIs created with a scorecard wizard are quite simple in nature, consisting of one Actual and one Target metric that utilize the measures available in one data source.

Nonetheless, scorecard wizards are a great tool to whip up a quick scorecard based on a particular data source. Each of the wizards follows a similar set of steps:

1. Configure scorecard metadata.
2. Select a data source.
3. Create/Add KPIs.
4. Add Measure Filters (optional).
5. Add Member Columns (optional).
6. Create scorecard.

These wizards offer an excellent way to quickly create both scorecards and a large number of KPIs in a few quick steps. In most cases, however, the business requirements for KPIs and scorecards will normally exceed the functionality provided by the wizards. The same is also true for the layout of the scorecard. Now that we have done everything "the hard way" up to this point, you should understand the processes covered by each step of each scorecard wizard flavor. Experiment with each wizard type to discover how they may help speed up some aspects of element creation.

Tech Tip:

The Fixed Values scorecard wizard is very helpful in putting together a "quick and dirty" proof-of-concept scorecard with ease. The Create KPI step can be a great time saver for creating a large number of simple KPIs and entering fixed sample values simultaneously.

Analysis Services KPIs

One of the scorecard wizards that contains special functionality is Analysis Services (SSAS). This wizard facilitates the creation of workspace KPIs based on KPIs defined in an SSAS cube. The important thing to remember about this process is that the SSAS KPI is not really "imported." In reality, KPI elements are created that simply reference the values produced by the cube-based KPIs using MDX.

Importing SSAS KPIs

Follow these steps to import definitions from the AdventureWorksPPS cube:

1. Make sure MyWorkspace.bswx is open in DD.

2. Right-click the **Scorecards** node in the workspace browser and select **New Scorecard**.

3. In the **Select a Scorecard Template** dialog, select **Microsoft** in the **Category** pane and then **Analysis Services** in the **Template** pane. Click **OK**.

4. Fill in the standard element metadata as per Table 8.2 and click **Next**.

Property	Value
Name	Import SSAS KPI
Default display folder location	Rational PPS\SSAS
Grand Read permission to all users...	Checked ✓

Table 8.2: Import SSAS KPI Scorecard Properties.

5. In the **Select a Data Source** step, select the **AdventureWorksPPS** data source. Click **Next**.

6. Select the **Import SQL Server Analysis Services KPIs** radio button. Click **Next**.

7. Check the boxes for **Channel Revenue**, **Gross Profit Margin**, and **Discount Percentage** KPIs. Click **Next**.

8. Click **Next** on the **Add Measure Filters** step.

9. In the **Add member columns** step, check the **Add column members** check box. Click the **Select Dimension** button and select **Date.Fiscal** in the **Dimension Selector** and click **OK**. Click the **Select Members** button and expand the **All Periods** member. Right-click the **FY 2004** member and select **Check Children**. Click **OK**.

10. Click **Finish** and then click **Close** on the **Confirmation** step.

11. Select the **Edit** tab and click the **Pivot** button located on the **Format** chunk. Your scorecard should look similar to that in Figure 8.13. Click **Publish All** and save the workspace.

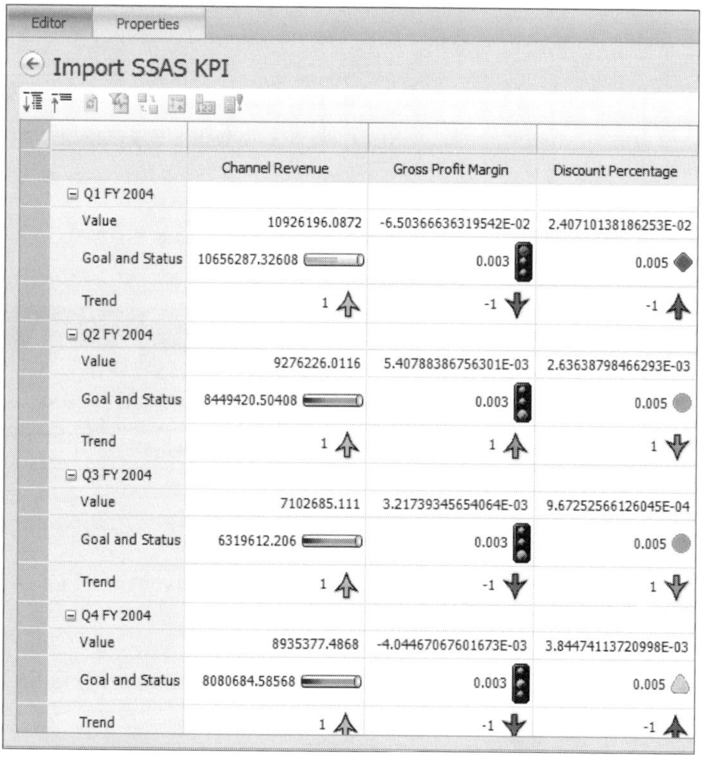

	Channel Revenue	Gross Profit Margin	Discount Percentage
Q1 FY 2004			
Value	10926196.0872	-6.50366636319542E-02	2.40710138186253E-02
Goal and Status	10656287.32608	0.003	0.005
Trend	1	-1	-1
Q2 FY 2004			
Value	9276226.0116	5.40788386756301E-03	2.63638798466293E-03
Goal and Status	8449420.50408	0.003	0.005
Trend	1	1	1
Q3 FY 2004			
Value	7102685.111	3.21739345654064E-03	9.67252566126045E-04
Goal and Status	6319612.206	0.003	0.005
Trend	1	-1	1
Q4 FY 2004			
Value	8935377.4868	-4.04467067601673E-03	3.84474113720998E-03
Goal and Status	8080684.58568	0.003	0.005
Trend	1	-1	-1

Figure 8.13: Imported SSAS KPIs in a Scorecard.

Aside from the newly created scorecard, the most interesting output from this process is three new workspace KPIs, along with several new indicators. Take time to examine the properties of the metrics contained therein. Imported SSAS KPIs use the **Band by stated score (advanced)** banding method for their thresholds. They also use MDX KPI functions to access the values in each of the Actual, Goal, Status, and Trend areas of the SSAS KPI object.

Note that there are no number formats applied to the **Value** and **Goal and Status** metrics (see Figure 8.13). This can easily be remedied by changing the Number Format property in the KPIs.

Scorecard Configuration

Now that the appropriate items have been dragged, dropped, and updated onto the working surface, the Reseller Improvement scorecard is beginning to take shape. The opportunity now exists to configure a number of different properties to ensure that the scorecard communicates the data it contains as effectively and efficiently as possible. While formatting and colors play a part, the most important aspect of this part of scorecard development is the configuration of Targets.

Target Settings

The display properties of each Target metric on a scorecard can be individually configured. This configuration is very much centered around what is to be displayed inside each cell for that Target in the scorecard. Figure 8.14 shows the **Target Settings** dialog, which is divided into four areas: **Values**, **Scoring**, **Indicators**, and **Overrides**.

The **Target Settings** dialog can be accessed by selecting the Target name header (in this case **Budget**) on the scorecard axis and clicking the **Properties** button on the **Scorecard Editor** chunk of the **Edit** tab.

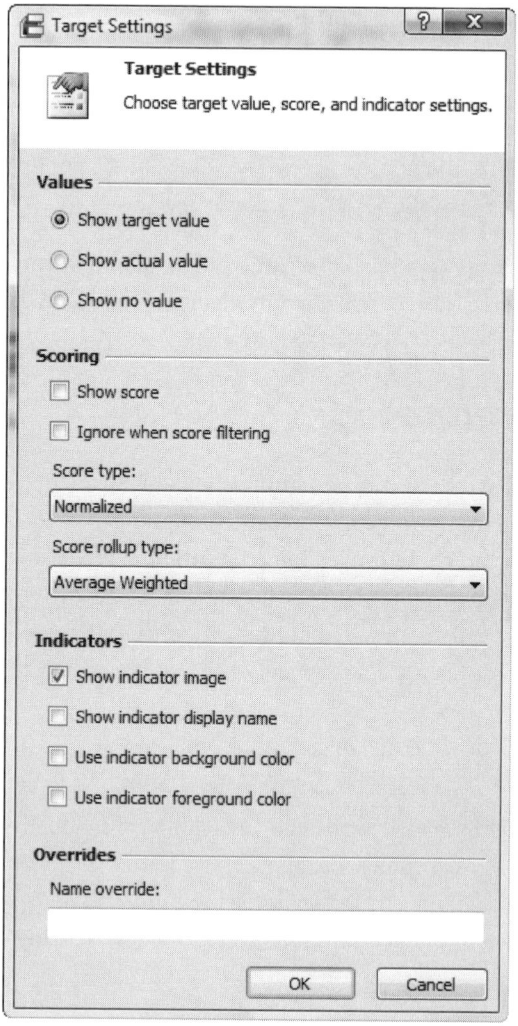

Figure 8.14: Target Settings Dialog.

Tech Tip:

No property settings can be configured for actual metrics. Actuals simply display the data they are linked to, nothing more. Target metrics contain all the configurable functionality.

Values

The value displayed in a Target is very important. Using radio buttons, we can either choose to **Show target value**, **Show actual value**, or **Show no value**. Naturally, the option chosen depends on the scorecard requirements. An understanding of the flexibility available here can assist in creating scorecards that communicate information efficiently.

For example, a particular scorecard requires that the Actual value be displayed with an image next to it depicting the Actual value's comparison to the Target. The value of the Target does not need to be seen. In this case, the **Show actual value** option is the perfect choice; instead of dragging both the Actual and Target metrics onto the scorecard, we can display required data in the one Target. Figure 8.15 shows the difference between fulfilling the above requirements using an Actual and a Target compared to one properly configured Target. We kill two birds with one stone and save valuable screen real estate.

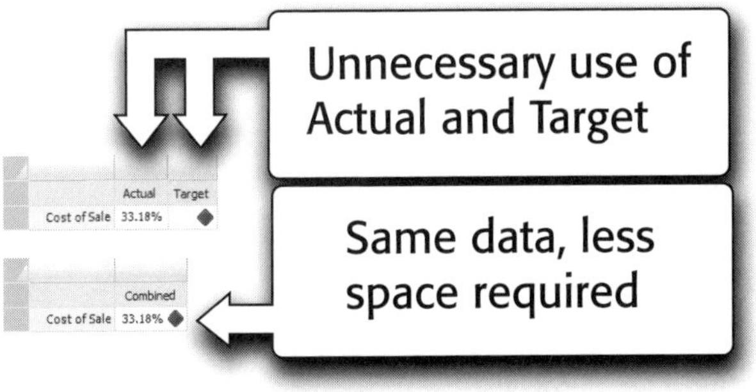

Figure 8.15: Efficient Target Configuration.

> **Note:**
>
> **There is no option to show both Actual and Target values within the one target metric.**

Scoring

The score is a percentage value calculated for each individual leaf KPI in a scorecard hierarchy. It is this score that allows KPI values to be rolled up, resulting in the all-important (hopefully green) image at the top level that indicates that the business is on track. Because KPI figures can consist of a variety of numeric data types such as dollars, percentages, and decimals, a consistent numeric format is needed in order for KPIs to be comparable, and hence rolled up.

The score can be displayed in a Target by checking the **Show Score** option. Irrespective of whether it is displayed or not, score is always calculated internally by the scorecard.

The **Score Types** dropdown determines the algorithm used to calculate the score. The options available are as follows:

- **Raw** uses the number that is calculated as a result of the banding method and calculation settings configured on the target threshold.
- **Normalized** begins with the raw score number calculated using the threshold settings. The raw score value, the number of levels in the Target indicator, and the threshold boundary values are used in a formula that calculates the score across a linear scale.

The normalized scoring method is the one that should be used when implementing any of the scorecarding methodologies such as Balanced Scorecard, Six Sigma, etc. The linear scale that is applied in this method ensures that the score is normalized across all KPIs. It is strongly advised *not* to use the raw scoring with the aim of rolling up KPI values. Because no normalization is applied to raw scores, inaccurate rollup numbers can result. Scoring is a quite complex topic and is discussed in detail in the bonus chapter on Scoring, available with the downloadable material for this book. See the last page in this book for information.

Tech Tip:

The Normalized score percentage may not make much sense to scorecard users when displayed in the scorecard. It is advisable when using this method to keep the score number itself hidden. Again, please refer to the bonus chapter on Scoring, which will help you understand the normalized score calculation process.

The selected option in the **Score Rollup Type** dropdown determines what will be displayed in objective KPIs in the scorecard hierarchy:

- **None** — No rollup is calculated; the target cell is left blank (Figure 8.16).

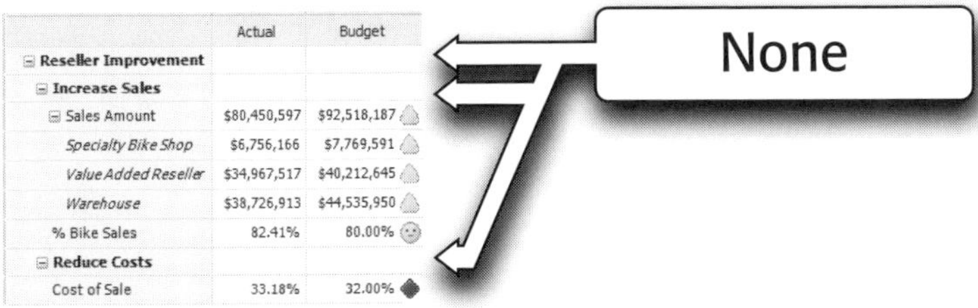

	Actual	Budget
Reseller Improvement		
Increase Sales		
Sales Amount	$80,450,597	$92,518,187
Specialty Bike Shop	$6,756,166	$7,769,591
Value Added Reseller	$34,967,517	$40,212,645
Warehouse	$38,726,913	$44,535,950
% Bike Sales	82.41%	80.00%
Reduce Costs		
Cost of Sale	33.18%	32.00%

Figure 8.16: No Rollup.

- **Average Weighted (default)** — Uses the calculated score combined with the weight assigned to each item in the hierarchy to drive the configured indicator display for the objective KPI (Figure 8.17).

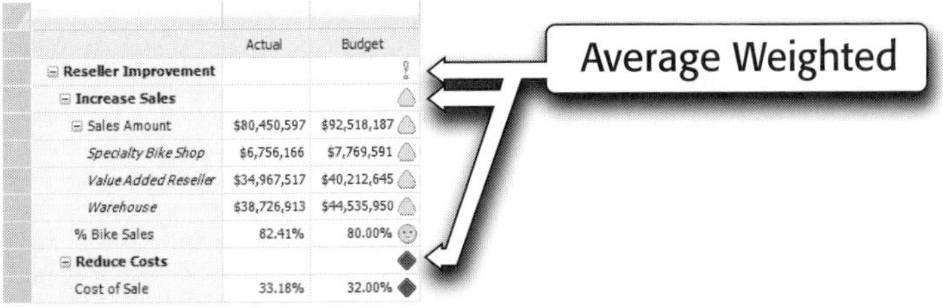

	Actual	Budget
Reseller Improvement		
Increase Sales		
Sales Amount	$80,450,597	$92,518,187
Specialty Bike Shop	$6,756,166	$7,769,591
Value Added Reseller	$34,967,517	$40,212,645
Warehouse	$38,726,913	$44,535,950
% Bike Sales	82.41%	80.00%
Reduce Costs		
Cost of Sale	33.18%	32.00%

Figure 8.17: Average Weighted Rollup.

- **Indicator Count** — Displays a count of indicator images located beneath each objective KPI (Figure 8.18)

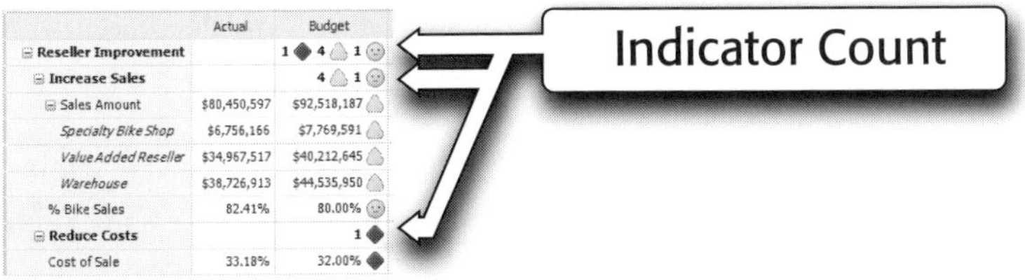

	Actual	Budget
Reseller Improvement		1 4 1
Increase Sales		4 1
Sales Amount	$80,450,597	$92,518,187
Specialty Bike Shop	$6,756,166	$7,769,591
Value Added Reseller	$34,967,517	$40,212,645
Warehouse	$38,726,913	$44,535,950
% Bike Sales	82.41%	80.00%
Reduce Costs		1
Cost of Sale	33.18%	32.00%

Figure 8.18: Indicator Count Rollup.

- **Worst Child** — Displays the configured Target information for the child KPI with the worst score (Figure 8.19).

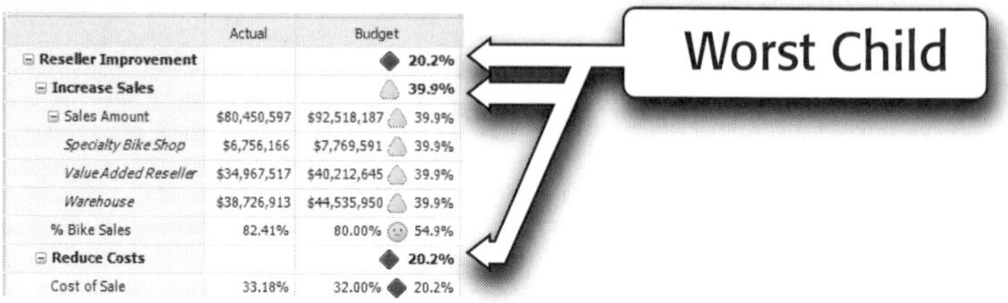

	Actual	Budget	
Reseller Improvement			20.2%
Increase Sales			39.9%
Sales Amount	$80,450,597	$92,518,187	39.9%
Specialty Bike Shop	$6,756,166	$7,769,591	39.9%
Value Added Reseller	$34,967,517	$40,212,645	39.9%
Warehouse	$38,726,913	$44,535,950	39.9%
% Bike Sales	82.41%	80.00%	54.9%
Reduce Costs			20.2%
Cost of Sale	33.18%	32.00%	20.2%

Figure 8.19: Worst Child Rollup.

Indicators

The **Indicators** section of the **Target Settings** dialog contains check boxes that allow the visibility to be set for all four properties configured in an indicator level. You'll remember from Chapter 6 that these were *image*, *display name*, *background color*, and *text color*. Because they are check boxes, any combination of indicator level properties can be displayed in a Target.

Overrides

This text box simply allows the display name of the Target as it appears in the scorecard to be changed.

Weight

Is one particular KPI more important than others? How much more? Do the KPIs grouped under a specific objective provide more value to the business in the context of the current scorecard? Configuring the **Score Rollup Weight** property on a KPI item facilitates the "balancing" of items within the scorecard hierarchy. The higher the number assigned relative to all other items on that level, the greater the importance of that item. The Normalized scoring method takes this weight into account when calculating score rollup. More detailed information on this process is covered in the Scoring bonus chapter.

The weight of a particular scorecard hierarchy item can be accessed by selecting the KPI name in the scorecard and clicking the **Properties** button. Figure 8.20 shows the **KPI View Settings** dialog. Note that the KPI display name can be changed if required.

Figure 8.20: KPI View Settings Dialog.

The default weight for all KPIs when added to a scorecard is 1. Weight is a property of the KPI and the role it plays in an individual scorecard.

Scorecard Toolbar Options

Each published scorecard exposes extra interactivity options to end users via the toolbar in the upper left corner of the scorecard. Using the **Toolbar Options** dialog (shown in Figure 8.21), the scorecard designer can choose to hide the toolbar altogether or expose specific buttons in the published scorecard. The functions exposed in this toolbar are detailed in Chapter 11, which covers the Dashboard Item web part.

View Options

The **View Options** dialog (Figure 8.22) is used to configure global settings on a scorecard. Data display settings such as how empty or error cell information is displayed can be set in the **Data Cells** section. Enabling or disabling scorecard comment functionality is also set in this dialog, as well as other view-based settings.

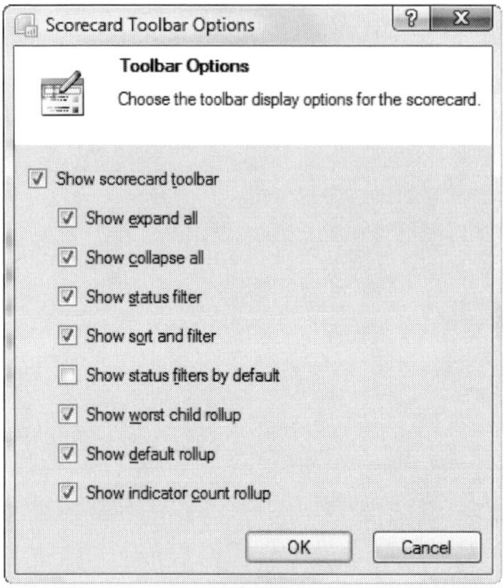

Figure 8.21: Scorecard Toolbar Options Dialog.

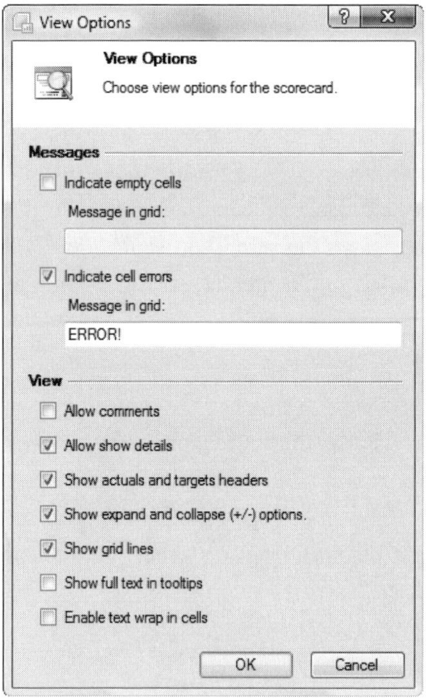

Figure 8.22: View Options Dialog.

Note:

Remember that in order to allow comments on a scorecard, the Monitoring server to which the scorecard is published needs to be configured to allow comments. This was covered in Chapter 4.

Formatting and Layout

You are no doubt familiar with the ability to format the font type, font weight, background color, etc. using standard Microsoft user interface paradigms and the tools housed in the **Font** and **Format** chunks. However, it is worth calling out just how much formatting flexibility all the tools in the **Edit** tab bring to the table (see Figure 8.23). Specific tools in various chunks become active depending on what part of the scorecard is selected. This provides simple visual clues as to what functionality is available.

Figure 8.23: Scorecard Edit Tab.

Tech Tip:

Font style can be set on an individual row or column basis. This opens the possibility of creative use of font styles such as Wingdings and Webdings. Naturally, most of the scorecard visualization functionality will be handled by indicators but the opportunity to be creative is there nonetheless. The ability to display special characters in the appropriate place based on data returned from a query or MDX formula can be quite powerful.

Reporting Services Deployment

Scorecard definitions can be deployed to a Reporting Services (SSRS) instance. Simply right-click on the scorecard in the workspace browser and select **Deploy ⇨ SQL Server Reporting Services** from the context menu (Figure 8.24).

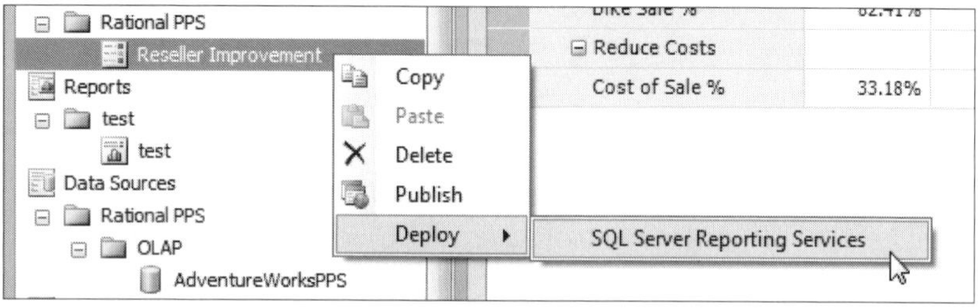

Figure 8.24: Deploy to Reporting Services Option.

A simple wizard will step through a deployment to either a Report Definition Language (.rdl) file (which can be saved locally) or the generated report can be deployed directly to an SSRS server.

Note:

To use deployed SSRS scorecards, the Reporting Services Scorecard Viewer must be installed on the SSRS server where the report is deployed. Editing the .rdl file in Visual Studio 2005 requires the Reporting Services plug in.

Summary

This chapter covered scorecards and the multitude of options and functionality available when creating elements of this type. Scorecards are built by dragging items from the details browser onto scorecard row and column axes in the workspace pane. The KPIs contained in a single scorecard can utilize data from multiple data sources. We created a scorecard using the data sources, indicators, and KPIs created in the previous three chapters. The building process is made easier by the ability to preview the scorecard inside the DD interface. A number of different scorecard wizards provide step-by-step functionality to quickly create scorecards and their constituent KPIs in several simple steps.

Chapter 9

Reports

Much of this book has focused on building scorecards and their constituent parts. When an end user views the content of our scorecard and sees a particular KPI that is not performing as expected, the first question is, naturally, "Why?" The *report* is the element by which we attempt to answer that question.

The term *report* is pretty non-specific when you think about it. To some, a report is a paginated document that provides static, organized, often summarized data on a specific business area or problem. To others, a report can be an interactive item that provides functionality to delve into the detailed records behind a certain figure. There are many other derivations of what people consider a report, but we'll just agree that it can mean different things to different people. It is beyond the scope of this book to define what a report is or isn't and why. For the purposes of the report element within PPS Monitoring, a report is a reusable element that can take many forms and provide access to both interactive and static data in a number of different ways. How's *that* for fence sitting?

Reports are elements unto themselves and therefore offer enormous flexibility in their use. In *The Rational Guide to Microsoft® Office Business Scorecard Manager 2005,* we often made reference to "scorecard-centric dashboards." In BSM, reports were built *into* the definition of KPIs and scorecard elements. This meant that in order for report data to be available, a scorecard was a mandatory part of every solution, in order to expose the reports that made up part of their definition. In PPS Monitoring, this has changed, so we are not bound by the scorecard-centric rules any more. Because almost all report types can stand on their own, there may not even be a need to create a single KPI, let alone a scorecard, in order to build a useful dashboard; you could just use reports.

Report Types

There are many options when it comes to the report types available:

- Analytic Chart & Analytic Grid
- SQL Server Report
- Strategy Map
- Excel Services
- Trend Analysis Chart *
- ProClarity Analytics Server Page
- Web Page
- PivotChart & PivotTable *
- Spreadsheet *

* Requires that Office 2003 Web Components (OWC) be installed on the client machine.

Tech Tip:

Several report types rely on OWC being installed on the client machine in order to deliver their content. The OWC product is not undergoing any further development and support for it will be removed in subsequent versions of PPS. With the exception of the Trend Analysis Chart, the OWC-dependant report types have been included in this release of PPS for backwards compatibility with BSM. In future releases, the Trend Analysis Chart report type will use a different charting engine, while functionality provided by Pivot and Excel report types will be provided by new components.

Report Endpoints

Reports will eventually be exposed to end users through dashboards. The content of a report within a dashboard is often required to be driven by a user's interaction with other objects on the dashboard. Some report types expose interfaces that are often referred to as *filters* or *parameters* in order to accept information and drive this contextual functionality. We will refer to these interfaces simply as *endpoints* from here on. Not only is this a nice generic term, it also meshes well with the upcoming chapter on dashboards.

When designing reports, it is important to think about what endpoints need to be made available. What information needs to be provided to drive the report behavior? The answer will determine what endpoints need to be configured or created. In this chapter, we will call out parts of a particular report type that are exposed as endpoints. If specific endpoint configuration is not detailed for a report type, then no action is required when designing these elements.

Analytic Chart and Analytic Grid

Analytic charts and grids are powerful report types that expose data from Analysis Services multidimensional data sources. The functionality available to the designer of the report and the end user thin-client interactivity means that this report type will be heavily featured in many dashboards. The functionality provided by these reports really underscores the advantages of having data stored in Analysis services cubes. Analytic chart and grid report functionality could easily take up an entire chapter.

Analytic chart reports support two base chart types, each with a few different flavors:

- **Bar Chart** — Standard, stacked, 100% stacked.
- **Line Chart** — Standard, with markers.

It appears that analytic grid and chart reports are two completely separate types, but they are not. Grid reports can be converted to charts and vice versa with the click of the **Report Type** button found on the **Format** chunk of the **Edit** tab (see Figure 9.1).

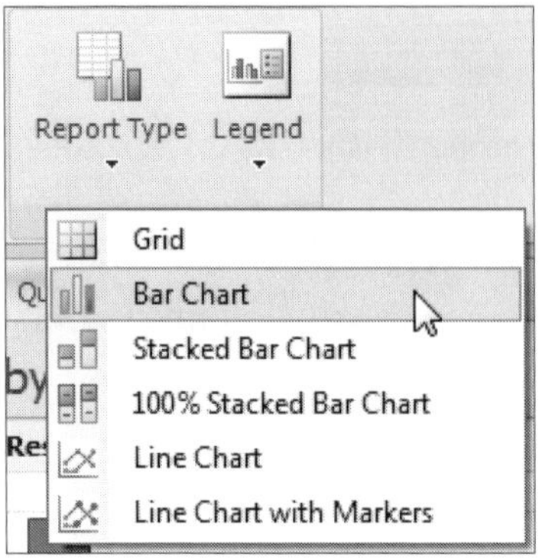

Figure 9.1: Report Type Options.

Both report types can be designed in two (well, two-and-a-half) different ways: drag and drop, custom MDX, or a combination of the two. The functionality requirements of the report will determine which method is used. The design interfaces for chart and grid reports are virtually identical. The only real difference is the format in which the report data is presented, and as mentioned earlier, this can be changed easily by both the designer or the eventual end user whenever needed.

Drag and Drop

The details browser provides access to all the available measures, dimensions, and named sets defined in the source cube. In the **Design** tab of the workspace pane cube, items can be dragged and dropped into **Series, Bottom Axis**, or **Background** areas for charts and similarly **Row**, **Columns**, and **Background** areas for grids in order to build out definitions. Figure 9.2 shows the details browser and the **Design** tab of an analytic chart and where available items are dropped onto axis areas.

Figure 9.3 shows the **Design** tab of the same report shown in Figure 9.2; the report type has simply been switched to **Grid**.

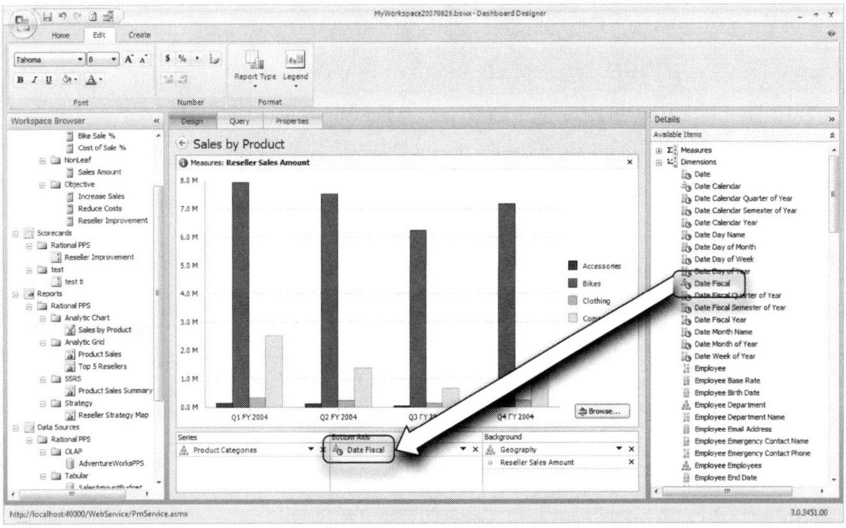

Figure 9.2: Analytic Chart Design Tab.

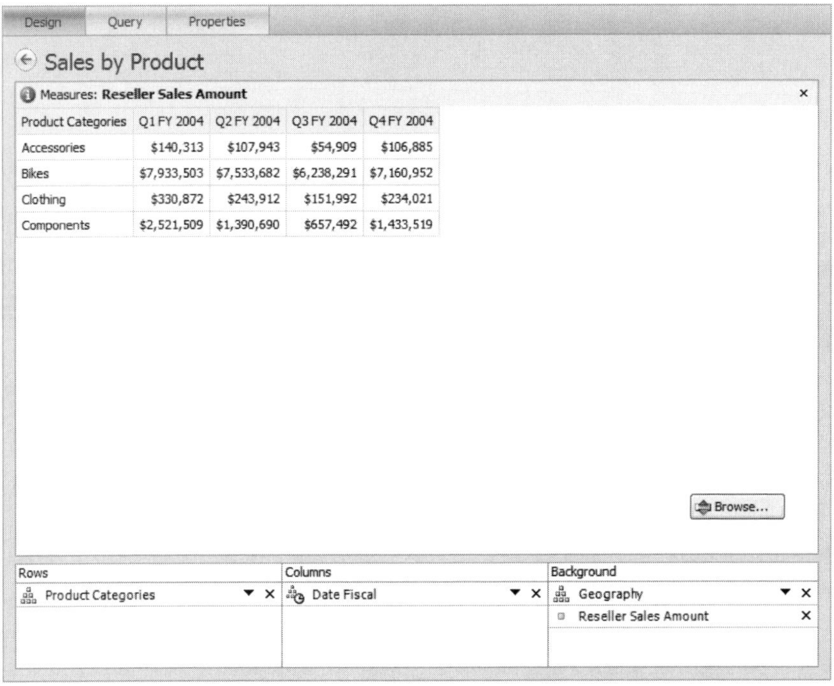

Product Categories	Q1 FY 2004	Q2 FY 2004	Q3 FY 2004	Q4 FY 2004
Accessories	$140,313	$107,943	$54,909	$106,885
Bikes	$7,933,503	$7,533,682	$6,238,291	$7,160,952
Clothing	$330,872	$243,912	$151,992	$234,021
Components	$2,521,509	$1,390,690	$657,492	$1,433,519

Figure 9.3: Analytic Grid Design Tab.

Member Selection

Once a dimension has been dropped into one of the axis areas of a report, a number of options are available to determine which members are displayed. Clicking the down arrow on an axis dimension will bring up the **Member Selector** dialog (Figure 9.4).

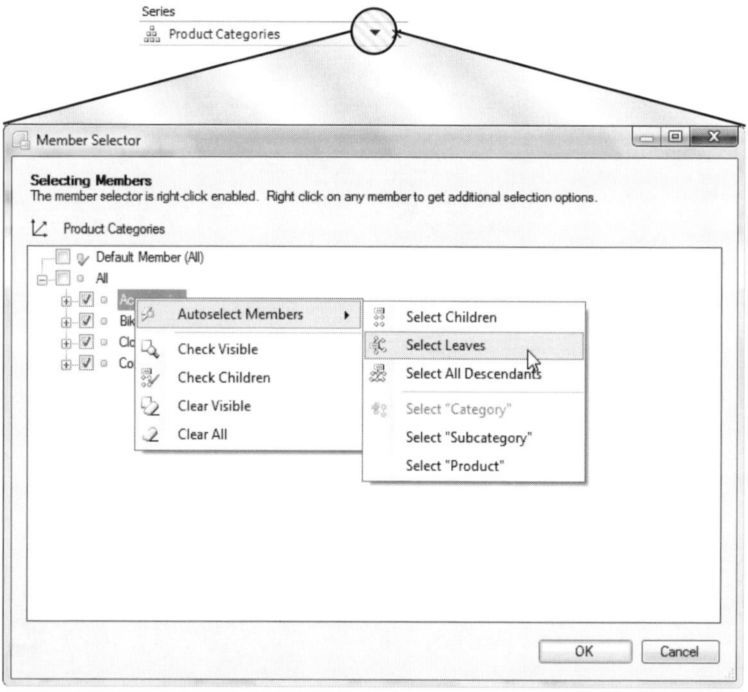

Figure 9.4: Dimension Member Selector.

The **Member Selector** dialog provides options for configuring which dimension members are to be displayed in the report. Static sets of members can be configured by manually checking the appropriate boxes next to the desired members. More dynamic functionality can be configured via the right-click contextual menu (shown in Figure 9.4). We have seen the **Check Visible** and **Check Children** options in previous chapters, but the analytic report version of this contextual menu includes an **Autoselect Members** option, which enables the selection of sets at specific levels. This can be very useful when the members of a particular dimension may change over time.

Create an Analytic Chart

Follow these steps to create an analytic chart report:

1. Ensure that MyWorkspace.bswx is open in DD.
2. On the **Create** tab of the ribbon, click **Analytic Chart**.
3. Fill in the element metadata as per Table 9.1 and click **Next**.

Property	Value
Name	Sales By Product
Default display folder location	Rational PPS\Analytic Chart
Grand Read permission to all users...	Checked ✓

Table 9.1: Sales By Product Metadata.

4. Select **AdventureWorksPPS** as the data source. Click **Finish** and then click **Close**.

Follow these steps to configure the chart:

1. Expand the **Dimensions** section of the details browser. Drag and drop the following dimensions into these areas.
   a. **Series:** Product Categories
   b. **Bottom Axis:** Date Fiscal
   c. **Background:** Geography
2. Expand the **Measures** section of the details browser. Drag and drop the **Reseller Sales Amount** measure into the **Background** axis.
3. Click the black down arrow on the right of the **Product Categories** dimension in the **Series** area to bring up the **Member Selector** dialog.
4. Uncheck the **Default Member (All)** item.
5. Right-click the **All** item and select **Autoselect Members ⇨ Select "Category."** Click **OK**.

6. Click the black down arrow on right of the **Date Fiscal** dimension in the **Bottom Axis** area to bring up the **Member Selector** dialog.

7. Uncheck the **Default Member (All Periods)** item.

8. Expand the **All Periods** member, right-click the **FY 2004** member and select **Autoselect Members** ⇨ **Select Children**. Click **OK**.

9. Click **Publish All**.

The preview of the chart should look like the one shown in Figure 9.2.

Create an Analytic Grid

Follow these steps to create an analytic grid report:

1. On the **Create** tab of the ribbon, click **Analytic Grid**.

2. Fill in the element metadata as per Table 9.2 and click **Next**.

Property	Value
Name	Reseller Sales
Default display folder location	Rational PPS\Analytic Grid
Grand Read permission to all users...	Checked ✓

Table 9.2: Reseller Sales Metadata.

3. Select **AdventureWorksPPS** as the data source. Click **Finish** and then click **Close**.

Follow these steps to configure the grid:

1. Expand the **Dimensions** section of the details browser. Drag and drop the following dimensions into these areas.

    a. **Rows:** Reseller Type

    b. **Background:** Date Fiscal, Geography

2. Expand the **Measures** section of the details browser. Drag and drop the **Reseller Sales Amount** and **Reseller Order Quantity** measures into the **Columns** area.

3. Bring up the **Member Selector** dialog for the **Reseller Type** dimension on the **Rows** area by clicking the black down arrow.

4. Right-click the **All Reseller** member and select **Check Children**. Click **OK**.

5. Press CTRL + F4 to publish all.

The **Design** tab should similar to the one shown in Figure 9.5.

Figure 9.5: Reseller Sales Design Tab.

MDX

The ability to write full-fledged MDX queries to populate a grid or chart with data is an incredibly powerful feature. It opens up a world of opportunities to the report designer. Once more, we stress the importance of skilling up on your MDX; the benefit of expertise in this area cannot be overstated.

There are two approaches that can be used when working with custom MDX in the **Query** tab:

- Use the MDX created by DD as a result of drag and drop activity in the **Design** tab as a base for further customization.
- Write your own MDX select statement from scratch.

Parameters

The configuration of parameters is supported in the **Query** tab. Surrounding a chosen parameter name in double angle bracket tokens (e.g., `<<MyParameter>>`) makes their existence known to the interface. Parameters will be exposed as endpoints when the report is used in a dashboard. Figure 9.6 shows a hand-coded MDX statement that contains one parameter named **Fiscal**. A **Parameters** section at the bottom of the **Query** tab can be used to manage or create parameters. Default parameter values can also be configured here to allow the report to be tested within DD.

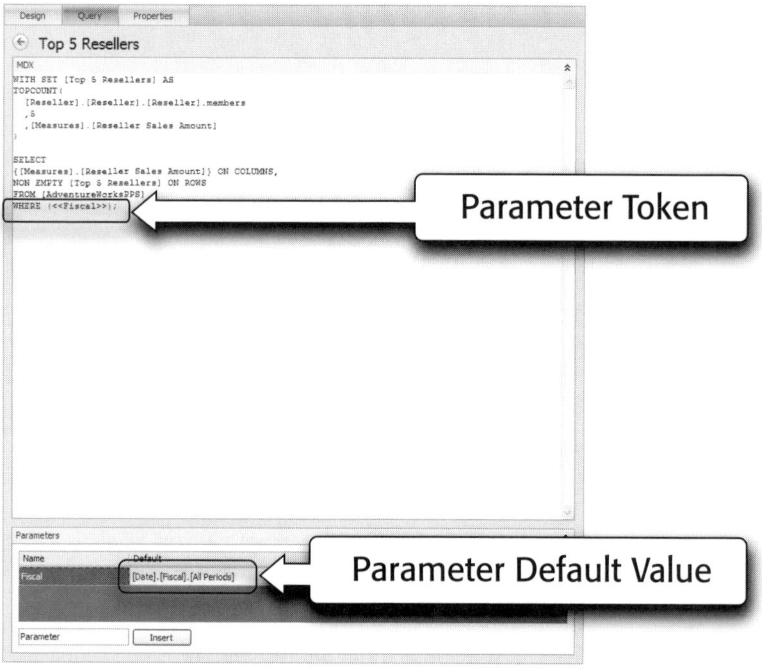

Figure 9.6: Query Tab with Parameterized MDX.

Create an MDX Analytic Grid

Follow these steps to create an analytic grid report using MDX:

1. On the **Create** tab of the ribbon, click **Analytic Grid**.

2. Fill in the element metadata as per Table 9.3 and click **Next**.

Property	Value
Name	Top 5 Resellers
Default display folder location	Rational PPS\Analytic Grid
Grand Read permission to all users...	Checked ✓

Table 9.3: Top 5 Resellers Metadata.

3. Select **AdventureWorksPPS** as the data source. Click **Finish** and then click **Close**.

Follow these steps to configure the MDX:

1. In the workspace pane, select the **Query** tab. Delete the default MDX stub code.

2. Type the MDX in Listing 9.1 into the query window (a text file containing this code can be found in this chapter's bonus material):

```
WITH SET [Top 5 Resellers] AS
TOPCOUNT(
  [Reseller].[Reseller].[Reseller].MEMBERS
  ,5
  ,[Measures].[Reseller Sales Amount]
)
SELECT
{[Measures].[Reseller Sales Amount]} ON COLUMNS,
NON EMPTY [Top 5 Resellers] ON ROWS
FROM [AdventureWorksPPS]
WHERE (<<Fiscal>>, <<Geography>>);
```

Listing 9.1: Top 5 Reseller MDX Code.

3. The Query window will detect the existence of the **Fiscal** and **Geography** parameters and will create corresponding items in the **Parameters** section.

4. To be able to test the query, a default value for the parameter must be defined. Type `[Date].[Fiscal].[All Periods]`into the **Default** property of the **Fiscal** parameter and `[Geography].[Geography].[All Geographies]` for the **Geography** parameter.

5. Click the **Design** tab to run the query. The result should look like Figure 9.7.

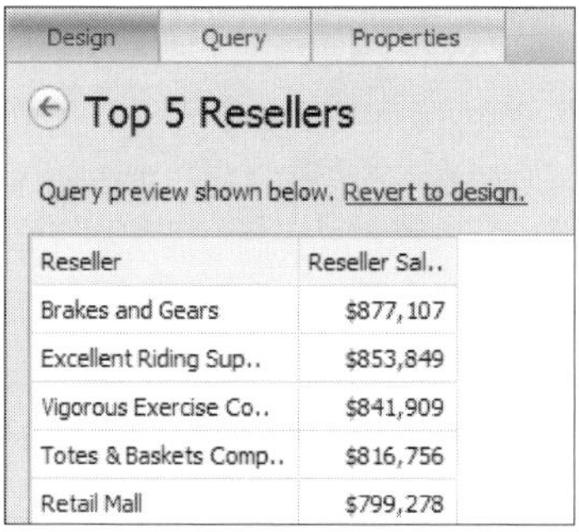

Figure 9.7: Top 5 Resellers Analytic Grid.

6. Click **Publish All.**

End User Interactivity

One of the major features of the analytic report types is the built in thin-client functionality available in the browser. Right-clicking an item in either a chart or grid presents a myriad of drill up/down, expand, pivot, and drillthrough capabilities.

It is assumed that you have a solid understanding of navigating OLAP structures, so we will not go into detail on each of the options available here. Instead we will point to Figure 9.8, which shows the functions available from the right-click menu. In particular, the **Drill Down To** option pretty much opens up the entire cube space to the user without having to leave the browser.

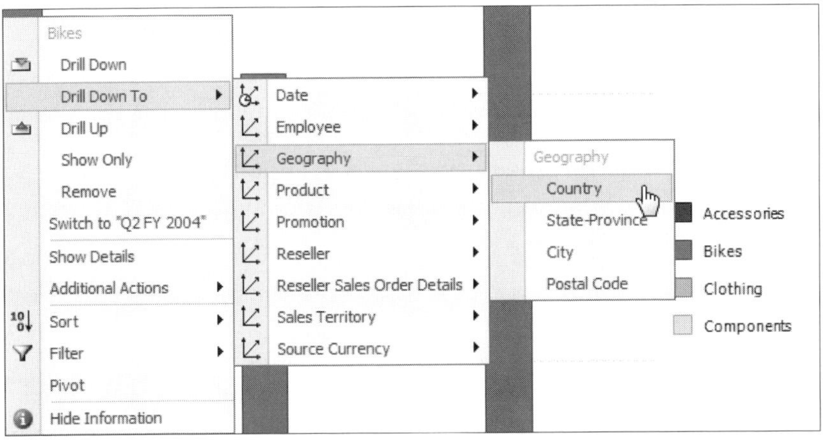

Figure 9.8: Dimension Right-click Options.

Further interactivity with the report is available via the toolbar at the top of the report window (Figure 9.9).

Figure 9.9: Analytic Report Toolbar.

The interactivity features of an Analytic report can be tested in DD by clicking the **Browse** button found at the bottom right corner of the **Design** tab. It is important to note, however, that if MDX in the **Query** tab is created from scratch or customized in any way, much of the interactive capability just mentioned will not be available. This is not a bug; it is by design. The report engine cannot support interactivity based on the limitless ways that custom MDX statements can create query-scoped objects and make calculations on the fly. The **Design** tab supports only objects that are defined in the cube. This ensures a controlled environment where interactivity can be supported. Please note that this is not meant to discourage the use of MDX in any way, but instead to set expectations: MDX customizations limit the interactive capability of the resultant report. Quite often, reports that require the use of custom MDX do not have as much of an interactive requirement.

Tech Tip:

It is easy to see whether the right-click interactivity functions in a report are limited. The Browse button will not be visible and a Revert to design link will be displayed in the top left of the screen. Clicking this link will revert the report to the point right before the MDX was modified manually.

Actions

Drillthrough, reporting and URL cell-level actions defined in the source cube are available from the **Additional Actions** item of the right-click menu. These actions will be available regardless of whether the report uses custom MDX or not. Naturally, the list of available actions depends on what part of the report has been clicked. An **Order Details** drillthrough action is defined on the AdventureWorksPPS cube. Try right-clicking on a measure cell in either of the two analytic grid reports created earlier and select **Additional Actions ⇨ Order Details** to display granular detail in a window similar to that in Figure 9.10.

Reseller Sales Amount	Reseller Order Quantity	City	State-Province	Country	Reseller	Product
567.8978	2	London	England	United Kingdom	Variety Cycling	Touring-3000 Blue, 50
283.9489	1	London	England	United Kingdom	Variety Cycling	Touring-3000 Blue, 54
283.9489	1	London	England	United Kingdom	Variety Cycling	Touring-3000 Yellow, 5
1135.7955	4	London	England	United Kingdom	Variety Cycling	Touring-3000 Yellow, 4
851.8466	3	London	England	United Kingdom	Variety Cycling	Touring-3000 Yellow, 6
283.9489	1	Croix	Nord	France	Finer Sporting Goods	Touring-3000 Blue, 54
283.9489	1	Croix	Nord	France	Finer Sporting Goods	Touring-3000 Yellow, 4
283.9489	1	Croix	Nord	France	Finer Sporting Goods	Touring-3000 Blue, 50
567.8978	2	Croix	Nord	France	Finer Sporting Goods	Touring-3000 Yellow, 5
762.9024	1	London	England	United Kingdom	Variety Cycling	Touring-1000 Yellow, 4

Figure 9.10: Drillthrough Action Records.

Tech Tip:

The Show Details option on the right-click menu can also be used to display granular detail behind a cell without the need to create a drillthrough action.

Endpoints

Any item present in the **Series**, **Bottom Axis**, or **Background** areas for charts or **Row**, **Columns** and **Background** for grids will be available as an endpoint. The background area is particularly useful for exposing endpoints on data that is not seen by the end user. Background items make up the WHERE clause of the generated MDX statement. For example, we placed the **Date Fiscal** and **Geography** attribute hierarchies in the **Background** for the Reseller Sales report. Neither date nor Geography information is visible on the report, but both these items will be available to us as endpoints when we use this report in a dashboard.

All defined parameters will be available as endpoints for reports created with customized MDX.

SQL Server Report

This report type can be configured to run and display any report deployed to a SQL Server Reporting Services (SSRS) instance configured as standalone or integrated into SharePoint. The user interface allows the designer to browse all published report names once the Report Server web service address has been entered in the **Server** text box (see Figure 9.11).

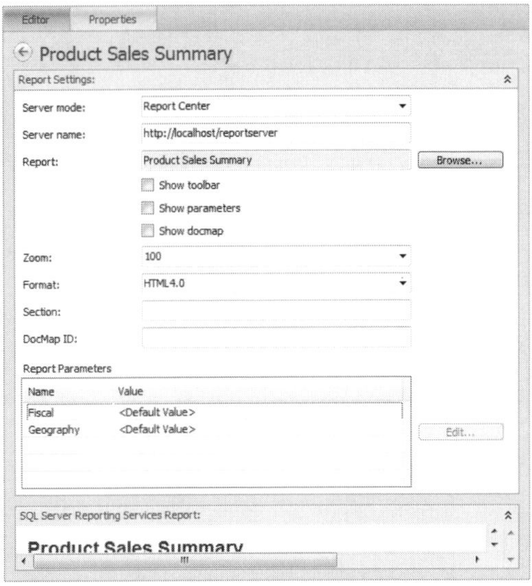

Figure 9.11: SQL Server Report User Interface.

Creating a SQL Server Report

To follow this exercise, you need to deploy the **Product Sales Summary** report (found in the downloadable bonus material for this chapter) to your report server. Once deployed, follow these steps.

1. Right-click the **Reports** node in the workspace browser and select **New Report**.

2. In the **Select a Report Template** dialog, select **SQL Server Report**. Click **OK**.

3. Fill in the usual element details as per Table 9.4 and click **Finish**, then click **Close**.

Property	Value
Name	Product Sales Summary
Default display folder location	Rational PPS\SSRS
Grand Read permission to all users...	Checked ✓

Table 9.4: Product Sales Summary Metadata.

4. In the **Server Mode** dropdown, select **Report Center**.

5. In the **Server URL** text box, enter the path to the report server where the report was been deployed. On a default SSRS installation, this path will be `http://<servername>/reportserver`.

6. Click the **Browse** button and select **Rational PPS Reports** ⇨ **Product Sales Summary** in the popup window.

7. Uncheck the **Show Toolbar** option.

8. Click **Publish All** and save the workspace.

Endpoints

Any parameters defined on the selected report will be available for configuration in the **Report Parameters** grid. These parameters are the endpoints that will be made available for this report type.

Strategy Map

Strategy maps provide a different way of communicating scorecard data. The purpose is not to provide detailed analytical capability, but instead to show a visual representation of the contents of a scorecard. This is the first example of a report that requires a scorecard as a data source. An example strategy map can be seen in Figure 9.12.

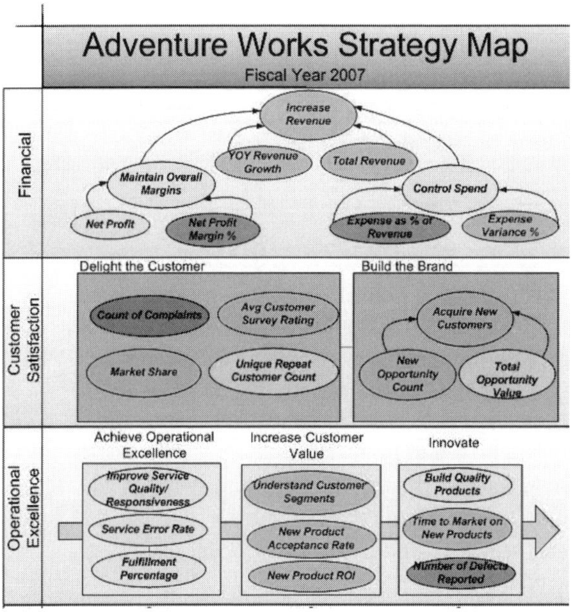

Figure 9.12: Sample AdventureWorks Strategy Map.

A strategy map report enables the shapes on a Visio document to be linked to the KPIs in a published scorecard. The simple linking process is performed within DD. A pre-existing Visio document can be used or one can be created from scratch within DD.

Note:

To configure a strategy map in DD, Visio 2007 must be installed.

Creating a Strategy Map

Follow these steps to create a Strategy Map report:

1. Click the **Strategy Map** button on the **Reports** chunk of the **Create** tab.

2. Fill in the usual element metadata as per Table 9.5. Click **Next**.

Property	Value
Name	Reseller Strategy Map
Default display folder location	Rational PPS\Strategy
Grand Read permission to all users...	Checked ✓

Table 9.5: Strategy Map Report Metadata.

3. In the **Select a Scorecard** pane, select the **Reseller Improvement** scorecard. Click **Finish** and click **Close**.

Configuring a Strategy Map

In this exercise, we will use a Visio document that has already been created. The ResellerStrategyMap.vsd file can be found in the bonus material for this chapter. Once you have the document saved locally, follow these steps to configure it:

1. Select the **Edit** tab in the ribbon and click the **Edit Strategy Map** button.

2. In the **Strategy Map Editor** (Figure 9.13), click **Open Visio File** and browse to the location of ResellerStrategyMap.vsd. Click **Open**.

3. In the strategy map, select the **Sales Amount** ellipse and click the **Connect Shape** button.

4. In the **Select a KPI** dialog, select the **Sales Amount** KPI. Click **OK**.

5. Repeat Steps 3 and 4 for all of the remaining items. Once complete, each of the ellipses and rectangles on the strategy map should be a light blue color, indicating that they are now associated with a KPI.

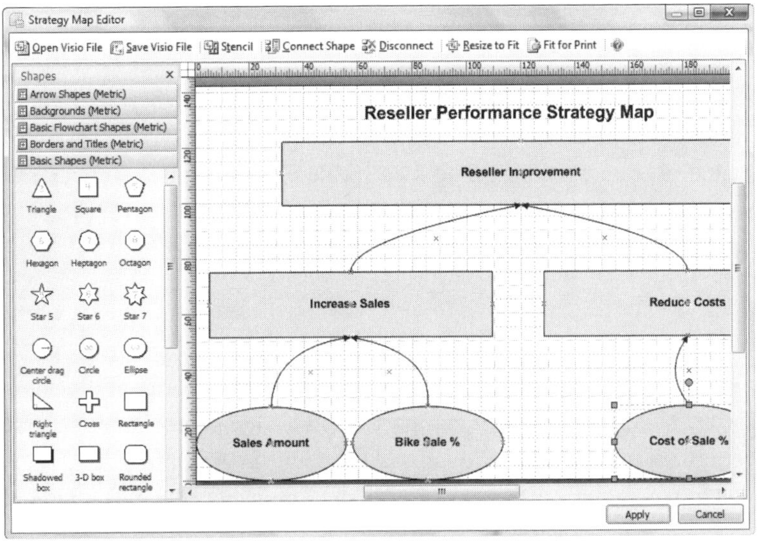

Figure 9.13: Strategy Map Editor.

6. Click **Apply**. Click **Publish All**.

The color displayed in each linked shape is driven by the level background color of the indicator element used by the configured target for the linked KPI. It is also worth noting that all metadata contained within the associated KPI (such as value, description, score, owner, etc.) can be shown in the strategy map using Visio functionality.

Tech Tip:

When a strategy map is displayed in SharePoint, it requires the installation of Visio 2007 viewer, which can be downloaded from `www.microsoft.com/downloads`**. This plug-in enables user interaction with the strategy map. Mostly, though, users do not really need this functionality. To remove reliance on the Visio viewer, check the Render as Image check box in the bottom right corner of the strategy map design surface. This option uses the Visio runtime on the server to generate an image of the strategy map, which is served up to the user.**

Trend Analysis Chart

This report type uses data mining functionality to predict the future value of KPI metrics contained in a scorecard. Using the SSAS Time Series algorithm, the KPI value for the next *n* periods is calculated and displayed in an OWC line chart. The actual values are displayed as a blue line, while the predicted values are represented as a continuation of that line colored red.

Trend Analysis Chart definitions must be based on a published scorecard element with time dimension members present on the column axis. The data in the scorecard can be sourced from either a tabular or multidimensional data source. Under the covers, the report creates a temporary mining model on the configured analysis server and uses the Time Series data mining algorithm to predict the values for the next *n* periods. The value of *n* is configurable in the report definition's **Forecast Period** text box. The report can also be configured to use a rolling window of *n* trailing periods.

In order for Trend Analysis Chart functionality to be available, there are some important configurations that must be made:

1. The **value** property of the **Microsoft Analysis Services Server name (for Data Mining)** server option needs to be set to the name of a SQL Server Analysis Services instance. This is configured in the DD **Options** ⇨ **Server** tab (see Chapter 4).

2. The Analysis Server instance configured in Step 1 must have its **DataMining\AllowSessionMiningModels** property set to **True**. This property is set through SQL Server Management Studio (refer to SQL Server Books Online for more details).

Creating the Supporting Scorecard

The scorecard that the report is built on can be simple—in fact, the simpler the better. Follow these steps to create a basic scorecard that will enable the prediction of the **Cost of Sale %** and **Bike Sale %** KPI Actuals:

1. Right-click the **Scorecards** node in the workspace browser and select **New Scorecard**.

2. In the **Select a Scorecard Template** dialog, select **Standard** in the **Category** pane and **Blank Scorecard** in the **Template** pane. Click **OK**.

3. Fill in the usual element details as per Table 9.6 and click **Finish**.

Property	Value
Name	Trend Chart Source
Default display folder location	Rational PPS\Trend
Grand Read permission to all users...	Checked ✓

Table 9.6: Trend Chart Source Metadata.

4. On the scorecard workspace pane interface, drag the **Bike Sale %** and **Cost of Sale %** KPIs from the details browser onto the rows axis.

5. The previous action brought all three metrics associated with both KPIs onto the scorecard, but we only want the Actual. Right-click the **Budget** metric heading and select **Delete**. Do the same for the **YTD** metric.

6. Drag and drop the **Date Fiscal** dimension onto the columns axis above the **Actuals** metric. In the **Member Selector** dialog, expand the **All Periods** node. Right-click the **FY 2003** member and click **Check Children**. Click **OK**.

7. Select the **Edit** tab on the ribbon and click the **Update** button. Click **Publish All**. Your simple scorecard should look similar to Figure 9.14.

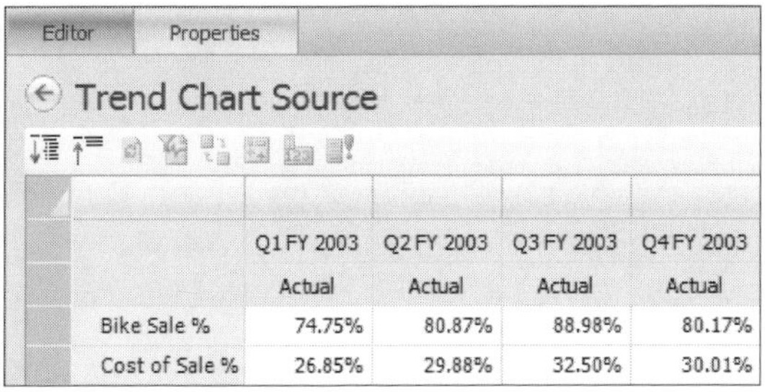

	Q1 FY 2003	Q2 FY 2003	Q3 FY 2003	Q4 FY 2003
	Actual	Actual	Actual	Actual
Bike Sale %	74.75%	80.87%	88.98%	80.17%
Cost of Sale %	26.85%	29.88%	32.50%	30.01%

Figure 9.14: Trend Chart Source Scorecard.

Configuring a Trend Analysis Chart

Now we'll use the new scorecard to create the report. Follow these steps:

1. Right-click the **Reports** node in the workspace browser and select **New Report**.

2. In the **Select a Report Template** dialog, select **Trend Analysis Chart**. Click **OK**.

3. Fill in the usual element details as per Table 9.7 and click **Next**.

Property	Value
Name	Forecast
Default display folder location	Rational PPS\Trend
Grand Read permission to all users...	Checked ✓

Table 9.7: Forecast Report Metadata.

4. In the **Select Scorecard** dialog, select the **Trend Chart Source** scorecard. Click **Next**.

5. In the **Select KPIs** step, check both the **Bike Sale %** and **Cost of Sale %** KPIs. Click **Finish**. Click **Close**.

6. After a few seconds of processing, two trend charts (one for each KPI) should appear in the workspace pane. At the bottom of the pane in the **Select Time Period** section, type 3 in the **Forecast Period** text box and hit the **Tab** button. The finished product should look similar to Figure 9.15.

Tech Tip:

The Time Series algorithm can only make predictions along existing time dimension members. In the example above, we cannot predict past Q2 FY 2005. The AdventureWorksDW relational database does not contain any time values greater than Q2 FY 2005 in the DimTime table.

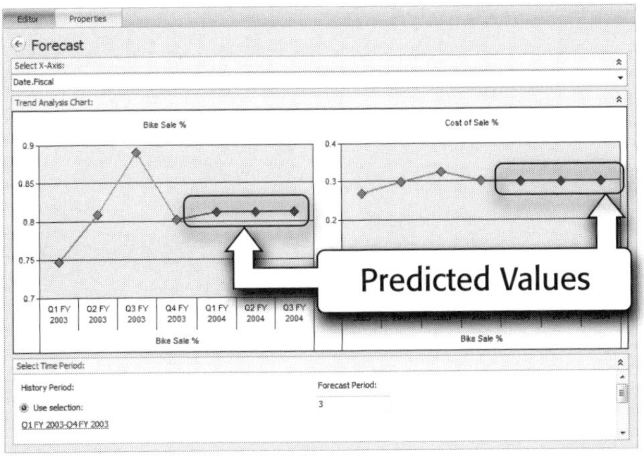

Figure 9.15: Trend Charts with Predicted Values.

ProClarity Analytics Server Page

The ProClarity stack acquired by Microsoft contained a huge amount of analytic functionality. Analytic views and charts were the first to be integrated into PPS. The remaining analytic types views—such as performance maps and decomposition trees (see Figure 9.16)—were not integrated into this product release because of time constraints.

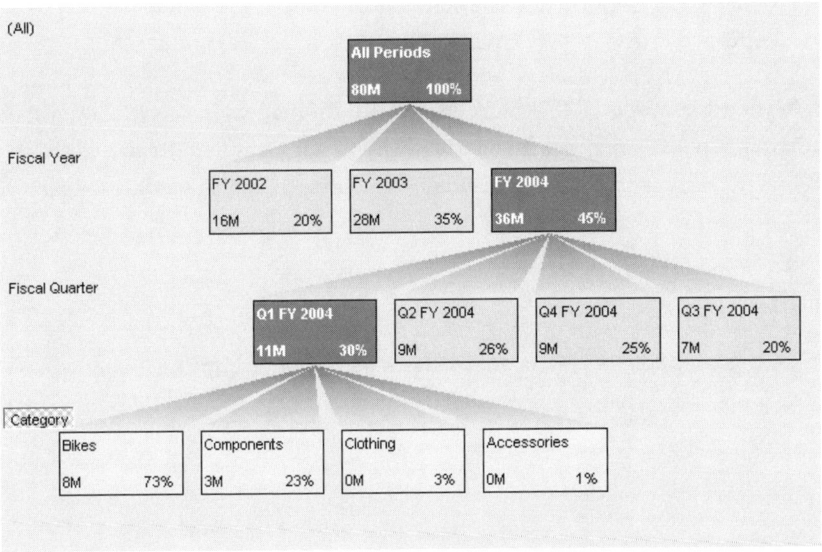

Figure 9.16: ProClarity Decomposition Tree.

Rest assured, in time many of these analytic view types (and certainly some new ones) will be fully integrated into the product for subsequent PPS releases. In the meantime, this report type enables analytic views that are deployed to a ProClarity Analytics Server (PAS), much like the SQL Server report covered earlier.

Configuration is performed by entering the PAS server URL in the appropriate text box (Figure 9.17)

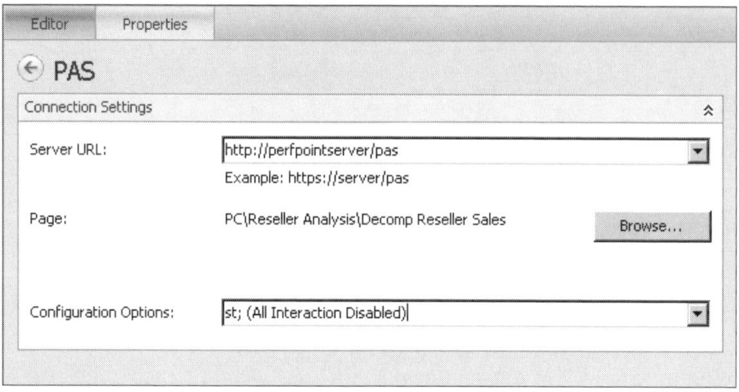

Figure 9.17: PAS Configuration.

Once connected, a PAS page can be selected from the PAS Browser, which lists all the published PAS pages by Briefing Book, as shown in Figure 9.18.

It is beyond the scope of this book to detail the functionality available in the ProClarity product suite, but it is a great way to augment the already baked-in PPS functionality with best-of-breed data visualization and analysis tools.

Note:

There is no extra licensing cost for the PAS software; it is included in the PPS license.

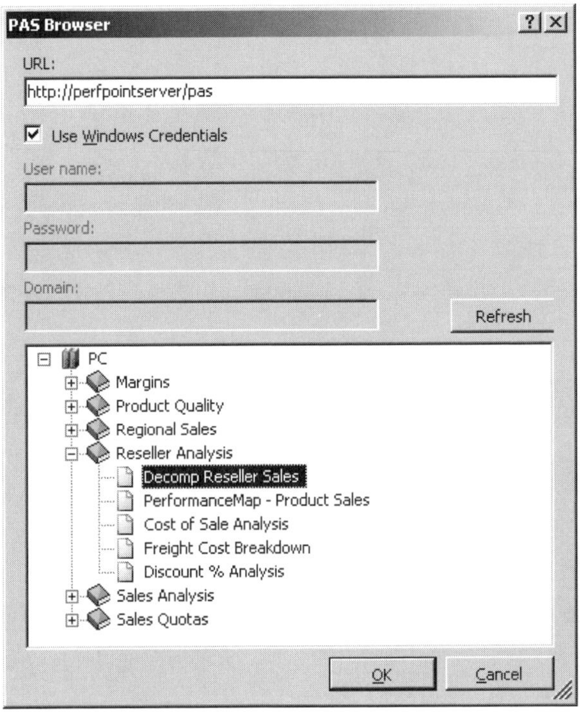

Figure 9.18: PAS Browser.

Endpoints

PAS pages do not need to be built with endpoints in mind.

Excel Services

Excel Services is a separately licensed product that is used in conjunction with MOSS. It enables the entire contents of Excel workbooks (or specific items defined within them) to be published to document libraries. Users can view and interact with these published workbooks in a thin-client environment, thanks to the Excel Services rendering engine.

Put simply, the Excel Services report type can be configured to display the contents of a published Excel Services item. The report is configured by providing the URL to the MOSS site that contains the document library where Excel Services items have been published (see Figure 9.19). The specific document library and workbook are then chosen along with the specific items defined within it.

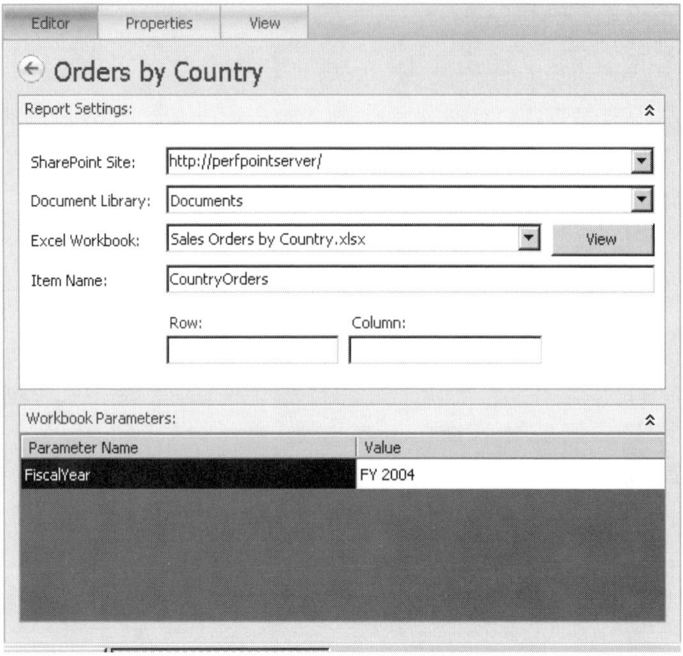

Figure 9.19: Excel Services Report User Interface.

Once configured, the report can be previewed in the **View** tab (Figure 9.20).

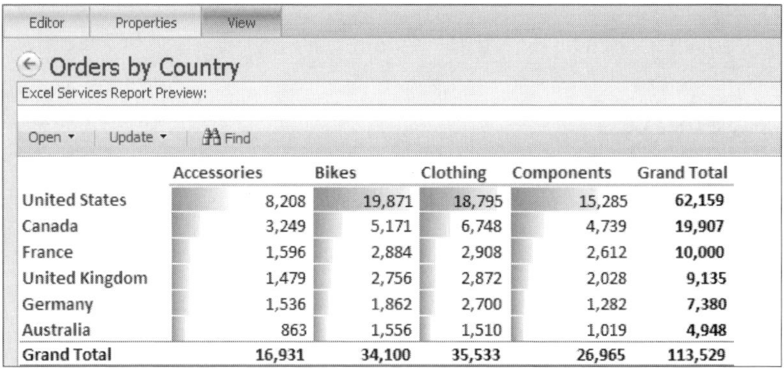

Figure 9.20: Excel Services Report Preview.

Endpoints

Objects published to Excel Services can be defined with parameters for interactivity. These parameter structures are exposed in the **Workbook Parameters** section of the report user interface and are subsequently available as endpoints.

Web Page

The Web Page report is very simple; it displays the web page referenced by the URL that has been entered into the URL text box (Figure 9.21).

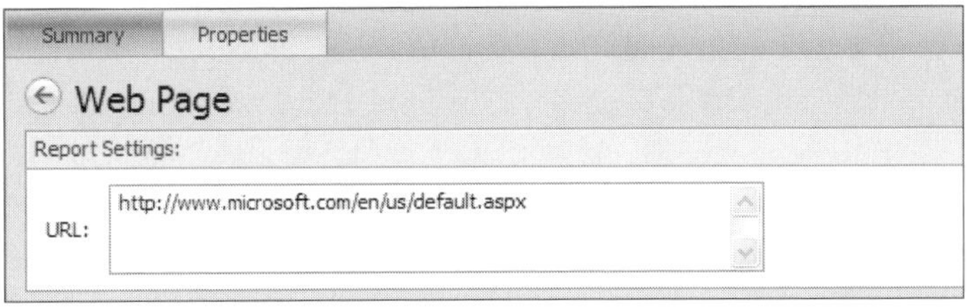

Figure 9.21: Web Page Report URL Text Box.

Any URL can be entered here. It could reference a document that exists in a SharePoint document library, a company web site, or anything. Using it to simply point towards a static URL is useful but still not dynamic. Enter the .NET developer. The web page could be considered the "catch all" report type. Just because the URL entered in the text box is not dynamic doesn't mean the URL can't redirect them somewhere else.

For example, AdventureWorks uses a third party, web-based reporting tool. Reports are rendered by a web service in response to receiving a URL containing embedded parameters. A web page report is created and the URL property is configured to point towards a custom .aspx page. This page contains code to parse out and utilize any contextual data passed to it by dashboard endpoints. Using this information, a URL is constructed on the fly and the user is sent there. The URL instructs the third party web service to render the appropriate report with corresponding parameter values. So long as the required contextual information is made available (and of course someone has built the .aspx page and written the code that does the work), the possibilities with this report type are limitless.

PivotChart and PivotTable

In BSM, PivotChart and PivotTable reports were one of the most commonly used report types because of the interactive functionality they provide. Usage of this report type was covered extensively in *The Rational Guide to Microsoft® Office Business Scorecard Manager 2005*. In PPS Monitoring, this report type is supported for backwards compatibility. However, analytic chart and grid reports provide a much more powerful and flexible alternative without the need for OWC. Consider using the analytic report type before the pivot.

This report type is commonly used to connect to Analysis Services multidimensional data sources. In a similar style to analytic charts and grids, available dimensions are dragged and dropped onto series, category, and filter axes. PivotChart reports support the creation of Column, Bar, Line, SmoothLine, Pie, XY (Scatter), Bubble, Area, Doughnut, Radar, Stock, and Polar charts. Figure 9.22 shows a stacked column chart. PivotTable reports are configured the same way, but display data in grid format.

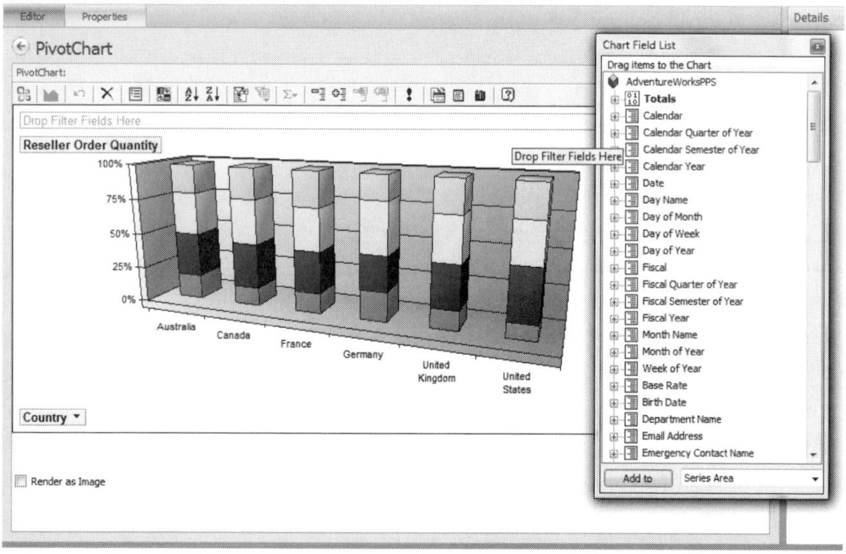

Figure 9.22: PivotChart and Field List.

Up until now, all data access has been routed through data source elements, which connect using the account defined in the PPSMonitoringWebService application pool. From a security perspective, Pivot reports are the exception to the rule in terms of data access—each requires a separate connection string to access the back-end data source. Once defined, the connection string is held as part of each report's definition.

Tech Tip:

Like strategy maps, PivotChart reports have a Render as Image option. When checked, this negates the need for OWC to be loaded on the client machine. The OWC runtime on the server is used to generate an image of the PivotChart, which is served up to the user. Naturally, this means that users will not be able to interact with the chart, because it will simply be a static image. This functionality is not available for PivotTables. It should also be noted that when Render as Image is used, the Application Pool account is used to connect to the data source.

Spreadsheet

This report enables the construction of an OWC Excel spreadsheet, which is stored on the Monitoring server. Basic models such as mortgage repayment calculators can be made available to end users to interact with. If you are using MOSS and Excel Services, the Excel Services report type is far better suited to this purpose.

Often, this report type is not actually used as a spreadsheet per se. Instead, the spreadsheet is used as a container for formatted, textual details about a specific part of a dashboard. This is useful when the amount of information the designer wants to convey may be a bit too much to fit in an element **Description** property, but too little to warrant a separate document.

Summary

The report element enables users to access and interact with data in a number of ways. We briefly examined each of the eleven different types of report element and stepped through the creation of several examples. Report types like SQL Server Report, Excel Services, and ProClarity Analytics Server Page offer a way of accessing published items for eventual exposure in a dashboard. Analytic charts and grids offer huge flexibility and interactivity features to the end user via the browser. Strategy Map and Trend Analysis reports bring very specialized functionality to the table and use scorecards as a data source. Web Page reports open the door to just about any kind of customization.

We have now covered five of the six elements. We have all the parts we need to build an example of the final element, the dashboard.

Chapter 10

Dashboards

Now it's time to create dashboards! This chapter concentrates on the dashboard element as implemented in PPS and how it ties together all the other elements in a reusable, highly-flexible object. A *dashboard* element is a collection of one or more scorecard or report elements arranged in a paginated layout utilizing custom filter objects and inter-item links to communicate contextual data. Dashboards are the vehicle to expose report and scorecard data to end users. If users wish to access content from either of those two elements, they *must* be contained in a published dashboard. Only then can they be surfaced through the PerformancePoint Dashboard Item web part (which is covered in the next chapter).

Dashboards are a very flexible element, and they present a great opportunity to deliver some really intuitive functionality to end users. BSM did not support an element of this kind. The creation of a BSM dashboard required a quite a bit of manual work inside SharePoint to satisfy user requirements. When the solution needed to be moved from, say, development to testing, all that manual WSS work had to be painstakingly duplicated (and documented). The dashboard element removes virtually all that manual labor, because pagination, layout, sizing, and inter-item communication are all part of the element definition itself. Much of the dashboard design and layout experience in DD feels very similar to performing tasks in SharePoint, only now you can build it once and then deploy the resultant element as many times as required.

Creating Dashboards

There are five main steps involved in creating and perfecting a dashboard element:

1. Defining the layout
2. Creating filters
3. Adding items
4. Configuring item links
5. Previewing and testing

Layout

Each dashboard can have one or many pages, each containing one or many zones. The configuration of pages and zones is done in the **Editor** tab in the dashboard workspace pane (Figure 10.1).

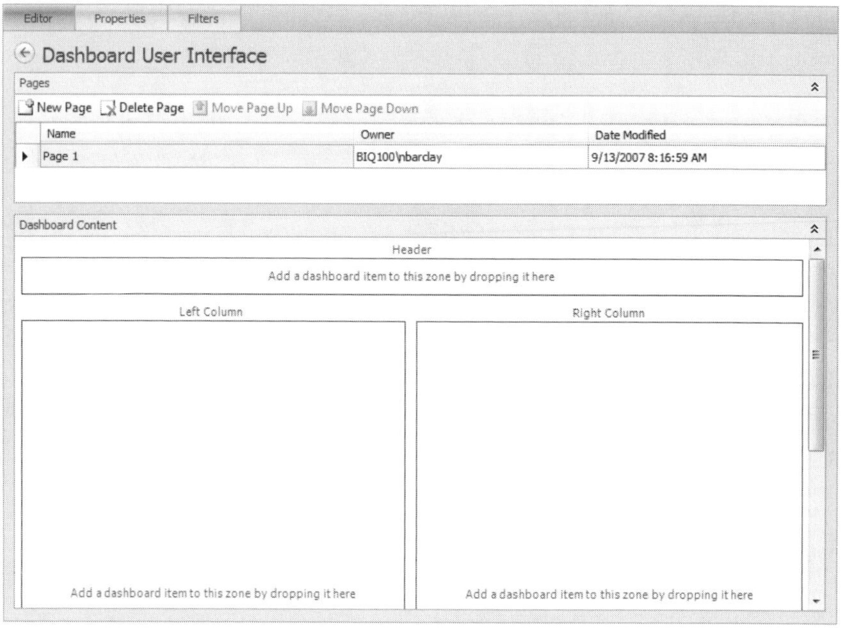

Figure 10.1: Dashboard User Interface.

Pages

The **Pages** area of the dashboard UI (see Figure 10.1) is where the creation or deletion, naming, and ordering of dashboard pages is performed. Selecting a particular line in the grid will display the page layout in the **Dashboard Content** area, which occupies the bottom two thirds of the **Editor** tab.

Zones

Each dashboard page is made up of one or many *zones*—these are the eventual containers into which dashboard items will be placed. When creating a dashboard page, designers can choose one of several page templates (shown in Figure 10.2).

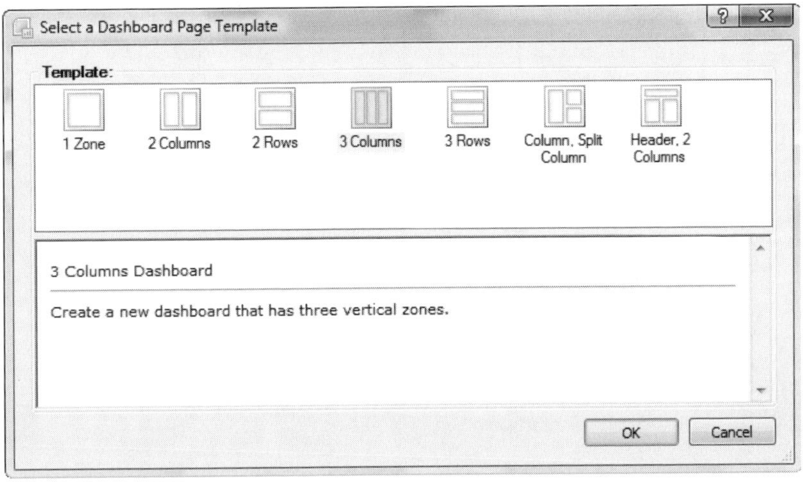

Figure 10.2: Dashboard Page Templates.

Adding, Deleting, and Splitting Zones

Just about any layout can be easily created by using the options available on the **Zone** button located on the **Dashboard Editor** chunk of the **Edit** ribbon tab. Another zone can be added to the left, right, above, or below the currently selected zone. The selected zone can also be split or deleted. These same options are available from the right-click contextual menu for each zone (Figure 10.3).

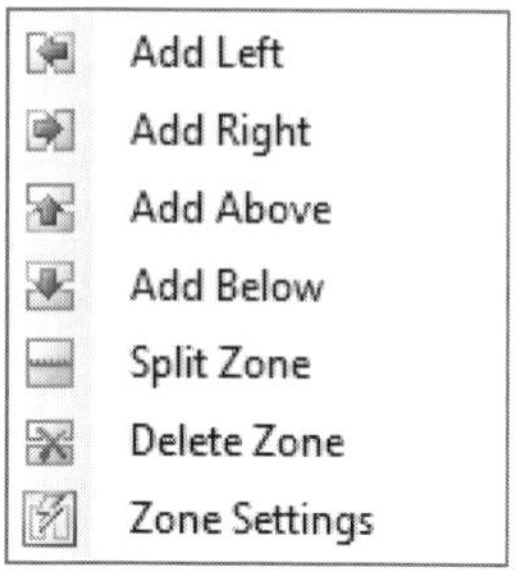

Figure 10.3: Zone Context Menu.

Zone Settings

Property settings for each zone can also be accessed through the **Edit** tab or right-click menu. The **Zone Settings** dialog is home to three tabs:

- **General** — The name given to the zone can be configured here. Pages created from templates have pre-configured zone names such as Left Column, Top Row, Header, etc. The zone names can be left as is or changed as required.

- **Size** — Width and height can be configured in pixels or as a percentage of the dashboard page (Figure 10.4).

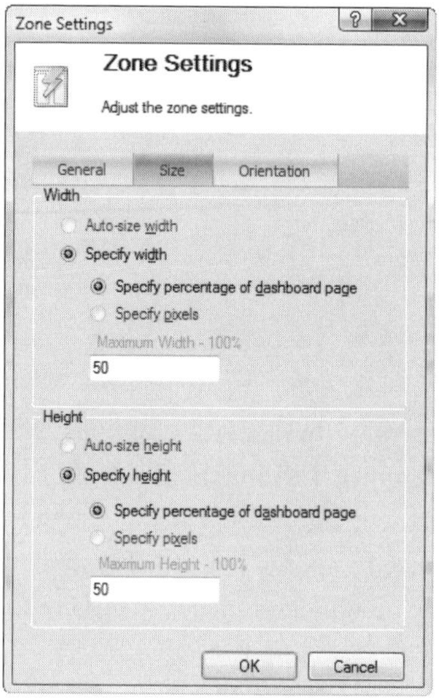

Figure 10.4: Zone Settings Size Tab.

- **Orientation** — A zone's orientation setting will determine how dashboard items will be arranged within it. There are three options:
    - **Horizontal** — Items will be arranged to the left or right of each other within the zone.
    - **Vertical** — Items will be arranged above or below each other within the zone.
    - **Stacked** — Items added to the zone will be stacked on top of each other. In the published dashboard, a dropdown list at the top of the zone will be available to choose which item is displayed at any one time.

Creating the Reseller Performance Dashboard

Follow these steps to create the Reseller Performance dashboard:

1. Make sure that MyWorkspace.bswx is open in DD and all elements contained therein are published. Click **Refresh**.

2. In the workspace browser, right-click the **Dashboards** item and select **New Dashboard**.

3. In the **Select a Dashboard Page Template** dialog, select the **Header, 2 Columns** template. Click **OK**.

4. Fill in the element metadata as per Table 10.1, then click **Finish**.

Property	Value
Name	Reseller Performance
Default display folder location	Rational PPS
Grand Read permission to all users...	Checked ✓

Table 10.1: Reseller Performance Metadata.

5. Right-click anywhere in the **Left Column** zone and select **Add Below** to add another zone beneath it. This new zone will be given a default name of **Zone 1**.

6. Left-click anywhere in the **Right Column** zone to select it. On the **Edit** tab of the ribbon, click the **Zone Settings** button. Select the **Orientation** tab and select the **Stacked** radio button. Click **OK**.

7. In the **Pages** section of the **Editor** tab, click the **New Page** button. Select the **2 Rows** template when prompted. Click **OK**.

8. On the newly created page, right-click the area inside the **Top Row** zone and select **Zone Settings**. In the **Zone Settings** dialog, select the **Size** tab. In the **Height** section, change the number in the **Maximum Height** textbox to **5**. Click **OK**.

9. Click **Publish All**.

Filters

A *filter* is an object defined within a dashboard element that contains a collection of values for users to select. The selected values can be passed to other dashboard items (scorecards or reports) in order to filter the data contained in them. There are six different types of filter, each of which provides a different method for populating the values it will contain. Filter types are MDX Query, Member Selection, Named Sets, Tabular Values, Time Intelligence, and Time Intelligence Post Formula.

Note:

A filter is *not* an element. Filters are classified as Second Class Objects (SCOs) and are part of the definition of an individual dashboard element. Metrics and their role within KPIs are also considered to be SCOs. The Monitoring architecture only considers the six elements to be First Class Objects (FCOs).

Filter Display Methods

The eventual look and feel of a filter in the dashboard can be configured in three different ways: *List*, *Tree*, and *Multi-Select Tree*. The display method is configured in a wizard step. Figure 10.5 shows how the same data would be displayed in a dashboard using each of the filter display methods.

Figure 10.5: Filter Display Methods.

MDX Query

This filter type requires an MDX formula that returns a set of members to dynamically populate filter values. Once more we see that the MDX language adds extra value and functionality. For example, the set formula could return the members of a specific attribute hierarchy. The MDX in the following code would populate the filter with all members of the Category attribute of the Product dimension:

```
[Product].[Category].members
```

Listing 10.1 shows a more interesting example—the names of the top 10 resellers for the USA based on overall sales.

```
TOPCOUNT(
 [Reseller].[Reseller].[Reseller].MEMBERS
 ,10
 ,([Geography].[Country].[United States], [Measures].[Reseller Sales
➲Amount])
)
```

Listing 10.1: Top 10 Reseller Set Formula.

Member Selection

Member Selection filters can be created using the data from either tabular or multidimensional data sources. The now familiar **Member Selector** dialog that we have used in previous chapters facilitates the manual selection of items, including a default member.

Named Sets

This filter type populates the filter with the values from a named set defined in a multidimensional data source. The **Select named set** dropdown will contain all the named sets defined in the selected SSAS data source. The MDX that defines the selected named set will be displayed in the **Named set expression** box (shown in Figure 10.6).

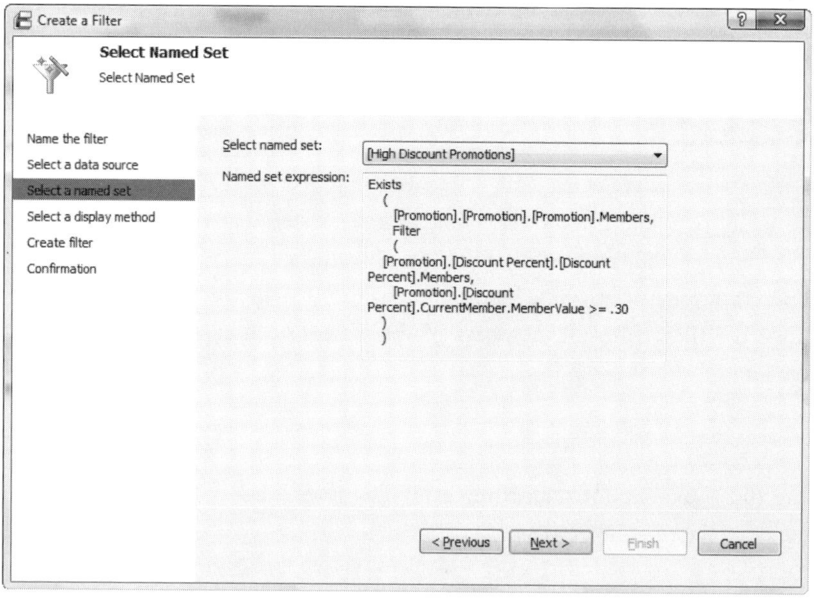

Figure 10.6: Select Named Set Dialog.

Tabular Values

The Tabular Values filter type sources data from a tabular data source. As discussed in Chapter 5, tabular data sources can range from SQL tables to SharePoint lists, manually entered values via Excel, and others. This presents a simple way to populate a filter with any value desired. Specific key and display value fields can be configured so that their specific values can be passed to other dashboard items. A parent key property can also be set up to create a parent-child style filter hierarchy, so long as the tabular data has been set up in this way.

Time Intelligence

Time Intelligence (TI) is a very powerful filter type and provides functionality many BI developers have been implementing manually up until now. We touched on TI in Chapter 5 because of the important initial configuration that needs to happen in the **Time** tab of multidimensional and tabular data sources. A single TI filter can be configured to calculate time periods for multiple data sources simultaneously.

When a data source's **Time** tab properties have been configured, TI filters can use the Simple Time Period Specification (STPS) language to dynamically reference specific members of the configured time dimension, using the current system date as a reference. This functionality makes it easy to satisfy the following types of dashboard user requests: "I want to see the numbers from last year / this month / next quarter / the first quarter of last year."

Time Intelligence Post Formula

A Time Intelligence Post Formula filter displays a fully-featured calendar control in the dashboard (see Figure 10.7). This calendar control is linked to the Monitoring server's internal master time dimension and hence is aware of the current date. Clicking the **Today** link found at the bottom of the control will automatically select the current date. The calendar control lets users pick a specific day.

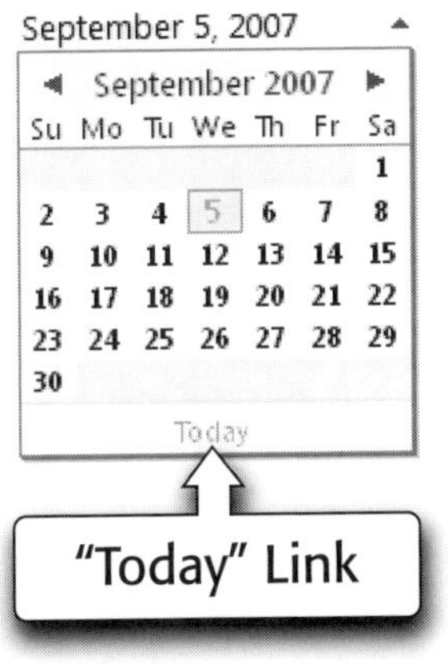

Figure 10.7: Time Intelligence Post Formula Filter Calendar.

The creation of this filter type is only the first of two steps. The second is to apply *filter link formulas* on other dashboard items, which use the selected day as a reference point to filter their data in their own way. For example, the dashboard user selects 5th September 2007; one dashboard item requires the month of the selected day, another needs to know the quarter that preceded the quarter that the selected date is in, and a third needs to know the year of the selected date. These calculations are made possible with filter link formulas, the details of which are covered later in this chapter.

Simple Time Period Specification

The Simple Time Period Specification (STPS) language was created by the PPS team to fulfill the desire of all BI developers: dynamic handling of time periods. Using the STPS expression language and the metadata configured in the data source **Time** tab, the Monitoring server can determine the member or set required from the time dimension. The STPS can use a combination of member values and functions, combined with numeric offsets, to return the appropriate time dimension members. The STPS is simple to learn and use and makes dealing with "current" time periods easy.

Member Values

In the **Time** tab of the AdventureWorksPPS data source, we configured *Time Member Associations* for each level of the Date.Fiscal hierarchy. We had a choice of Year, Trimester, Semester, Quarter, Month, Week, Day, Hour, Minute and Second. This metadata informs the Monitoring server which levels of the time dimension represent years, quarters, etc. Each of the period names is considered a *member value*. When used in the STPS, a member value by itself represents the "current" member for the configured time dimension level. For example, at the time of this writing the current month is September 2007. An STPS formula of `Month` is all that would be needed to reference the correct month member of an appropriately configured time dimension. Offset numbers can be combined with member values. For example, `Month-1` would reference August 2007, `Month+2` would reference November 2007, and so on.

> *Note:*
>
> **Keep in mind that we are working with AdventureWorksDW data in this book. Because this database only contains data up until August for calendar year 2004, STPS will not find any information for a "current" period, because it uses the system clock as a reference. The STPS can only reference existing members of a time dimension.**

Member Functions

Member functions can be combined with member values to reference individual members or sets of members in a time dimension. The familiar functions of `Parent`, `Children`, `FirstChild` and `LastChild` can be appended to member values separated by a period. For example, `Year.Children` will return a set of members for the level configured beneath the year in the data source **Time** tab. Usually, this would be Quarters, so the example function would return a set of quarters for the current year. Adding an offset number to the member value like `Year-1.Children` would return a set of last year's quarters and so on.

`First` and `Last` round out the member functions list and can be combined with any member value, such as `FirstMonth`, `LastQuarter`, `FirstMinute`, `LastSecond`. For example, for a calendar time dimension where each year starts in January, the STPS formula of `Year.FirstMonth` would reference the member for January 2007.

Table 10.2 contains more examples to demonstrate just how flexible and easy working with the STPS can be.

Type	STPS	Description
Member Value with Offset	`Month+2`	Two months from now
	`Day-1`	Yesterday
	`Year-1`	Last year
Range	`Month-7:Month-1`	Rolling six month set (last 6 full months)
Parallel Period	`(Year-1).Month`	This month last year
	`(Month-3).Day`	This day 3 months ago month

Table 10.2: STPS Formula Examples.

Type	STPS	Description
Period to Date	`Year.FirstMonth:Month`	Year-to-date (by month)
	`Month.FirstDay:Day`	Current month-to-date
	`(Year-1).FirstMonth:` ➲`(Year-1).Month`	Last year year-to-date (by month)

Table 10.2: STPS Formula Examples (continued).

Creating a Time Intelligence Filter

Follow these steps to create a Time Intelligence filter:

1. Make sure the **Reseller Performance** dashboard is selected in the workspace browser.

2. In the workspace pane, select the **Filters** tab and click the **New Filter** button in the **Filters** section.

3. In the **Select a Dashboard Filter Template** dialog, select **Time Intelligence**. Click **OK**.

4. Enter `Fiscal` in the **Name** text box and click **Next**.

5. In the **Select a Data Source** step, click the **Add Data Source** button, and select the **AdventureWorksPPS** data source. Click **OK**, then click **Next**.

Tech Tip:

The Select a Data Source step allows multiple data sources to be configured. The TI filter acts as a translator of sorts because it understands the specific makeup of each data source's time dimension. Dashboards that contain items referencing multiple data sources can share one TI filter. When a user selects Current Year, the TI filter will work out what is considered the current year for each data source and make that value available.

6. The **Enter Time Formula** step is where we use the STPS. Because AdventureWorksDW relational database contains data from several years ago, we will have to make a small concession when it comes to the "current" and past years when using the STPS. We also cannot be sure *when* you will be reading this book. For simplicity, we have not tried to work any date magic with the sample database. As a result, the STPS formulas used here will need to take this into account. Using the STPS `Year` formula will not return any reference because no fiscal year member greater than 2005 exists. Instead, we will use `Year-n` so that the Current year filter item is 2004. Click the **Add Formula** button twice and fill in the **Formula** and **Caption** sections using the values in Table 10.2.

Formula	Caption
Year-4	Current year
Year-5	Last year
Year-6	2 years ago

Table 10.2: STPS Formulas.

7. Click the **Preview** button and observe that the TI engine generates MDX tuples for each TI calculation (Figure 10.8). Click **Close**, then click **Next**.

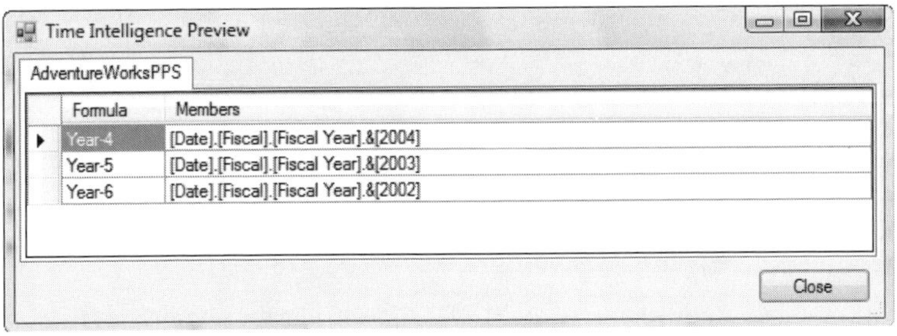

Figure 10.8: TI Formula Preview.

Note:

Depending on when you are reading this book, you may need to go back and adjust the offset numbers in the STPS formulas so that the Current Year returns [Date].[Fiscal].[Fiscal Year].&[2004].

8. In the **Choose Display Method** step, select **List** (Figure 10.9).

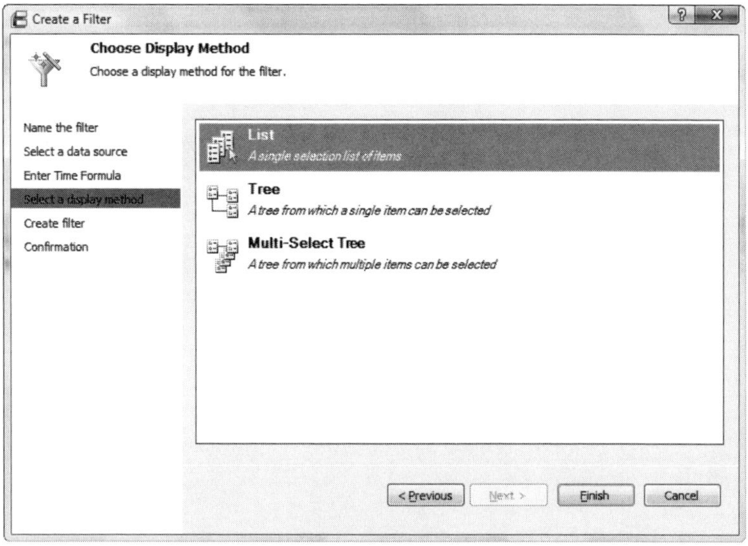

Figure 10.9: Choose Display Method Step.

9. Click **Finish** and click **Close** on the confirmation step.

Creating an MDX Query Filter

Follow these steps to create an MDX Query filter for Geography:

1. Select the **Filters** tab in the **Reseller Performance** dashboard workspace pane.

2. Click the **New Filter** button. In the **Select a Dashboard Filter Template** dialog (Figure 10.10), select the **MDX Query** filter template. Click **OK**.

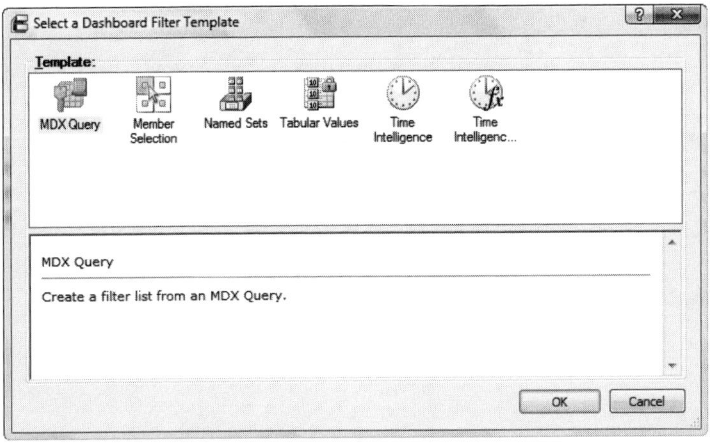

Figure 10.10: Select a Dashboard Filter Template Dialog.

3. Enter `Geography` in the **Name** text box and click **Next**.

4. In the **Select a Data Source** step, select **AdventureWorksPPS** and click **Next**.

5. Enter the following MDX into the **MDX Formula** text box and click **Next**.

```
DESCENDANTS(
  [Geography].[Geography].[All Geographies]
 ,[Geography].[Geography].[Country]
 ,SELF_AND_BEFORE)
```

6. Select **Tree** in the **Choose Display Method** step. Click **Finish**, then click **Close**.

7. Click **Publish All** and save the workspace.

Items

In much the same way as it has done for both scorecards and reports, the details browser provides a convenient list of the items available for use in a dashboard. All reports and scorecards that exist in the currently open workspace will be listed, as will any filter definitions that have been created inside the currently active dashboard. Figure 10.11 shows the contents of the dashboard details browser grouped under scorecards, reports, and filters.

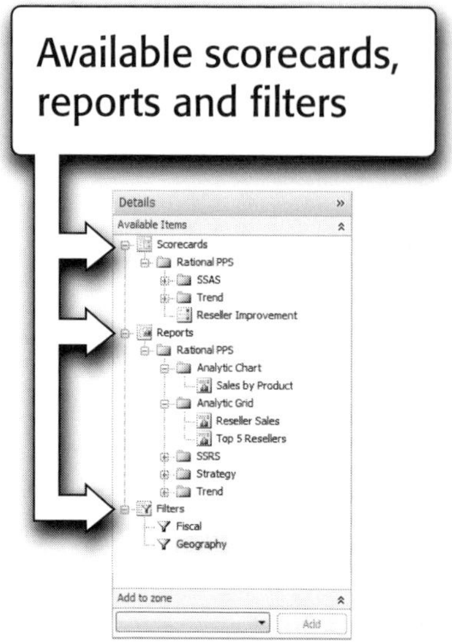

Figure 10.11: Dashboard Details Browser Items.

Items are dragged and dropped from the workspace browser onto the desired zone in the workspace pane. Figure 10.12 shows the Reseller Improvement scorecard being dropped into the zone named *Left Column*.

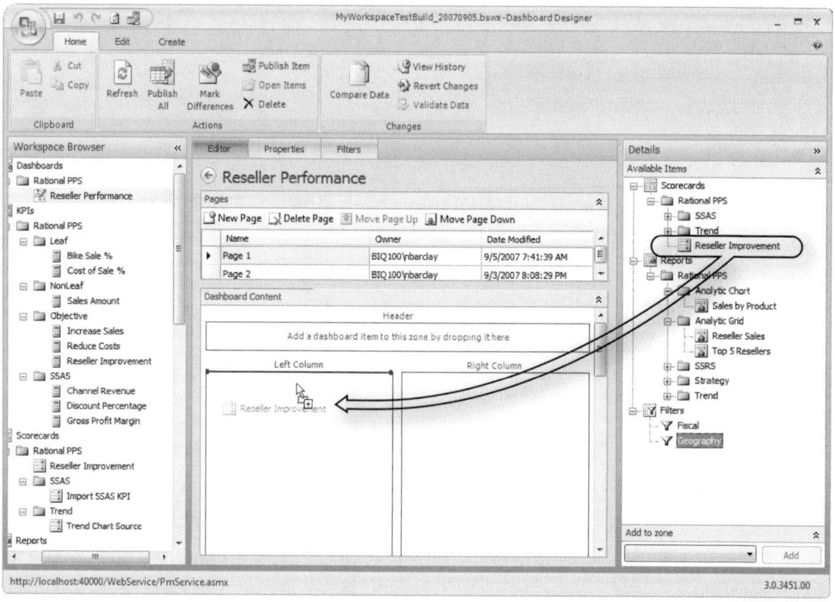

Figure 10.12: Drag and Drop Item Placement.

Drop guides provide visual clues as to whether an item will be placed above/below or to the left/right of any other items already present in that zone. The above/below, left/right settings are determined by the orientation property of the zone. Just like web parts, dashboard items can be easily dragged and dropped to other zones if required.

Items can also be added to dashboard pages by selecting the item and picking a zone name in the **Add To Zone** dropdown list (located at the bottom of the details browser). Much of this should feel familiar to those who have laid out and configured web parts on a SharePoint page. In fact, each dashboard item will eventually be contained in its own instance of the Dashboard Viewer web part. We will cover this in the next chapter.

Adding Items to the Reseller Performance Dashboard

Follow these steps to add items to the Reseller Performance dashboard:

1. Select the **Edit** tab in the workspace pane and ensure that **Page 1** of the dashboard is selected in the **Pages** section.

2. In the details browser, locate the **Reseller Improvement** scorecard under **Scorecards > Rational PPS > Reseller Improvement**.

3. Drag **Reseller Improvements** from the details browser and drop it into the **Left Column** zone.

4. Use the contents of Table 10.3 to drag and drop all required items onto the appropriate zone or page.

Page	Zone Name	Item Type	Item Name
Page 1	**Header**	Filter	Fiscal Geography
	Right Column	Report > Analytic Chart	Sales by Product
		Report > Analytic Grid	Reseller Sales Top 5 Resellers
	Zone 1	Report > Strategy	Reseller Strategy Map
Page 2	**Top Row**	Filter	Fiscal Geography
	Bottom Row	Report > SSRS	Product Sales Summary

Table 10.3: Reseller Performance Dashboard items.

5. Click **Publish All** and save the workspace.

Item Properties

Once present in a dashboard zone, each individual item's properties can be accessed by either selecting the item itself and clicking the **Edit Item** button on the **Dashboard Editor** chunk of the **Edit** ribbon tab, or by clicking the black down arrow located in the top right corner (Figure 10.13).

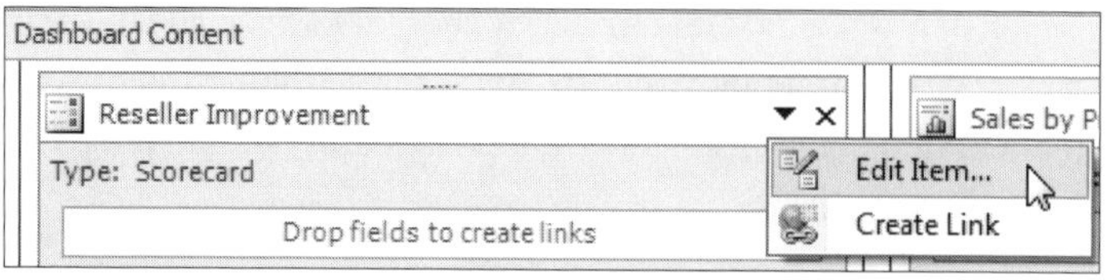

Figure 10.13: Item Contextual Menu.

The **Edit Item** dialog contains two tabs:

- **General** — Contains options to control each item's **Display Position** in relation to any other zone items, **Caching** options and the ability (like several report types in the previous chapter) to **Render as Image**.

- **Size** — Enables the configuration of width and height settings of the item within the zone; this is very similar in nature to the zone settings.

Links

Links are created to pass either data or display instructions from one dashboard item to another. This link information is used by the target item to alter the data it contains or change the way it is displayed. It is important to understand the role each item type can play in a dashboard when it comes to establishing links.

- **Filters** only provide outgoing links. They are able to pass links to any scorecards or reports on the dashboard, but not other filters.

- **Scorecards** are the only item of the three that can both accept incoming links and provide outgoing links. The outgoing link can only be passed to other scorecard or report items.

- **Reports** can only accept incoming links from either scorecards or filters.

Figure 10.14 provides a simple view of available link data flow paths between dashboard items.

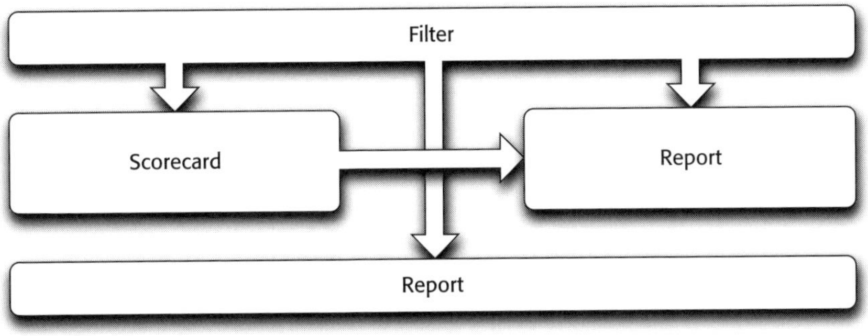

Figure 10.14: Item Link Information Flow.

Outgoing Links

When placed in a dashboard zone, filter and scorecard items contain lists of all outgoing link fields available for use. There are two kinds of outgoing link: *filter links* and *display condition* links.

Filter Links

Filter links pass textual or data values to their targets. They are represented by an icon with a picture of filter and a green arrow pointing "out" (Figure 10.15).

Figure 10.15: Filter Link Icon.

Within each dashboard item, filter links are grouped together in an indented list. For example, in Figure 10.16 the **Display Value**, **KPI ID**, **Name**, **Description** and **Person Responsible** filter links are grouped under the **KPI Row** item. Each is a property of a KPI; their values are available to be passed to another permissible item on the dashboard (either another scorecard or a report).

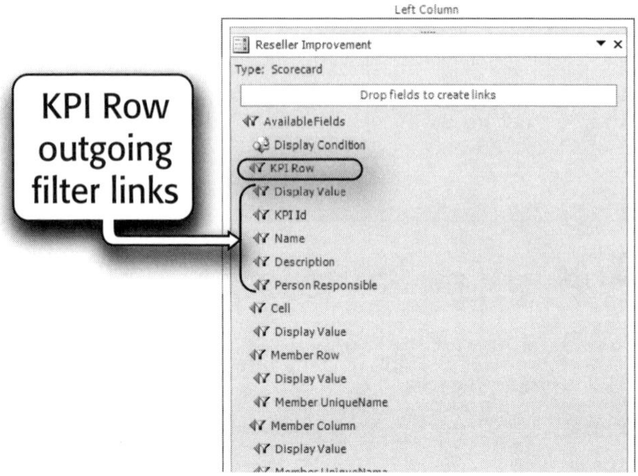

Figure 10.16: Scorecard Outgoing Filter Links.

Display Condition Links

Scorecard and filter items both have one **Display Condition** link. Unlike filter links, they do not pass any textual data to their target. Instead they pass a *display* or *hide* command to their target item based on user interaction with the source item. Display condition links sourced from a filter facilitate the setting of conditional visibility of the target items, based on the filter value that is selected. For example, a specific North American-based report can be set to be visible when *United States* or *Canada* is selected in the filter; the report is hidden if any other country is selected. Scorecard display condition links allow the same functionality using the individual KPIs contained in the scorecard. Clicking the name of a specific KPI could display a customized report specific to it.

Linking Dashboard Items

The outgoing links represent *what* information we are going to transfer. The actual process of linking dashboard items determines *where* we are going pass that information. Each dashboard item contains a white rectangle containing the text **Drop fields to create links**. This is the *incoming links drop box*. Once an incoming link is created on a dashboard item, it will be listed in this box.

One way to create a link between two dashboard items is to drag the outgoing link from the source item and drop it into the incoming links box on the target item (Figure 10.17).

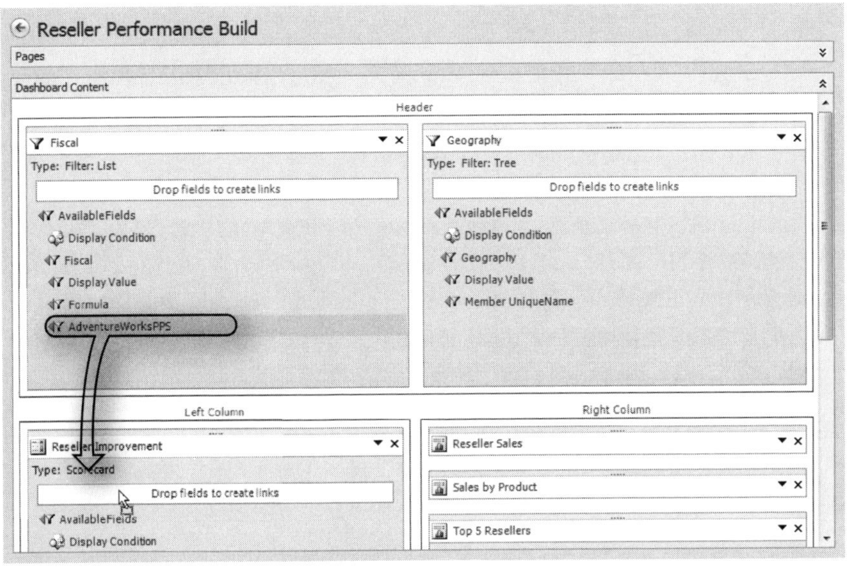

Figure 10.17: Drag and Drop Item Links.

Larger dashboards containing many items can be difficult with the drag and drop method. Links can also be created using button clicks only. The **Create Link** button can be found on the **Edit** tab; it will become active when a dashboard item is selected. A **Create link** item can also be found on the each dashboard item by clicking the black down arrow.

Once a link has been created, there are a few more configuration settings to take care of. The interface used to make these configurations will vary depending on whether a filter link or display condition link have been created.

Tech Tip:

The dashboard design interface is smart—it knows what outgoing and incoming links can be configured to which items. If you try to configure an invalid dashboard item link, it simply won't let you hook it up.

Filter Link Editor Dialog

The properties of a filter link are configured using the **Filter Link Editor** dialog, which consists of two tabs: **Link Items** and **Link Options**.

Link Items

This tab contains two dropdown menus, one for the **Filter** (source) and one for the **Linked dashboard item** (target) as shown in Figure 10.18. Items in the **Filter** dropdown contain references to the items available to use as a link source. The **Linked dashboard item** dropdown lists all dashboard items that are available to receive an incoming link.

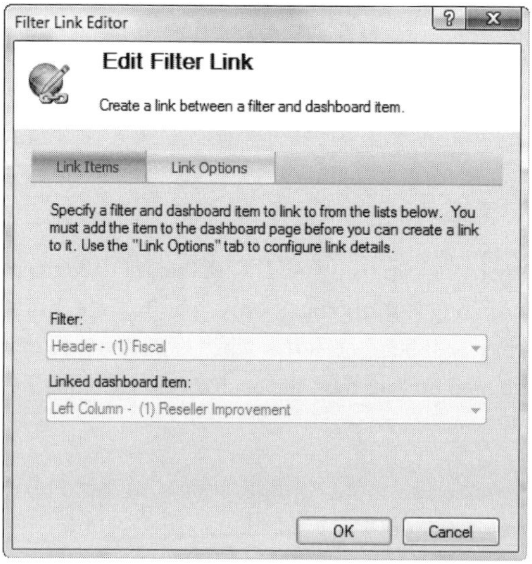

Figure 10.18: Link Items Tab.

When the filter link has been dragged and dropped onto the target, these dropdowns will already be configured (see Figure 10.18) and cannot be changed. If using the button click method for creating links, the **Linked dashboard item** dropdown will be active and must be configured.

Tech Tip:

The Edit Filter Link tab dropdowns show the available dashboard items using a three-part name in the following format: `<ZoneName>-(<ZoneDisplayPosition>)<ItemName>`**. For example, Header – (1) Fiscal refers to the item named Fiscal located in position 1 in the zone named Header.**

Link Options

The **Link Options** tab (see Figure 10.19) enables configuration of precisely the part of the target item that will receive the link data being sent to it. The **Dashboard item endpoint** dropdown will contain different values depending on whether the target item is a scorecard or a report. Available scorecard endpoints where link data can be applied are: **Filters**, **Rows**, or **Columns**. For reports, the endpoints listed will depend entirely on the type of report the dashboard item represents. This is the place where you will see the report endpoints that were configured in the previous chapter. As mentioned in Chapter 9, not all reports need to have specific endpoints configured.

Figure 10.19: Link Options Tab.

The **Source value** dropdown contains a list of all available filter links from the source item. The item selected in this dropdown contains the value that will be passed to, and used by, the **Dashboard item endpoint**.

The other option available in the **Link Options** tab is the **Filter Link Formula** button. We'll cover this a little bit later. Filter link formulas deserve their own special section.

Creating Filter Links

Follow these steps to create a filter link from the **Fiscal** filter (source) to the **Reseller Improvement** scorecard (target):

1. In the **Pages** section of the **Reseller Performance** dashboard workspace, ensure that **Page 1** is selected.

2. Hover over the **Fiscal** filter item at the top left of **Page 1** to display the item contents.

3. Hover over the **AdventureWorksPPS** filter link. When the four-arrow cursor icon appears, click, drag, and then drop it into the **Reseller Scorecard** incoming links drop box.

4. The **Edit Filter Link** dialog will automatically display. Click the **Link Items** tab and notice that both dropdowns are populated and disabled; the drag and drop process from the previous step has automatically completed this part of the configuration.

5. Click the **Link Options** tab and make sure that the **Dashboard item endpoint** dropdown is set to **Filters**. The **Source value** dropdown will already be populated with **AdventureWorksPPS** because that is the filter link we chose. Click **OK**. Note that the incoming links box now contains an item named **Fiscal** with a filter link icon with the green arrow pointing "in" (Figure 10.20).

6. Click **Publish All**.

Figure 10.20: Incoming Links Box with Link Item.

Now that we have completed one example, there are quite a few more links that must be established in order to completely hook up our dashboard items. For efficiency's sake, we will not list the information required to set up the link. These details are listed in Table 10.4 and will also be sufficient if you wish to create links using the **Create Link** button in lieu of the drag and drop method.

Source Item	Target Item	Filter Link	Dashboard Item Endpoint
Filter: Geography	**Scorecard:** Reseller Improvement	MemberUniqueName	Filters
Filter: Fiscal	**Report:** Reseller Sales	AdventureWorksPPS	Date Fiscal
Filter: Geography	**Report:** Reseller Sales	MemberUniqueName	Geography
Filter: Fiscal	**Report:** Sales By Product	AdventureWorksPPS	Date Fiscal
Filter: Geography	**Report:** Sales By Product	MemberUniqueName	Geography
Filter: Fiscal	**Report:** Top 5 Resellers	AdventureWorksPPS	Date Fiscal
Filter: Geography	**Report:** Top 5 Resellers	MemberUniqueName	Geography
Filter: Fiscal	**Report:** Reseller Strategy Map	AdventureWorksPPS	Page (*see warning below)
Filter: Geography	**Report:** Reseller Strategy Map	MemberUniqueName	Page (*see warning below)
Filter: Fiscal	**Report:** Product Sales Summary	AdventureWorksPPS	Fiscal
Filter: Geography	**Report:** Product Sales Summary	MemberUniqueName	Geography

Table 10.4: Dashboard Filter Link Settings.

Caution:

The RTM build of DD contains a bug that does not allow Strategy Maps to accept multiple filter links on Page or Filters endpoints. You will find that the user interface will not allow both incoming Fiscal and Geography filter links to use the Page endpoint. This will be fixed in a subsequent service pack. The workaround involves manually editing the workspace XML. If you are not comfortable performing these steps, you can use the completed workspace for this chapter (available with the downloadable bonus material). Alternately, you can simply hook up just one of the filters to the Page endpoint. This will not break anything; the strategy map will simply not change in response to user interaction with both Fiscal and Geography filters.

Here's how:

1. **Create both filter links using either Page or Filter endpoints.**
2. **Save and close the workspace.**
3. **Make a backup copy of the workspace (just in case).**
4. **Open the workspace file with Notepad or your favorite XML editor and search for "StrategyMap" to find the appropriate `ReportView` node.**
5. **Find the `EndPoints` collection and ensure the `AcceptsMultipleFilterLinks` property for both Page and Filters endpoints is set to `True`.**

```
<ReportView … TypeName="StrategyMap" …>
    …
  <EndPoints>
   <EndPoint UniqueName="Page" DisplayName="Page" AcceptsMultiple
➲FilterLinks="True" />
   <EndPoint UniqueName="Filters" DisplayName="Filters"
➲AcceptsMultipleFilterLinks="True" />
   </EndPoints>
</ReportView>
```

Save and close the document and reopen it in DD. You should now be able to set the Page endpoint on both incoming links for the Strategy Map item.

Display Condition Dialog

When a *display condition* link is configured from a target item, the **Display Condition Editor** dialog will appear (Figure 10.21). Selecting a source item property in the **Conditional field** dropdown (e.g., Display Value) will populate the main list box with data. The desired check boxes can then be selected to control visibility. When a user interacts with the items for which the check boxes are selected, the target item will be made visible on the dashboard. Conversely, the boxes that are not checked will cause the target item to be hidden if or when the corresponding items are clicked by the end user.

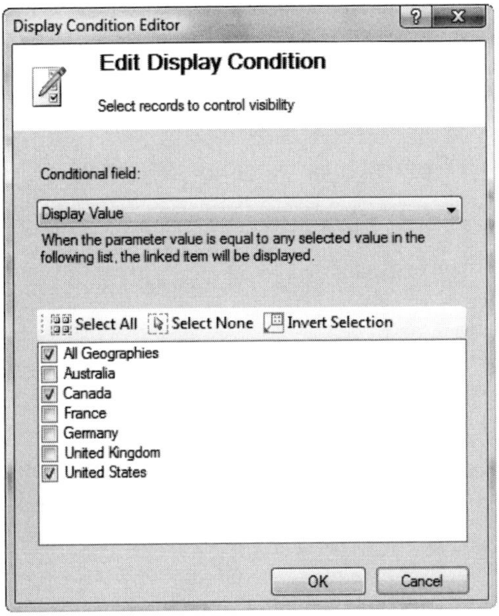

Figure 10.21: Display Condition Dialog.

Creating a Display Condition Link

Follow these steps to create a display condition link that will only display the **Product Sales Summary** report when certain members of the Geography filter are selected:

1. In the **Pages** section of the **Reseller Performance** dashboard workspace, ensure that **Page 2** is selected.

2. Hover over the **Geography** filter item. Drag and drop the Display Condition link into the **incoming links drop box** of the **Product Sales Summary** item.

3. The **Edit Display Condition** dialog will automatically appear. Select **Display Value** in the **Conditional field** dropdown.

4. Select the check boxes for **All Geographies**, **Canada** and **United States** items. Click **OK**.

5. Click **Publish All** and save the workspace.

Filter Link Formulas

Filter link formulas are a very powerful addition to filter links. Is short, they provide a simple way to customize the filter values passed to any individual dashboard item on the fly. The extra functionality that this feature can add to dashboards cannot be overstated. The potential applications for filter link formulas could easily be a chapter unto itself.

Filter link formulas use MDX or STPS to return either a tuple or a set. In much the same way that MDX parameters are configured for analytic chart and grid reports, a placeholder text string surrounded by double angle brackets (`<<SourceValue>>` or `<<DisplayValue>>`) is required to reference the value being passed into the filter link formula.

For example, a user has asked for a dashboard where the embedded scorecard will display data for the selected month. The report that is to be located next to the scorecard on the dashboard needs to contain all data from the current fiscal year, using the selected month as a reference point. There can only be one filter controlling this behavior. This is a perfect scenario for a filter link formula. To fulfill requirements, we must configure a filter link formula on the report item that uses the month value supplied to it by the filter in order to return the prior year. The following MDX would achieve this goal:

```
EXISTS([Date].[Fiscal].[Fiscal Year], <<SourceValue>>)
```

When configuring a link sourced from a Time Intelligence Post Formula filter, the STPS is used. A useful post on configuring filters of this kind using the STPS can be found on the Performance Point Team blog: `http://blogs.msdn.com/performancepoint/default.aspx`.

Creating a Filter Link Formula

In this exercise, we will configure a filter link formula that will return a set of quarters based on the year selected in the **Fiscal** filter. The members of that set will be applied to the **Sales by Product** report, resulting in those quarters being displayed along the bottom axis.

1. Locate the **Sales by Product** report at the top of the **Right Column** zone on **Page 1** of the dashboard.

2. In the **incoming links drop box,** right-click the **Fiscal** filter link and select **Edit Filter Link** (Figure 10.22).

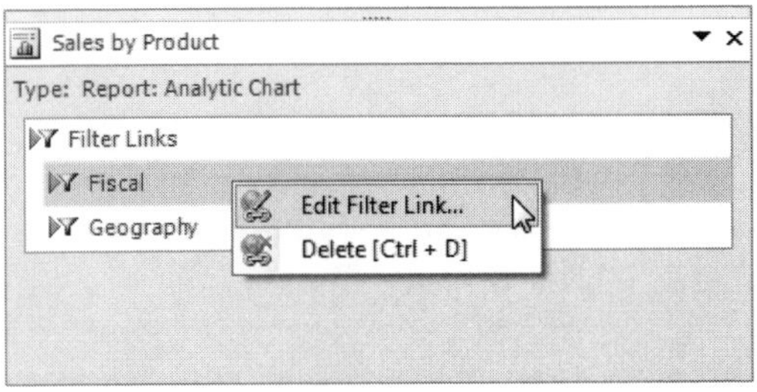

Figure 10.22: Filter Link Contextual Menu.

3. In the **Edit Filter Link** dialog, click the **Filter Link Formula** button.

4. Enter `<<SourceValue>>.children` into the **Formula Editor** text box. Click **OK**.

5. Click **Publish All** and save the workspace.

Dashboard Preview

Now that we have built and configured our dashboard, the time has come to test it. Eventually end users will interact with dashboards via SharePoint, which requires the dashboard to be deployed to a SharePoint server. We will cover this in the next chapter. At this point in the development cycle, the **Dashboard Web Preview** site comes in very handy. Instead of deploying to SharePoint, we want to deploy the dashboard to a preview site and make sure it functions as we want it to. The preview site will emulate the behavior of the dashboard as if it had been deployed to SharePoint. For those who wish to develop and test complete dashboarding solutions without the need to access a SharePoint instance, the dashboard preview site is a brilliant feature.

Preview the Reseller Performance Dashboard

Follow these steps to preview the dashboard we have just created:

1. Make sure the latest version of the **Reseller Performance** dashboard is published by clicking **Publish All**.

2. Make sure the **Reseller Performance** dashboard is selected in the workspace browser.

3. Select the **Edit** ribbon tab and click the **Preview** button in the **Deploy** chunk. This will launch the **Deploy Dashboard to a Preview Site** wizard.

4. The **Select a Dashboard** dialog will contain the names of all dashboards published to the currently connected Monitoring server. Select the **Reseller Performance** dashboard. Click **Next**.

5. On the **Specify the location** step, click **Finish**. An instance of Internet Explorer will be launched and the dashboard will be displayed (Figure 10.23).

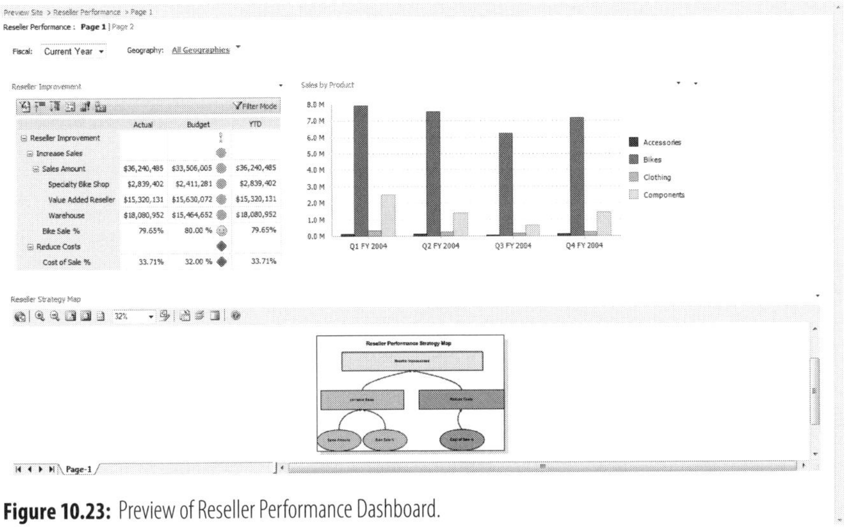

Figure 10.23: Preview of Reseller Performance Dashboard.

Now that a dashboard has been set up on the preview site, try browsing to `http://<machinename>:40000/Preview/`. The preview site page will contain links to the pages of all dashboards that have been deployed to it (Figure 10.24). Each dashboard element will have its own box containing links to each of its pages.

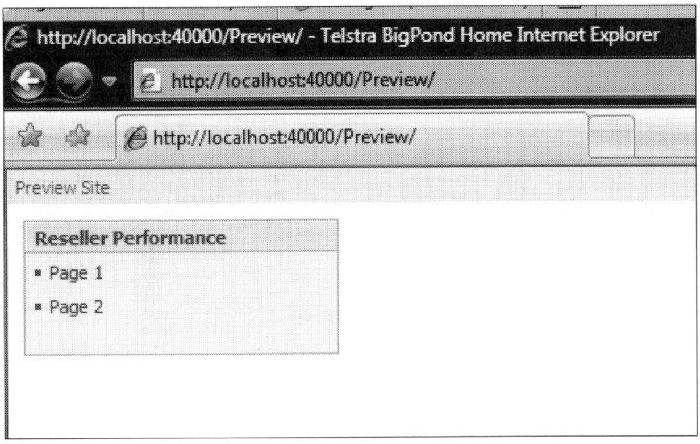

Figure 10.24: Dashboard Preview Site.

Note:

Remember that a link to the preview site can also be located through Monitoring Central: http://<machinename>:40000/Central.

Summary

This chapter provided enough detail on dashboard functionality to get you started, but also offered insight on just how much flexibility this element can provide. The amount of functionality available to the person designing the dashboard is huge. Half of this book could have been written about dashboards alone.

The layout of a dashboard in DD is performed in much the same way as web parts are added to a SharePoint page. A dashboard is used to create customized interaction between scorecard, report, and filter items. Filters are objects created as part of an individual dashboard definition. There are many different options for configuring the values a filter contains. Links are created to pass contextual information between dashboard items to control their behavior. Once built, dashboards can be easily deployed to preview sites for testing without the need for a SharePoint installation. The Simple Time Period Specification (STPS) language provides a simple but powerful way to configure dynamic time intelligence functionality.

This brings us to the end of Part III of this book. We have now covered all six of the Monitoring elements. If you are not convinced by now that SSAS and MDX skills are worth developing, you never will be.

In Part IV, we will look at dashboard functionality within SharePoint and discuss security topics. The free, downloadable bonus chapters elaborate on element management, scoring, and designing effective performance management solutions (see the last page in this book for information).

Part IV

Implementation and Management

RATIONAL PRESS

Chapter 11

Working with Dashboards in SharePoint

So, elements have been created, dashboards have been previewed and tested and everything has been published to the Monitoring server; the main part of the design work is over. Now it is time to expose your creations to the world and provide the business with the data it needs to move onward and upward.

This chapter details how to deploy dashboards (not publish, but *deploy*) to SharePoint. This will be a good time to view, through the eyes of the end user (in SharePoint) what was built in the previous chapters and what interesting functionality is available. We will also take a closer look at the functionality provided by the *PerformancePoint Dashboard Item* web part itself and the options it provides for exposing specific items from published dashboards.

It is important to distinguish between *publishing* and *deploying. Publishing* is the process of sending a new or altered element definition to the Monitoring server. This XML definition is then stored in the monitoring system database. *Deploying* creates structures either in SharePoint, Reporting Services, or a dashboard web preview site that references published element definitions in order to expose their data.

Deploying to SharePoint

Once published, dashboards can be *deployed* to SharePoint using DD. Dashboards are deployed to *document libraries.* There are no specific settings that need to be configured for a document library to be able accept dashboards deployments, but creating a specific document library for the purpose of centralizing groups of dashboards can help to organize your work. Nonetheless, the default document library that is auto-created with any SharePoint site will suffice. Dashboards deployed to document libraries can be managed like any other document library item. However, the items created in the document library by the deployment engine are simply links to pages; they are not documents.

Dashboards only need to be deployed to SharePoint once. When that deployment is complete, any published updates to the dashboard itself (or the elements that make it up) will be automatically be available in SharePoint.

Tech Tip:

In order to *deploy* a dashboard, all elements that make up the dashboard must first be *published* to the Monitoring server.

Deploying a dashboard to SharePoint is a simple, wizard-driven process which does the following:

1. Creates a SharePoint page for each page defined in the dashboard and applies a master page layout definition to each.

Note:

The deployment wizard presents a list of available master page templates. The selected master page is applied to all dashboard pages. During the initial Monitoring server configuration process, a master page named *PerformancePointDefault* is added to the master pages gallery on the specified site collection alongside the *default* master page. If you are looking to maximize dashboard screen space, the *PerformancePointDefault* master page is a good choice. If deploying to Microsoft Office SharePoint Server (MOSS), a number of pre-built master page templates will also be available. For more information on master pages and their application, consult MSDN or TechNet.

2. Creates a folder within the target document library that contains links to each page within the dashboard.

3. Configures a PerformancePoint Dashboard Item web part for each dashboard item present on each page.

As detailed in the previous chapter, creating dashboard pages, configuring zones, and adding items in DD is a very similar process to doing so in SharePoint. This similarity is not a coincidence; the dashboard element was designed so that much of what was manual work in SharePoint (in the BSM days) is now contained within the element definition itself. Dashboard page zone layouts and item locations are used by the deployment engine to create each SharePoint page with the same zone layout, along with adding and configuring the required number of dashboard item web parts.

Deploying a Dashboard to SharePoint

Please keep in mind that the exercises in this chapter assume a vanilla install of WSS. If you're using MOSS, you may find that the names of certain items or functions may differ slightly.

Follow these steps to deploy the **Reseller Performance** dashboard to SharePoint:

1. Open MyWorkspace.bswx in DD. Click the **Refresh** button.

2. Select the **Reseller Performance** dashboard in the workspace browser. This is to ensure that the **Edit** tab of the ribbon now contains the dashboard buttons we need.

3. Select the **Edit** tab and click the **SharePoint Site** button on the **Deploy** chunk.

4. In the **Select a Dashboard** step, select **Reseller Performance** (see Figure 11.1). Click **Next**.

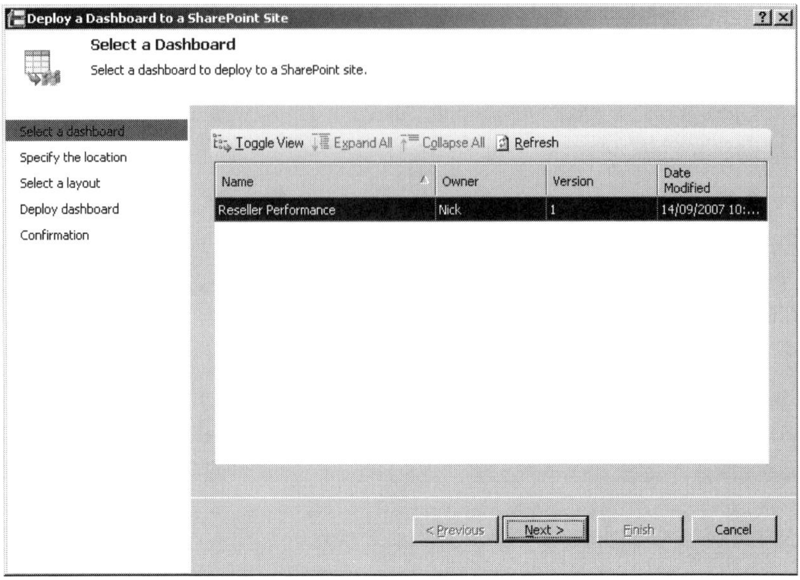

Figure 11.1: Select a Dashboard Step of Deployment Wizard.

5. In the **Specify a Location** step, type the URL of the SharePoint site collection used in the installation chapter in the **SharePoint site URL** combo box. On a vanilla SharePoint install, this will be `http://<servername>/`. Press the **Tab** key.

6. Tabbing off the **SharePoint site URL** combo box will fill the **Document Library** dropdown with all available document libraries. We will use the default document library created with the site. Select **Shared Documents** in the **Document Library** dropdown list (see Figure 11.2). Click **Next**.

7. In the **Select a Layout** step, select **PerformancePointDefault** in the **Master page** dropdown. Leave the **Include the page list for navigation** check box selected.

8. Click the **Finish** button to deploy the dashboard and automatically launch Internet Explorer. The deployed dashboard should look similar to Figure 11.3.

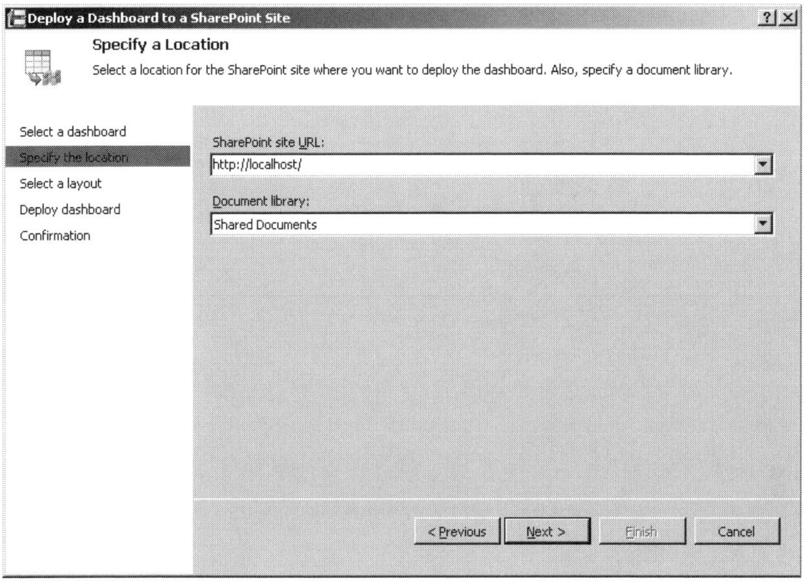

Figure 11.2: Specify a Location Step.

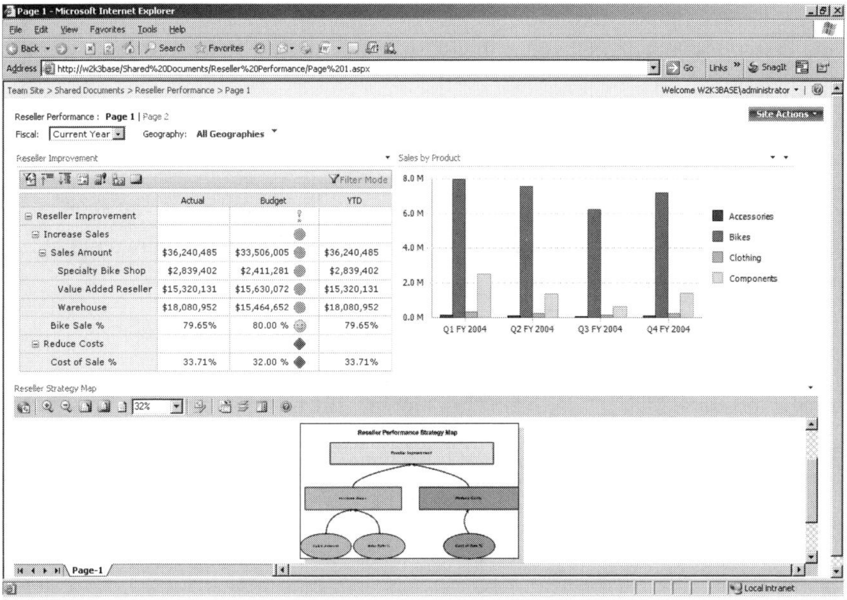

Figure 11.3: Deployed Reseller Performance Dashboard.

The Shared Documents document library will now contain a Reseller Performance folder. Clicking that folder will show the links to the two pages created by the deployment wizard (Figure 11.4).

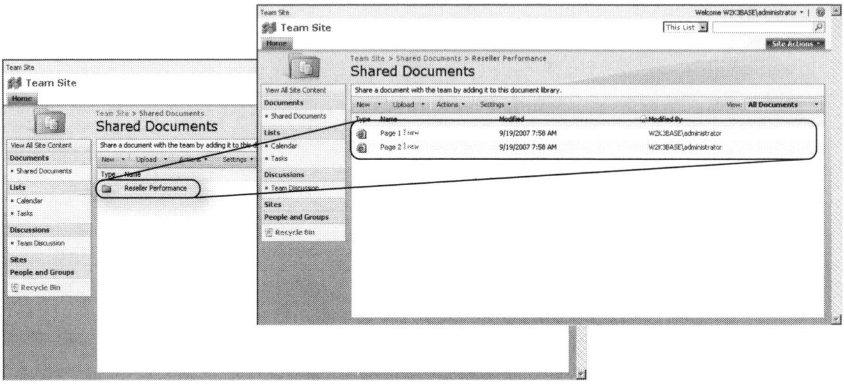

Figure 11.4: Shared Documents Contents.

Observation

Now that we have a deployed dashboard, it is a good time to look at just some of the functionality available for users.

The Scorecard Toolbar

Situated across the top of the Reseller Improvement scorecard is the scorecard toolbar, which provides five groups of functions for end-users, as shown in Figure 11.5.

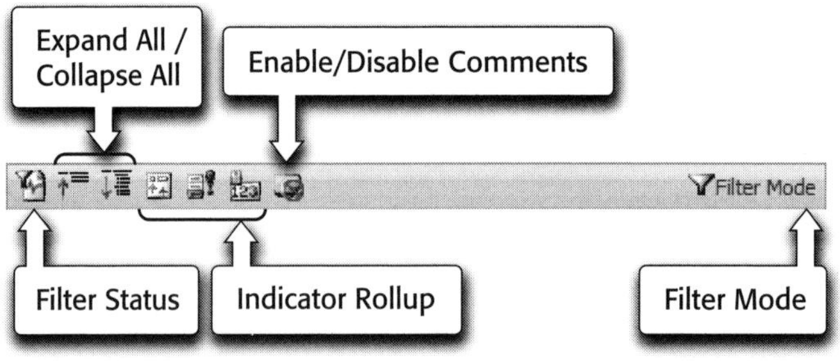

Figure 11.5: Scorecard Toolbar.

Let's review each of these functions.

Filter Status

Toggles a dropdown list that permits users to filter rows of the scorecard using the *display name* property of the indicator level associated with the score for leaf KPIs, as seen in Figure 11.6.

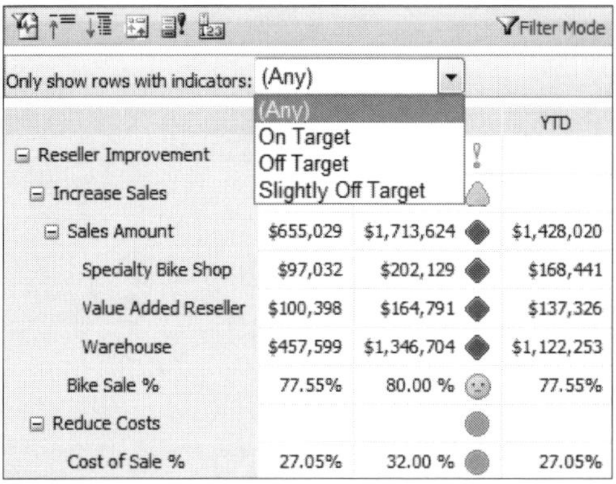

Figure 11.6: Filter Status Toolbar Dropdown List.

Tech Tip:

Status (or score) filters can be configured to contain the indicator level display name text for certain target metrics in a scorecard. This is configured on the scorecard element in DD by checking the Ignore when score filtering property in the target options dialog.

Collapse All / Expand All

The **Collapse All** and **Expand All** toolbar items are complementary, allowing the user to reduce the number of rows to top-level items, or display all of the leaf-level (usually KPI) rows in a scorecard.

Indicator Rollup

The default indicator rollup is configured in the dashboard itself, but users can use these three buttons to change the rollup display to *Average Weighted* (default), *Worst Child*, or *Indicator Count*. The function of each of these rollup types was detailed in Chapter 5.

Filter Mode

Clicking the **Filter Mode** button exposes dropdown lists on each column, permitting users to sort and filter the scorecard rows illustrated in Figure 11.7. Clicking the **View Mode** toolbar item hides the sorting dropdown lists and returns the scorecard to its original state.

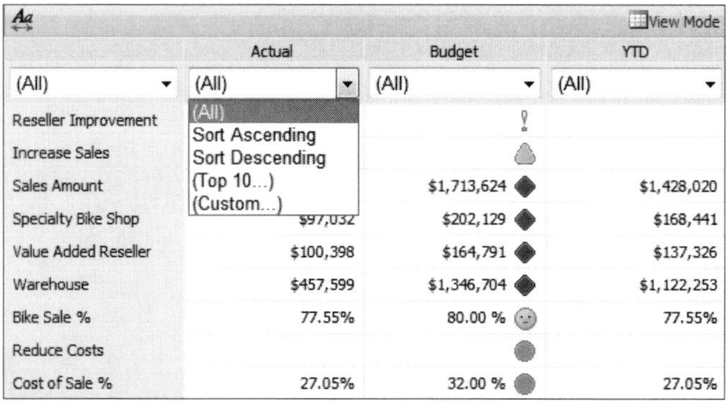

Figure 11.7: Filter Status Toolbar Dropdown List.

> ***Tech Tip:***
> **The buttons displayed in the scorecard toolbar and the visibility of the toolbar itself may be configured in the toolbar options of each scorecard element in DD.**

Enable / Disable Comments

Each data cell in a scorecard can be associated with one or more comments (also known as annotations). This feature enables users to record their thoughts or action points pertaining to the data displayed in that particular cell.

In order for a scorecard to support comments, and display the **Enable / Disable Comments** button in the toolbar, two properties need to be configured.

1. The **Enable Comments** item in the **Server Options** dialog in DD must be set to **Yes** on the Monitoring server that the scorecard is published to.

2. The **Allow comments** check box in the **View Options** dialog of the scorecard element must be checked and the scorecard republished.

Although we have not configured the **Reseller Improvement** scorecard to allow comments, your experience with DD should be ample preparation to make these adjustments should you see fit.

In a comment-enabled scorecard, right-clicking the desired cell and selecting **Comments** will bring up the **Scorecard Comment** dialog (Figure 11.8) where comments can be viewed or added by clicking the **Add Comment** link. For security reasons, comments can only be deleted using DD.

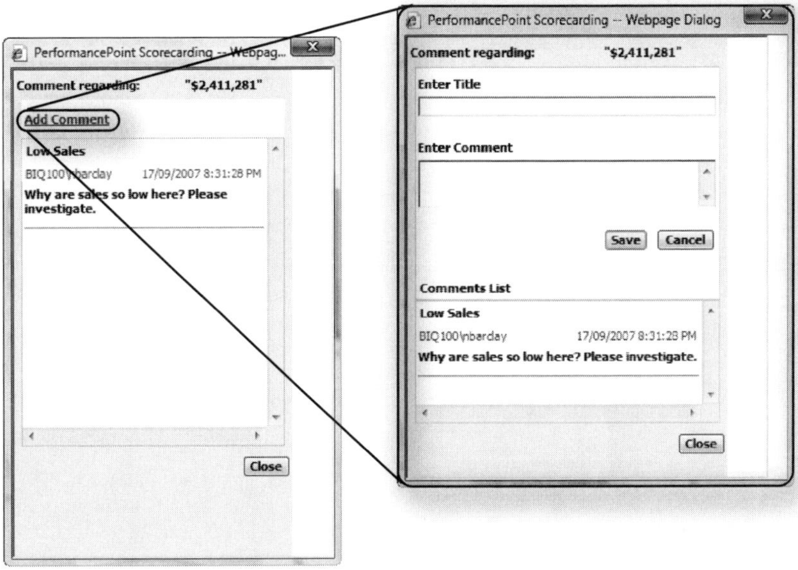

Figure 11.8: Scorecard Comment Dialog.

Scorecard cells that have a comment associated with them will be flagged with a small red triangle in the upper-right corner, as seen in Figure 11.9.

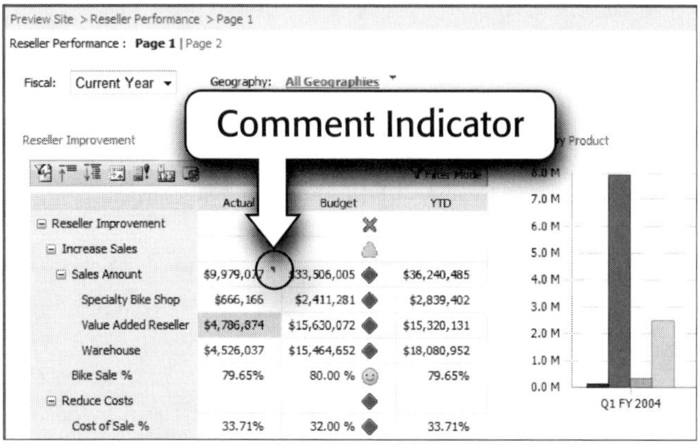

Figure 11.9: Cell Comment Indicator.

Item Functions

You'll see the familiar black down arrow in the top right corner of each dashboard item web part that contains either a report or scorecard. Clicking it will reveal the item's contextual menu, as seen in Figure 11.10. The options available beneath the *Help* item will depend on whether the item is a report or a scorecard.

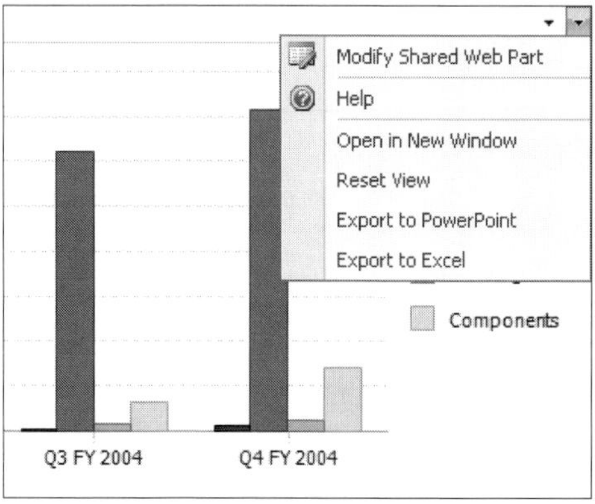

Figure 11.10: Dashboard Item Context Menu.

Let's explore each option the dashboard user can take advantage of.

- **Open in New Window** — Opens an instance of the report or scorecard in a new window. This window can then be maximized, providing far more space for the user to explore the data contained therein. This functionality is particularly valuable when it comes to plumbing the depths of an analytic chart or grid report, as seen in Figure 11.11. Opening analytic chart or grid reports in a new window will expose the analytic report toolbar at the top left of the window. It is worth noting that while embedded in the base dashboard page, the same pivot, sort, drill, exclude, change chart type functionality is available from the right-click contextual menu.

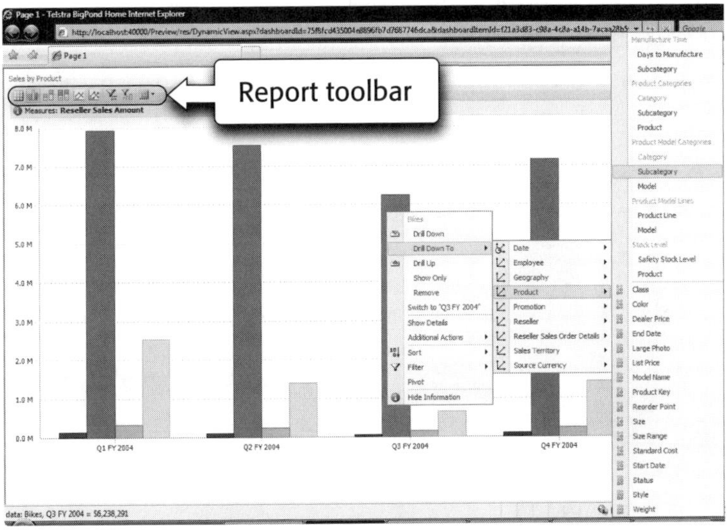

Figure 11.11: Analytic Report in New Window.

Opening a report of any type (or a scorecard) in a new window simply gives the user more room to move (analyze). Clicking the name found in the top left of each dashboard item performs the same **Open in New Window** functionality.

Tech Tip:

When opened in a new window, analytic report types make use of the *Forward* and *Back* browser buttons. Have you drilled down on the wrong dimension? Press the *Back* button to undo your last step and *Forward* to redo.

- **Reset View** — Resets the item to its original published state. This is great for users who really like to drill right to the bottom of a report but can't remember how they got there. "How do I start from the beginning again?" Use Reset View.

- **Export to PowerPoint / Excel** — Exports a disconnected copy of the current view of the item to either Excel or PowerPoint 2007, including contextual metadata and a hyperlink to the dashboard, as seen in Figure 11.12.

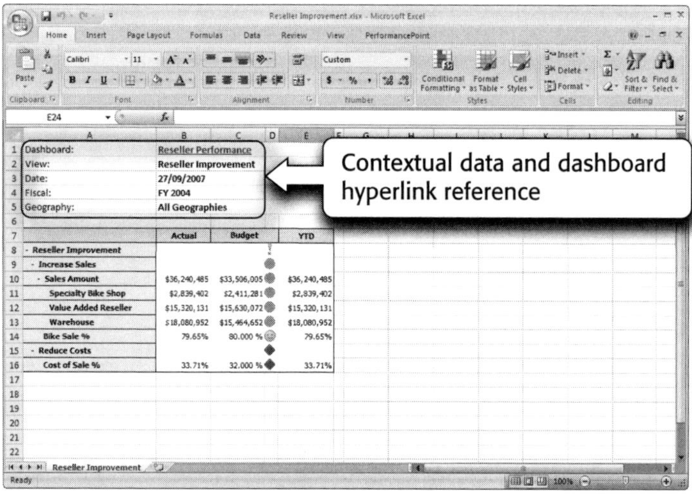

Figure 11.12: Exported Scorecard in Excel 2007.

Scorecards can be exported to both Excel and PowerPoint 2007. For report items, the ability to export to either application depends on the type of report. For example, analytic reports can be exported to both, but a Reporting Services report can only be exported to Excel. Only the **Export to** options available for a particular item will be visible in the contextual menu.

Stacked Zone Dropdowns

When a dashboard zone has been configured with an orientation of *Stacked* and multiple items are placed within it, only one item at a time will be visible. Only one web part is needed to contain a stacked zone and will have a second black arrow located just to the left of the contextual menu arrow. This arrow reveals a dropdown list with all items contained in the stack, as seen in Figure 11.13. Selecting an item will make it visible.

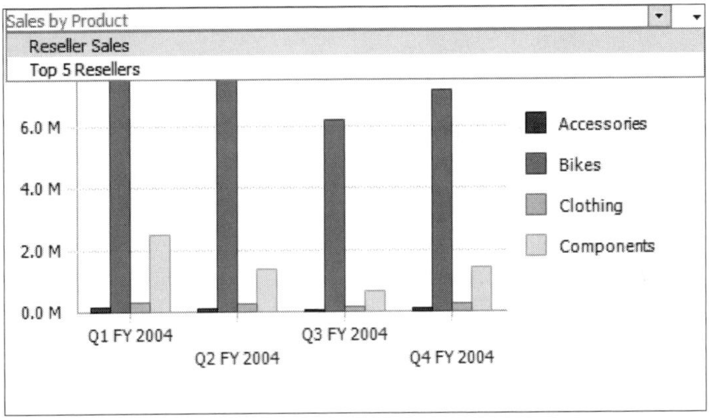

Figure 11.13: Stacked Zone Dropdown.

An item's Display Position property as set in the dashboard in DD determines the order of items in the dropdown. The item at the top of the stack (i.e., visible by default) will have its item Display Position property set to 1; the second item will be set to 2, and so on.

PerformancePoint Dashboard Item Web Part

The PerformancePoint Dashboard Item web part is a very simple web part to use and configure. The SharePoint portion of the Monitoring installation and configuration involves the addition of this web part to the chosen site collection.

A common assumption is that the PerformancePoint Dashboard Item web part encapsulates an entire dashboard element (i.e., one web part is needed for one dashboard). This is incorrect. As its name implies, each individual item that exists in a dashboard definition requires one instance of the web part to make its contents available to end users via SharePoint.

Note:

At this point it may be worth flipping back to Chapter 2 and taking another look at the element hierarchy diagram. The experience gained through building examples of each element should provide more perspective on the content of that diagram. Data is exposed to users through report and scorecard elements contained in published dashboards. Dashboard items are exposed via the PerformancePoint Dashboard Item web part.

Configuration of an instance of the web part could not be easier. Aside from the standard web part configuration options, there are only two properties that must be configured:

- **Dashboard** — Contains a hierarchical list of dashboard elements published to the Monitoring server. Figure 11.14 shows the **Select a Dashboard** dialog containing one published dashboard.

- **Dashboard Item** — Contains the item hierarchy for the dashboard selected in the dashboard property. The item hierarchy will be organized by pages and the items contained on each page, as in Figure 11.15.

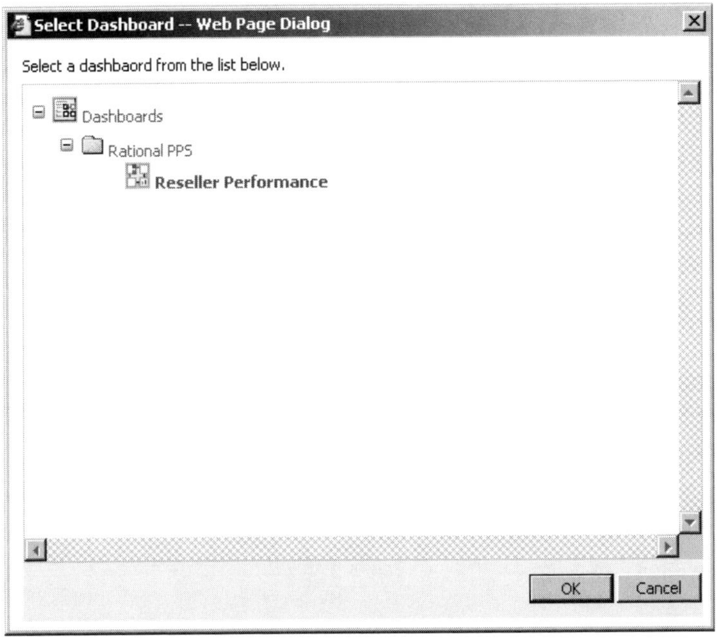

Figure 11.14: Select a Dashboard Dialog.

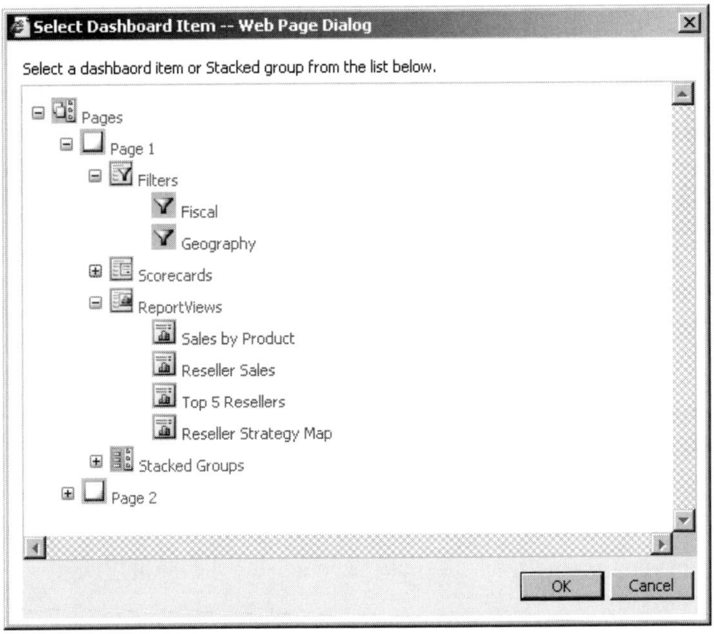

Figure 11.15: Select a Dashboard Item Dialog.

Note:

Stacked groups also appear as an available item as long as a stacked zone exists on the chosen dashboard. This is the exception to the "one item per web part" rule. Stacked groups and the items contained therein can be exposed using one instance of the dashboard item web part. The reports contained in those groups can also be configured in isolation by drilling into the ReportViews node of the hierarchy.

The need to "hook" dashboard item web parts to each other is not required in SharePoint. Because of the hard work already done in DD by creating links, the items already know how they relate to each other. For example, if a certain scorecard is linked to a filter, all that is necessary is to add two web parts to the same page, one pointing to each item. As long as the links have been defined in the published dashboard, the web parts will take care of the rest.

Tech Tip:

The dashboard item web part has been architected to be efficient in rendering its target dashboard item. The web part works within the Monitoring server memory space (in-proc) but does not communicate directly with the web service itself. Instead, the web part accesses the Monitoring system database for the item definition and then connects to the data sources.

Configuring Dashboard Item Web Parts

Let's configure the scenario described above. Management really likes the dashboard you have created and they are looking forward to using it. However, the **Reseller Improvement** scorecard is of particular importance to them. They want it to be embedded on the team's main SharePoint team site page. In that context, they are not interested in being able to slice the scorecard by geography, but they *do* want to be able to slice the data using the fiscal filter.

Adding Web Parts

Follow these steps to add two dashboard item web parts to a SharePoint page. Note that this example assumes a default SharePoint Team Site page layout.

1. If you are not already on the page, open **Internet Explorer** and browse to `http://<servername>/default.aspx`. In the top right of the screen, click **Site Actions** ⇨ **Edit Page**.

2. In the **Left** zone of the site, click the **Add a Web Part** bar at the top of the zone.

3. In the **Add Web Parts** dialog, scroll to the **All Web Parts Miscellaneous** section and select the check box next to the **PerformancePoint Dashboard Item** web part (Figure 11.16). Click **Add**.

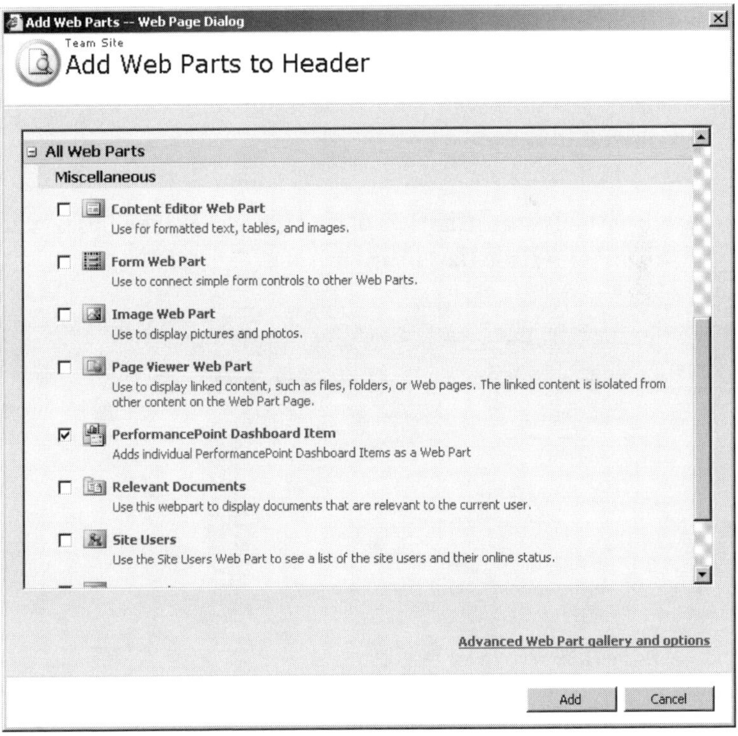

Figure 11.16: Add Web Parts Dialog.

4. Repeat the previous two steps to add another instance of the dashboard item web part to the **Left** zone.

Configuring Web Parts

Follow these steps to configure the web parts:

1. Click the **Click here to open the tool pane** link on the web part named **PerformancePoint Dashboard Item[2]** (Figure 11.17).

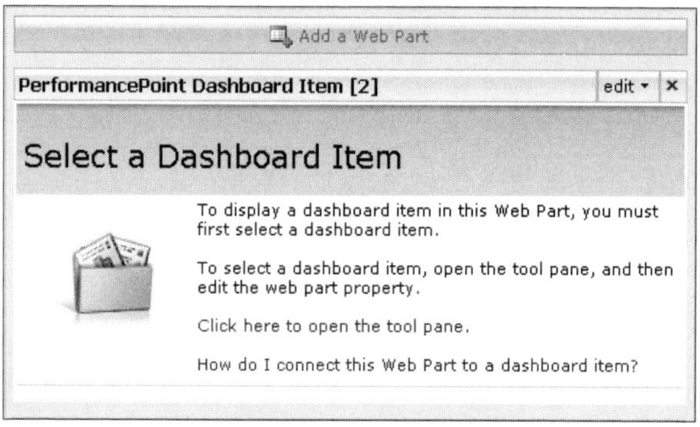

Figure 11.17: Dashboard Item Web Part Edit Mode.

2. In the tool pane on the right of the screen, click the ellipses button to the right of the **Dashboard** text box (Figure 11.18).

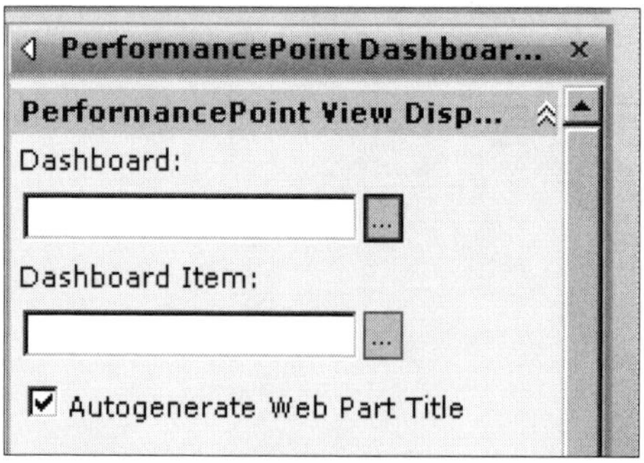

Figure 11.18: Web Part Tool Pane Options.

3. In the **Select Dashboard** dialog, select **Dashboards ⇨ Rational PPS ⇨ Reseller Performance**. Click the **Reseller Performance** dashboard. Click **OK**.

4. In the web part tool pane, click the ellipses button to the right of the **Dashboard Item** text box.

5. In the **Select Dashboard Item** dialog, drill down to **Pages** ⇨ **Page 1** ⇨ **Filters** ⇨ **Fiscal**. Click the **Fiscal** filter item. Click **OK**.

6. At the bottom of the web part tool pane, click **OK**.

7. Perform the same steps again for the second web part, only this time in the **Dashboard Item** dialog drill down to **Pages** ⇨ **Page 1** ⇨ **Scorecards** ⇨ **Reseller Improvement**. Click the **Reseller Improvement** scorecard and click **OK**.

8. Click the **Exit Edit Mode** link just under the **Site Actions** button in the top left of the screen. Your page should look similar to Figure 11.19, containing the scorecard and fiscal page filter.

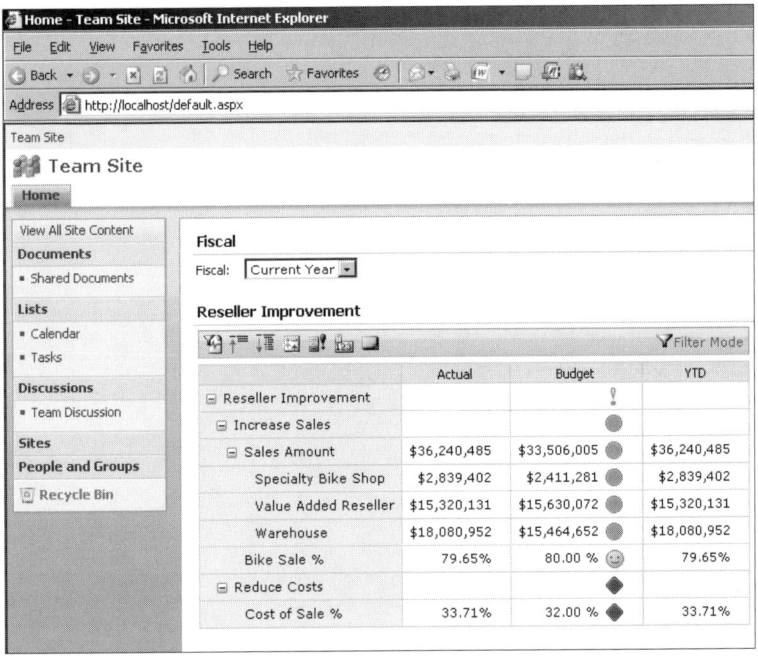

Figure 11.19: Reseller Improvement Scorecard and Fiscal Filter.

Try the using the page filter to slice the scorecard data. Both web parts know how they relate to each other because of the links defined in common dashboard element they are located in; no manual web part configuration is required.

Summary

Once a dashboard element has been designed, tested, and published, it is ready for use in SharePoint. Individual dashboard items are exposed within SharePoint using the PerformancePoint Dashboard Item web part. Published dashboard definitions can be deployed to SharePoint using a DD wizard. The deployment process will automatically create pages and configure web parts in accordance with the dashboard element definition; links to these pages will be created in a document library. Alternately, individual or groups of related dashboard items can be exposed in SharePoint by manually adding and configuring individual dashboard item web parts to SharePoint pages. The configuration of these web parts is minimal, because the dashboard item interactivity links have already been established in the published dashboard.

Chapter 12

Security

Like metadata, security is an aspect of software development that can easily be glossed over. Sometimes this can result in sudden unemployment or, at the very least, the wrong information getting into the wrong hands. Conversely, if not understood and managed appropriately, security can not only let the wrong people in but keep the right people out.

Because PPS can access data from a wide variety of data sources and deliver its content via SharePoint, there are also security considerations for those areas as well as the Monitoring server itself. Determining the levels in a BI system where security is best enforced is up to its creators and administrators.

Role-Based Security

Monitoring is secured using roles at both the server and element levels. Windows users or groups are simply assigned to the role best suited to their business requirements.

Application security is checked when users publish elements to the server. There are four basic operations: *Create*, *Read*, *Update*, and *Delete*. Roles are provided to grant these permissions to various users.

Server Roles

Server role membership is managed in the **Permissions** area of the DD options **Server** tab (see Chapter 4). The privileges granted to members of these roles apply globally to the specific Monitoring server instance they are granted on. Figure 12.1 shows the **Permissions** dialog.

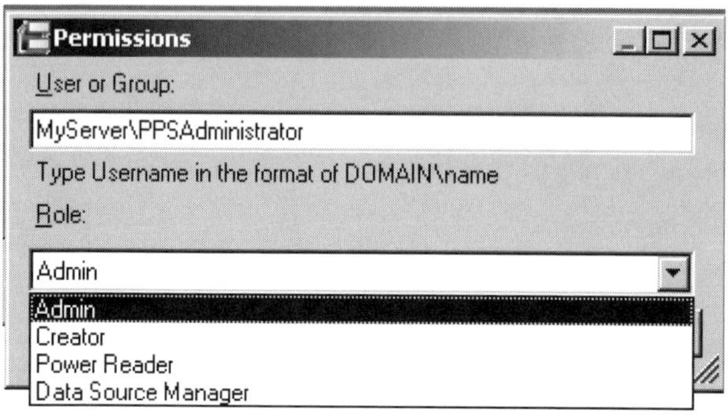

Figure 12.1: Permissions Dialog.

Admin (Create, Read, Update, Delete)

As would be expected, members of this role have complete control over the Monitoring server, as well as full access to all published elements and the source data associated with those elements, based on the permissions provided to the **PPSMonitoringWebService** application pool account. Members have full read, create, edit, delete, and publish permissions for all elements as well as access to the **Server Options** console. By default, the administrator group on the machine that hosts the Monitoring server is automatically made a member of this role.

> *Tech Tip:*
> **In order to deploy dashboards and their constituent elements to either SharePoint or Reporting Services, the appropriate permissions on those respective applications need to be granted.**

Creator (Create)

Members can create KPI, scorecard, report, indicator, and dashboard elements, but *not* data sources.

Data Source Manager (Create)

This role is almost the opposite of creator. Members can create data sources on the Monitoring server.

Power Reader (Read)

Members of this role have read-only access to all published elements on the Monitoring server through SharePoint. Members can also open the element definitions from the Monitoring server and view them in DD. They cannot, however, alter or publish any elements. This role is well-suited for services that need to access elements published to a Monitoring server.

Element Roles

Each individual element can have specific security defined. Element-level security can be configured in the **Permissions** area (Figure 12.2) of each element's **Properties** tab. Users or groups can be assigned to either the Editor or Reader roles.

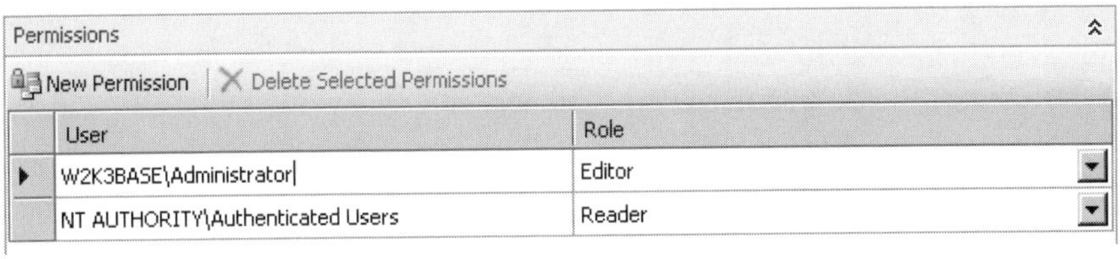

Figure 12.2: Element Properties Tab Permissions Area.

Editor (Update, Delete)

Members of this role may edit all metadata related to any element on which this permission has been granted. Users creating new elements on the server are automatically added to the editor role for those elements. It is the editor role membership that grants the user the ability to delete an element. If they are removed from the editor role later, they will lose their editor permissions on the element. In this way, create and update permissions can be separated so that ownership can be passed on to new users.

Reader (Read)

This role grants users read-only access to the element. Members of this role may view elements in SharePoint for which this permission has been granted. It also enables users to open element definitions from the Monitoring server and view them in DD. They cannot, however, publish or alter and republish any element definitions.

Tech Tip:

Whenever an element is created using DD, an option to Grant Read permissions to all authenticated users is available. This simply adds the NT AUTHORITY\Authenticated Users group to the reader role for that element. Naturally, this option is unchecked by default. Depending on the security requirements of the element, it may be much simpler to grant all domain users read access with this option. As we'll see later in this chapter, there are several areas where security can be enforced.

Data Source Security

Too often the inability of an all-power administrative user to connect to a specific data source is misdiagnosed. Understanding the ways in which the Monitoring server connects to data sources is very important.

Application Pools

The Monitoring security model is designed so that, by default, all user requests from the web application layer are carried out by a single user account. This is the account configured in the respective application pools.

There are three different application pools that are set up during the Monitoring installation:

- **PPSMonitoringWebService** — Primary Monitoring web service.
- **PPSMonitoringCentral** — Monitoring central and DD install sites.
- **PPSMonitoringPreview** — Dashboard web preview site.

Each application pool is configured to use the account chosen during the Monitoring server configuration process. This account can be changed at any time in IIS manager console. It is strongly recommend to use a specific domain account as the application pool identity. As a best practice, the account should only be assigned to the IIS_WPG group on the machine where the Monitoring server is installed.

It is also recommended that the **SharePoint - 80** application pool where the Monitoring server is installed use the same identity account as the one used for the Monitoring server's application pools. This is to ensure that if the default configuration is used, reports and scorecards are executed under the same user context. If using per-user connections security, using the same account is recommended to simplify configuration of Kerberos (per-user connections are covered in the next few pages). If you cannot use the same account, use one with equivalent security access.

Figure 12.3 shows the standard request flow using the application pool identity to connect to data sources.

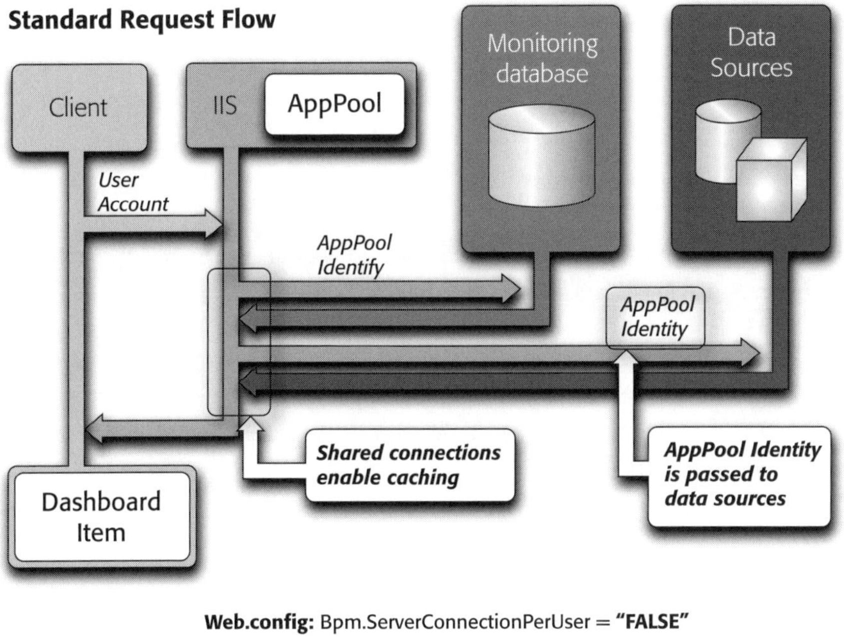

Figure 12.3: Standard Request Flow.

Per-User Connections

In order to pass user credentials to be authenticated against the data source (as opposed the application pool identity), per-user connections must be enabled. This is achieved by changing the value of the `Bpm.ServerConnectionPerUser` key from `False` to `True` in the `appSettings` node of three web.config files.

The first two web.config files are located at %Program Files\Microsoft Office PerformancePoint Server\3.0\Monitoring \PPSMonitoring_1 in the WebService and Preview directories. The most important is the WebService directory file. Altering the Preview web.config file will simply assist in the dashboard testing process by enabling per-user connections on the dashboard web preview site. The third `Bpm.ServerConnectionPerUser` key alteration needs to be made in the SharePoint web.config file, found in the %Inetpub\wwwroot\wss\VirtualDirectories\80 directory.

Tech Tip:

Multiple Monitoring instances can be set up on a single server. The PPSMonitoring directory containing WebService and Preview directories will be suffixed with _1 for the default instance, _2 for the second instance and so on.

Once these settings have been changed, user credentials are passed through for authentication against data sources (see Figure 12.4).

If the data sources are located on separate machines from that running SharePoint, security such as Kerberos needs to be set up to avoid the double-hop issue. An article on enabling SharePoint to use Kerberos can be found in Microsoft knowledge base article #832769 at `http://support.microsoft.com/Default.aspx?id=832769`.

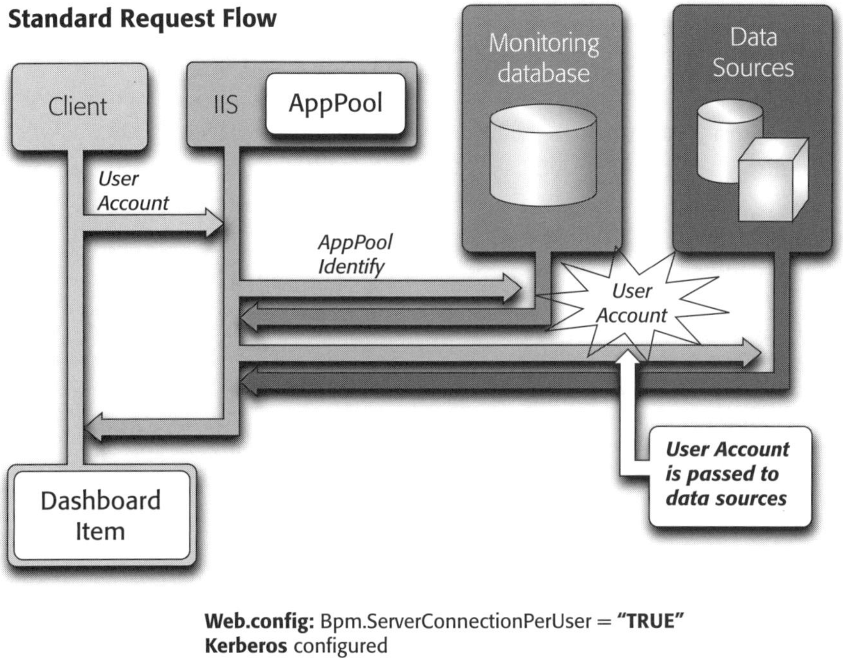

Figure 12.4: Per-user Connections Override.

Note:

OWC PivotTables and PivotChart or SQL Server Reporting Services reports do not access their data via the default PPSMonitoringWebService application pool account. Connections to the pivot data source or to the report server are made with the current user's credentials, regardless of whether per-user connections have been enabled. If the user has not been granted the appropriate access to the SSRS reports or pivot data sources, the reports may not be able to retrieve the required data. The exception to this rule is if pivot reports have their Render as Image property set to true; in this case, the application pool account is used.

Caching

Once a single user has requested it, the data for a specific dashboard is held in the Monitoring server cache. Once cached, any subsequent requests for data from the same dashboard will not require a round trip to the back-end data source. Naturally, if the cache period has expired, the next request will need to be re-cached.

There are three areas where cache settings can be configured:

- **Monitoring server** — The cache interval in minutes property in the **Server Options** dialog.
- **Data source** — Cache interval in minutes, located on the **Editor** tab.
- **Dashboard item** — Each item can be set to be cached or not cached in the **Edit Item** dialog.

Caching intervals (in minutes) can be set at both the server level or at a more granular level in each individual data source. The cache interval settings in a data source will override the server settings for actual data; metadata will still be cached using the server interval. When using Monitoring's default security model of the IIS application pool account for data access, the server-side caching of scorecards and reports is possible (see Figure 12.3). The exception to this rule is when per-user connections are enabled. Because each user is making his or her own request of the back-end data source, caching will function on a per-user basis; this can severely impact performance. The benefits of caching versus making per-user connections to data sources should be carefully considered.

Connection Strings

Many of the supported data source types let you specify connection strings to access data. These connection strings are not encrypted, so specifying username and password credentials as part of a data source connection string is strongly discouraged. These unencrypted connection strings can be viewed by anyone who has a workspace containing the data source definition or editor permissions on the item.

Element Security

As we have seen in the last several chapters, scorecards and dashboards are built using other elements, such as KPIs and indicators. The element hierarchy that was introduced in Chapter 2 shows the simple but necessary relationship that elements have with each other. Understanding this relationship will help you figure out why a specific part of a dashboard or scorecard may appear to be missing for certain users.

In order for a user to view the complete definition of any published scorecard or dashboard in SharePoint, the user must (as a minimum) be a member of the reader element role on each and every element that is used. If a user has not been assigned the appropriate permission for a particular element, it will not be visible to them.

For example, a scorecard is built using a number of KPIs, each of which uses the same published indicator for its Target metrics thresholds. The user is a member of the reader role for all KPIs and the data sources that the scorecard uses, and the scorecard itself. However, this user is *not* a member of any element role for the indicator. As shown in Figure 12.5, when this user attempts to view the scorecard in SharePoint, the KPI numbers are displayed but the indicator image is missing.

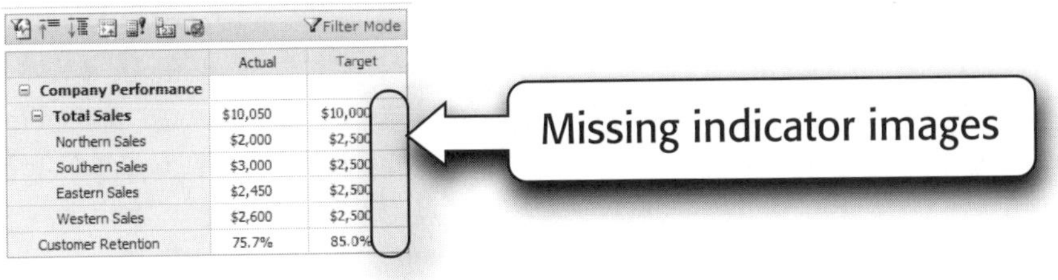

Figure 12.5: Scorecard Missing Indicator Images.

Generally, if a user asks why a certain part of a scorecard or dashboard is missing, the first place to check is the permissions granted on the elements that make it up.

Not displaying the elements in question is an elegant way of handling element permission oversights. This is a great improvement over BSM's behavior in this area. BSM's implementation was an "all or nothing" situation—that is, if a user was missing permission for just one element contained in a scorecard definition, an error was returned.

Note:

Remember, even though scorecards and dashboards are collections of other elements, they are still elements unto themselves. If a user has not been granted at least reader access to these parent elements, they will see nothing.

User Driven Visibility

As detailed earlier, a Monitoring server's security settings can be altered to pass user credentials back to the data source as opposed to using the default of the application pool account. The graceful invisibility behavior of elements to which a user does not have permission offers a potential middle ground. Administrators who do not want to turn on per-user connections but wish to have certain dashboard and scorecard content driven by the identity of the current user may find this functionality useful.

A common request is for scorecard content to be driven by a user's credentials. For example, the company CEO wishes to see a scorecard containing leaf KPIs for all four North, South, East, and West sales regions. Certain regional managers should see the same scorecard made up of only the KPIs for the regions they are responsible for. Using element security, the regional managers will see a scorecard that contains all four regional KPI names. However, only the metric numbers for the KPIs they have permissions to view will be visible. Score and rollup calculations for the scorecard will be made, based on the KPIs to which they have permission. Figure 12.6 shows the scorecard as seen by the North East region manager. Note that the **Western Sales** and **Southern Sales** leaf KPI names are still visible, but their metric numbers are not. The metric numbers are also removed from the sum of children calculation settings on the **Total Sales** non-leaf KPI. The **Company Performance** objective KPI also rolls up the score accordingly.

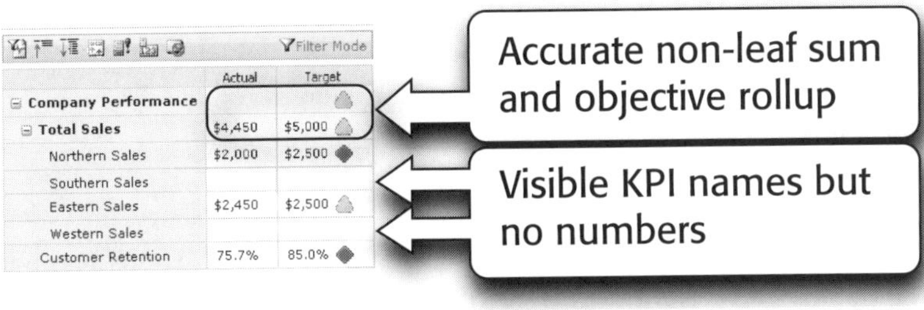

Figure 12.6: Missing KPIs Based on User Identity.

Note:

The functionality used here is *not* based on data source permissions, only element permissions. All we are doing is showing or hiding elements, based on the user's credentials. If user-based data security is required, the per-user connection option is the way to go.

Testing Security

A good way to test or troubleshoot element security is to view published dashboards in SharePoint while impersonating a particular user. SharePoint 2007 provides an elegant method for testing security, by allowing those with appropriate privileges to **Sign in as Different User**. This option can be found at the top right of each SharePoint page, as shown in Figure 12.7.

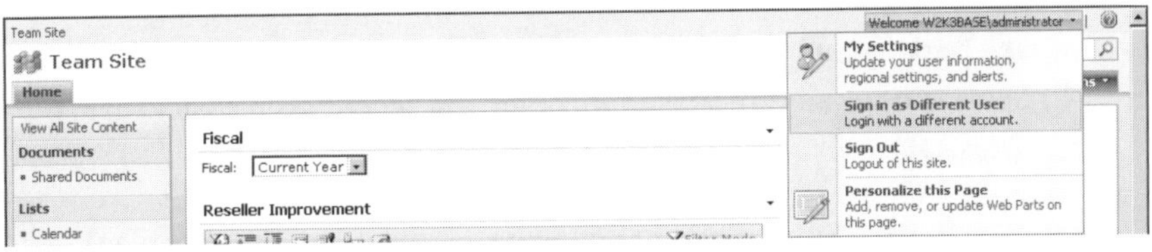

Figure 12.7: Sign in as Different User Option.

You will need a user account to impersonate, preferably one with low privileges or at least with membership to the same Windows group as the user account you're trying to troubleshoot. Depending on how your Monitoring environment is set up, you may create a local user or use an existing domain account. For more information on creating a user, consult your Windows Help and search for "create user account."

Be sure that the chosen account has at least *Visitor* access to the SharePoint site. This can be done in SharePoint by navigating to **Site Actions** ⇨ **Site Settings** and clicking the **People and Groups** link under the **Users and Permissions** heading. For more information, consult SharePoint Help and search for "sharepoint groups and users."

Change and Test Security

Armed with the knowledge of how element permission should affect our dashboard display, we will make some alterations to an element and observe these changes as another user. The following steps assume that you have set up a low-privileged user and granted them access to the SharePoint site.

1. Open MyWorkspace.bswx in DD. Select the **Sales Amount** KPI in the workspace browser and select the **Properties** tab in the workspace pane.

2. In the **Permissions** area at the bottom of the page, select the entry for **NT Authority\Authenticated Users** and click the **Delete Selected Permissions** button. Click **Publish All**.

3. Open up IE and browse to the team site where you embedded the scorecard and filter items as individual web parts. In the top right of the screen, click the **Welcome <domainname>\<username>** link and select **Sign in as Different User**. When prompted, enter the domain\username and password of the test account you wish to use. Click **OK**.

4. Note that the **Sales Amount** non-leaf KPI and its children are blank (see Figure 12.8). All other sections of the scorecard are visible, and the rollup calculation has taken the missing KPI into account.

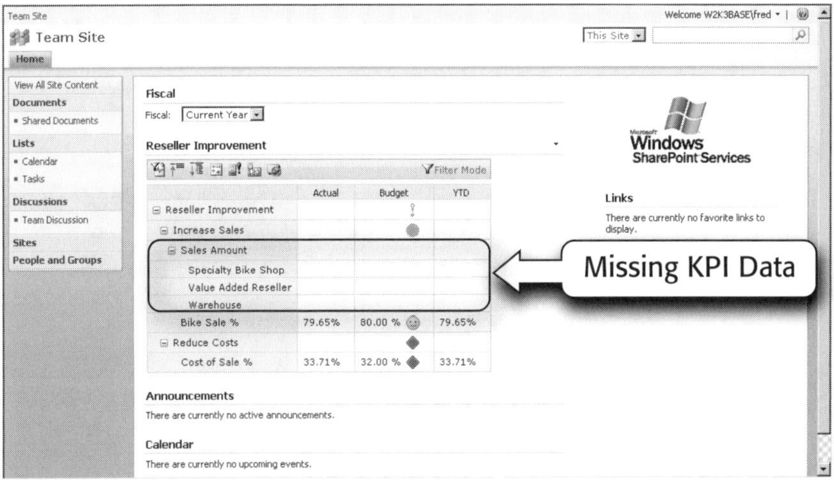

Figure 12.8: Missing KPI Data.

This technique is a great way to experiment with different security contexts. This kind of activity also lets you practice using *Revert Changes* functionality for rolling the changes made to any elements back to a previous state. We will roll back our changes to the Sales Amount KPI in Bonus Chapter A.

> *Note:*
>
> **Notice that in that exercise we simply republished the altered KPI definition and the changes were immediately visible in SharePoint. No redeployment or changes to the dashboard item web part were required.**

Application Security

As mentioned earlier, there are many layers in a BI ecosystem in which security can be enforced aside from the server and element role-based models.

- **SharePoint Services** — Site or page level security. Users or groups can be given access to a particular site and also restricted to specific items in document libraries.

- **Internet Information Services (IIS)** — Users and groups can be restricted from accessing the contents of an entire virtual directory if need be.

- **SQL Server Analysis Services** — The role-based security control available in SSAS is very powerful. If passthrough authentication (per-user connections) is to be used to access OLAP data sources, consider investing time into discovering how to best leverage this security functionality.

- **Other data sources** — Data access security will depend on the type of data source being connected to.

Summary

This chapter examined ways to manage security. Monitoring offers a role-based security model at both the server and element level. By default, a Monitoring server connects to all data sources using an application pool identity account. If per-user connections to data sources are required, the default behavior can be altered. Permissions defined on individual elements can also provide some quite simple security by not showing elements (or element data) that a user does not have permissions for. The **Sign in as Different User** function in SharePoint presents a useful way to test security access for specific users or groups.

BI implementations are made up of many different layers, of which Monitoring is only one; there are many other places within a performance management ecosystem where security can be configured.

FREE Bonus:

To access these free bonus materials, register your book at www.rationalpress.com.

- **Bonus Chapter: Element Management**
- **Bonus Chapter: Designing an Effective PM Solution**
- **Bonus Chapter: Scoring**
- **Bonus Material: Guide to Further Resources**

Part V

Extras

Index

Don't forget these Rational Guides to Business Intelligence

mann
PUBLISHING GROUP

For more information about these and other titles from Rational Press, visit *www.rationalpress.com*

RATIONAL PRESS

IMPORTANT NOTICE
REGISTER YOUR BOOK

Bonus Materials

Your book refers to valuable material that complements your learning experience. In order to download these materials you will need to register your book at `http://www.rationalpress.com`.

These bonus items are available after registration:

- Bonus Chapter: Element Management
- Bonus Chapter: Designing an Effective PM Solution
- Bonus Chapter: Scoring
- Bonus Material: Guide to Further Resources

Registering Your Book

To register your book, follow these steps:

1. Go to `http://www.rationalpress.com`.
2. Create an account and login.
3. Click the **My Books** link.
4. Click the **Register New Book** button.
5. Enter the registration number found on the back of the book (Figure A).
6. Confirm registration and view your new book on the virtual bookshelf.
7. Click the spine of the desired book to view the available downloads and resources for the selected book.

Figure A: Back of Your Book.